p 73 madness of Rufeti's father.

THE WISDOM OF ECCENTRIC OLD MEN

The Wisdom of Eccentric Old Men

A Study of Type and Secondary Character in Galdós's Social Novels, 1870–1897

PETER ANTHONY BLY

McGill-Queen's University Press
Montreal & Kingston • London • Ithaca

© McGill-Queen's University Press 2004
ISBN 0-7735-2802-4

Legal deposit fourth quarter 2004
Bibliothèque nationale du Québec

Printed in Canada on acid-free paper that is 100%
ancient forest free (100% post-consumer recycled),
processed chlorine free.

This book has been published with the help of a grant
from the Canadian Federation for the Humanities and
Social Sciences, through the Aid to Scholarly Publications Programme, using funds provided by the Social
Sciences and Humanities Research Council of Canada.

McGill-Queen's University Press acknowledges the
support of the Canada Council for the Arts for our
publishing program. We also acknowledge the financial
support of the Government of Canada through the Book
Publishing Industry Development Program (BPIDP) for
our publishing activities.

National Library of Canada Cataloguing in Publication

Bly, Peter
    The wisdom of eccentric old men: a study of type and
secondary character in Galdós's social novels, 1870–1897 /
Peter Anthony Bly.

Includes bibliographical references and index.
ISBN 0-7735-2802-4

    1. Pérez Galdós, Benito, 1843–1920 – Characters – Men.
2. Pérez Galdós, Benito, 1843–1920 – Characters – Older
people. I. Title.

PQ6555.Z5B73 2004   863'.5   C2004-902681-X

This book was typeset by True to Type in 10/12 Sabon

IN MEMORIAM

Paul Ian Bly (1944–1999)
for Tush from Tosh

Contents

Preface

The frequent appearance of a specific type of secondary character – the eccentric old man – in Benito Pérez Galdós's social novels was first noted by his most perceptive contemporary critic and close colleague, Leopoldo Alas (Clarín), in his 5 July 1883 review of *Doctor Centeno* [*El doctor Centeno*]: these characters were, he claimed, a "race of peaceable madmen" ["raza de locos pacíficos"], and Galdós knew very well how to create them (*Galdós* 115). With the explosion of Galdós studies in the late 1960s, this figure received more attention from critics. José F. Montesinos (*Galdós* 2:14) declared that these old men, though not entirely clinical cases, were dominated by a mania or eccentricity. Always ready to identify such characters in his subsequent discussion of Galdós's contemporary social novels ("The Series of the First Epoch" ["La Serie de la Primera Época"] [1870–78], and "The Contemporary Series" ["La Serie Contemporánea"] [1881–1915]), as well as the historical novels, or *The National Episodes* [*Los episodios nacionales*] (1873–79; 1897–1912), Montesinos, however, did not provide a systematic study of the type. In fact, the most detailed examination to date is that by Alfred Rodríguez ("El 'Don Simplísimo'"), but, unfortunately, his study group, like that of the two other critics who have treated this subject in some depth – Margarita O'Byrne Curtis and Roberto G. Sánchez – is restricted to only a few examples. Valuable monographic studies of certain individual eccentrics do exist, as we shall see in the respective chapters, but, generally, they do not relate their subjects to others in our group.

Consequently, the aim of this book is to fill what I perceive as a gap in Galdós studies. I propose not only to examine in greater depth those characters reviewed by the above-mentioned critics but also to enlarge the composition of the grouping, which would have been even more extensive if the whole Galdosian corpus had been examined. I have confined my research to those contemporary social novels written between 1870 and 1897 because this period is generally considered the most important in Galdós's oeuvre, and it provides a convenient chronological frame within which to study the treatment of this figure, which, while not found in every novel written between these two dates, appears in a sufficient number as to demand our attention.

To further enhance the value of this study, I have examined relevant comments that Galdós made in personal letters, book reviews, or other journalistic writing from the start of his career in Madrid in 1865, after his arrival from Las Palmas in 1862, as well as reviewing his other creative writings during the same period. The evidence, where available and germane (see Alan E. Smith "Catálogo" and de la Nuez), of changes in the manuscripts and galley proofs of the novels in question has also been included in order to cast more light on the evolution of this technique of characterization.

Galdós's treatment of this type cannot be viewed in isolation; it has to be related to the tradition of literary characterization in Spain in which he grew up and studied, as well as to the wider European current of nineteenth-century realism in which he so willingly immersed himself. But before these questions are addressed in the introduction, it is imperative to clarify what is meant by the key terms of this study, "secondary character" and "eccentric type," especially when one of my claims will be that the normal meanings of these words are given an additional dimension in the creation of these old crackpots.

When it is often stated that Galdós's greatest characters, both principal and secondary, are female (e.g. Montero-Paulson 15 and López-Baralt 157) – some of whom can be easily classified as eccentric or mad – the selection of an exclusively male group for analysis may strike female readers of this book as an example of typical male chauvinism by a male critic. Even if it were possible to avoid genderized textual readings and to achieve the objective of such male feminist critics as Robert Scholes – encapsulated in his rather defensive question: "is there any difference between reading *as* a woman and reading *like* a woman?" ("Reading" 217) – I will maintain that these Galdosian eccentrics, whose own sexual identity is a matter for debate in some cases, enable readers to obtain both a more sympathetic view of the social and emotional condition of the female characters with whom most of them primarily interact, and, simultaneously, a more critical awareness of the harmfulness of the traditional patriarchal attitudes to which the principal male characters subject these women. In other words, these eccentrics, for the most part, allow readers of both sexes "to read women better through excursionary readings" of the respective novels, as Lou Charnon-Deutsch (187) enjoined a decade ago.

The first question that the title of this book may raise in some readers' minds and which launches the introduction is the relevance of such a study in an age when the importance of characters in modern fiction is no longer of great interest to critics. Strange as it may seem, a great number of the eccentrics to be studied are presented by Galdós as having a certain association with literature, which inevitably prompts reflection on the relationship of the literary text to the contemporary reality from which the characters are supposedly re-created. David Galef's justification for such a study, more basic, is very convincing: "the analysis of minor figures will inevitably reveal the painstaking construction of the work: how the author intends to get from alpha to omega, or what contrasts he has in mind, or what thematic principles he is stressing" (22).

This book is primarily aimed at regular students and readers of Galdós's work, who, it is hoped, will find something new or perhaps eccentric to provoke their interest. To help others who cannot read Spanish and who may want to widen their knowledge of the nineteenth-century European novel, original French and Spanish quotations are preceded by an English paraphrase or a full translation. The latter are taken from published works (see "Works Cited"), or, when they are not available in print, I have provided my own. In order to facilitate consultation of editions of Galdós's work that are not cited at the back of the book, the relevant part, chapter, and sub-chapter numbers (if applicable), are given: viz.: I, 6, i. In the case of references to the manuscripts, volume and folio numbers are given thus: f. 1:268. The same style is preferred for references to the galleys, except that the letter "g" replaces that of "f," and, where necessary, the appropriate part is given: viz.: g. part I; 1:268. Since the opus of critical studies on Galdós's work, the realist novel, and characterology is voluminous, only the most pertinent studies are cited, and then, generally, with brevity. In the case of references to novels by other authors, chapter numbers are added in parentheses, where appropriate.

This study would have taken much longer to appear but for the generosity of Queen's University, Kingston, Ontario, in granting me a sabbatical leave from 1998 to 2000. A research grant awarded by the Social Sciences and Humanities Research Council of Canada allowed me to carry out bibliographical and manuscript research in the Biblioteca Nacional in Madrid and the Casa-Museo Pérez Galdós in Las Palmas de Gran Canaria. To the Directora of the latter, Doña Rosa

María Quintana Domínguez, I am particularly grateful for placing the available materials at my disposition. I should also like to thank the InterLibrary Loan Service Department of the Joseph S. Stauffer Library, Queen's University, for obtaining a number of books and articles from other institutions. A special thank you is due to Dr Pilar Esterán Abad for her invaluable help in deciphering some of the folios of Galdós's manuscripts.

I am also very grateful to the editors of McGill-Queen's University Press, in particular Kyla Madden and Joan McGilvray, for their kind help and advice in the preparation of this study for publication.

To my wife, Margaret, I owe, as always, my deepest gratitude for her understanding and support of this project during its various stages.

THE WISDOM OF ECCENTRIC OLD MEN

Introduction

TWENTIETH-CENTURY PERSPECTIVES ON CHARACTERS IN THE NOVEL

In nineteenth-century European realist novels, by which we mean those written in England, France, Portugal, Russia, and Spain in the half-century between 1835 and 1885, more or less, character succeeded in reversing the subordinate ranking that Aristotle had originally accorded it in the drama by becoming the principal element by which a novel's mimetic reproduction of contemporary phenomenal reality was judged. Character was the intersection "where the multiple levels and components of the text" met (Suleiman 173); they had to have the same external, physical features, as well as display the same behavioural and emotional habits that the readers did in their own lives: in short, fictional characters had to be like real people.[1] This supremacy of the character, appropriate in view of its etymology,[2] provoked a reaction from the young writers of the following century: James Joyce, Marcel Proust, Miguel de Unamuno, and Virginia Woolf, for example, set out to demolish the traditional character of nineteenth-century realism, and succeeded so well that later writers followed their example. In 1961 author and critic Nathalie Sarraute exulted in its demise, noting that in contemporary fiction character had lost its two most fundamental attributes: personality and name. Secondary characters – the focus of this study – had been reduced to "mere excrescences, quiddities, experiments" (Sarraute 216). For another semiotic critic, Hélène Cixous, in 1974, this decline represented a liberation from the eternal need to relate a literary text to the real world (385). For a feminist critic of the 1980s, Christine Brooke-Rose, this hostility could be expressed in sexual terms: all characters were like stray phalluses wandering through the reader's mind (193).

Nevertheless, the simple truth is that any novel, whether nineteenth-century realist or modern, does deal with the stories of human beings, and, therefore, character cannot be completely ignored. Semiologists like Roland Barthes in the 1960s attempted to fuse character into the linguistic text of the discourse: characters, principal as well as secondary, now became "actants" whose interest consisted, not in the complexity of their psychology, but in their role in determining the "major articulation of the praxis (desire, communication, struggle)" (107). In reality, however, this amounted to repeating what Henry James had declared in *The Art of Fiction* in 1888: "What is character but the determination of incident? What is incident but the illustration of character?" (reproduced in Martin 116).

In the last twenty years, some theorists, especially those working in English and American literature, have attempted to forge a middle ground between these two largely opposing views of character in fiction and to create a theory of character. For James Phelan (282) there is no problem in this synthesis: characters can be like real people, play an important thematic function, and still remain artificial verbal constructs. Martin Price (37) insists that the characters' existence is predicated exclusively on the needs of the novel and that therefore they are inventions. Seymour Chatman has argued for a recognition of character as an autonomous being with a paradigm of "traits" – a structuralist word that he now applies to a "relatively stable or abiding personal quality" – and not as a mere plot function (126). Likewise, Thomas Docherty (xiii) believes in a more flexible view of character that is determined by the act of reading and can change meaning accordingly, a position that Aleid Fokkema (13) sees as common to postmodern writers, some of whom, if preferring to reject the word "character" as outdated in favour of "subject," are still prepared to use it for life-like examples. This situation, Brian Rosenberg maintains, demonstrates how the term "character" still survives because of its historical relevance or because there is no other word to easily replace it. Unlike the postmodernists, he maintains that character, like every verbal element in the novel, "draws its import and role from some degree of reference to or reminiscence of a world outside" (11). This, however, is not the same as saying that the novel necessarily mirrors the outside world. He goes to the core of the division in character studies between structuralist and mimetic critics when he raises the question of the definition of terms: "one's argument rests on what one means by such elusive words as 'character' and 'text'" (133). They are, indeed, polysemic and ambiguous terms. This problem is not made any easier by the fact, as Roger Fowler (27) indicates, that "character" is "perhaps the most mimetic term in the critical vocabulary, and hence one of the most difficult to contain within the fictional environment; yet it is an essential condition of fictional existence that a character is so contained." Rawdon Wilson (749) is even more adamant: "Character, then, is a concept (and therefore a term) that the study of literature cannot do without." For a modern critic of the nineteenth-century realist novel, this really has never been a difficult question, for, as Shlomith Rimmon-Kenan lucidly declared: "even if we grant the 'death' of character in contemporary literature, can we also retrospectively 'kill' him in nineteenth-century fiction?" (31), when character was a fundamental, unquestioned instrument used by the novelist. Certainly, this study, like those of most recent writers on Galdós's work, aligns itself with the trends in general characterological studies of the last twenty years: characters inevitably involve references to the human condition in the real, contemporary world beyond the printed text, but they are also, and primarily, literary creations that have to be examined in the light of the totality of the narratives in which they appear. How far Galdós anticipated this current approach to characterology will be one of the important findings of this study. First, however, we must focus on the definition of the sub-group of characters that we have identified in our title as "secondary."

DEFINITIONS

So, what is a secondary character? We can start by saying what it is not: it is not a principal character, nor is it a cameo figure or bit part, who is merely a name or a phrase and who flits once or twice across the stage of the narrative. The truth is that literature of all kinds, not just the nineteenth-century realist novel, has accustomed us, as Barthes remarked (108), to arrange the characters of any text into a hierarchy, emphasizing the one or two at the top – the so-called heroes, heroines, or principal, main characters – with those below designated as secondary or minor characters. Such a classification inevitably begs questions about the relationship between the two groups, for their identification is mutually dependent. Another structuralist critic, Jonathan Culler (235), is also inclined to believe that readers are conditioned by literary tradition to hierarchize the characters in a novel from very early on in the reading process. Ordering and hierarchization are, thus, fundamental processes in the creation and reception of any novel, but they can be susceptible to subversion by both narrator and reader. For example, secondary characters might well be presented in more vivid terms than their principals, as is often the case in Charles Dickens's novels, and, consequently, deserve to be labelled as principals (Galef 11). In such instances, they go beyond their nominal function of animated scenery and become symbolic or plot necessities, perhaps best appreciated once the reading of the novel is completed. Our group of Galdosian eccentrics may well fit into such a special category.

Characters can also be classified according to their respective "flatness" or "roundness," that is to say, whether they are simple, two-dimensional characters endowed with very few traits and highly predictable in behaviour, or whether they are complex, multidimensional, and capable of surprising actions. This method, first propounded by E.M. Forster in his famous study, *Aspects of the Novel*, is somewhat mechanical and simplistic, but as susceptible of inversion as the "principal/secondary" hierarchization: Forster himself had allowed for some variation from the norm with "flat" characters moving towards "roundness" when they displayed unexpected traits. There is no doubt that normal "flat" characters are intensely useful for both narrator and reader: they do not make excessive demands on either and can be instantly reintroduced in the narrative without any further explanation (Muir 26). Yet, paradoxically, if they can prove to be more memorable than the true-to-life, principal characters, it is because they can force the reader to meditate on the nature of human behaviour, for instance (Rosenberg 13), or connect with the reality that they inhabit in an intricate and inevitable way (Martin 117).

Another label to differentiate minor characters is that of the "ficelle," invented by Henry James in his 1908 preface to *The Portrait of a Lady*: this character is like the wheels of a coach that do not belong to the body of that vehicle, or, adapting the metaphor further, is like a passenger who "is for a moment accommodated with a seat inside" the coach (James, *Theory* 224). In other words, the "ficelle" discharges a specific function, like that of a foil to the protagonist. W.J. Harvey (58) contrasts this sort of minor character with what he calls the "card," or a character who is a "character" in the often familiar sense of that word, that is, he or she is an essentially comic person who does not change at all or is static, not learning from life's experiences. Even so, the "cards" can still be more complicated and enigmatic than the accepted principal characters, and it is the reader, not the character, who is aware of this added dimension of complexity. They are capable of taking over the whole novel, as so many of Dickens's secondary characters, like Mr Micawber, do. Other critics may not use Harvey's label, but they do concur that the minor characters who are comic are the most successful and, in fact, contribute through their interaction with the principals to the fictional reproduction of life's complexity (Forster 75–6). For Mary McCarthy (287), the minor characters are the real characters in any novel, precisely because, unashamedly and unselfconsciously, they do not change, as their superiors do. It is in this static, rigid, automatic nature that, in the opinion of Henri Bergson (156), lies the comic appeal of the minor character; this privileging of humour is an important feature in Galdós's creation of his eccentric old men.

So far, we have referred to these figures as "characters," whether secondary, flat, ficelle, or card. "Type" – often interchangeable with "character" in the critical language of Galdós, his colleagues, and modern critics – will now be used, because, despite its notoriously confusing overuse – C-A. Sainte-Beuve referred to it in 1865 as "a pretty awkward word" ["un assez vilain mot"] (245) – it will help us to better understand Galdós's continuous experimentation through his novels with this particular figure.

In Greek and Latin, "type" originally meant an "impression," a visual image. However, by the fourth century AD, the word had been appropriated by Christian theologians, and some of this metaphysical meaning was retained by German and French thinkers of the late eighteenth and early nineteenth centuries (by when, incidentally, the older term "prototype" had given way to "type") to express the ontological energies of fate and failure as exemplified by such universal figures as Don Quixote and Hamlet, who were only to be found in literature (Lukacs, "Intellectual" 61). Meanwhile, scientists were advancing a different meaning of "type": in zoology, the one could now represent the many, a usage that was soon applied to the cataloguing of contemporary society by profession, social class, or moral quality, as evidenced in Honoré de Balzac's 1846 "Avant-Propos" to his Comédie humaine.[3] The thoughts of Balzac – one of Galdós's acknowledged mentors – on the relationship between the individual and the type, best expressed in a private letter in 1834 to Madame Hanska, are of great interest to this study, for they anticipate Galdós's elaboration of the secondary male eccentric. Balzac differentiated between "typified individuals" ["les individualités typisées"] (like César Birotteau) and "individualized types" ["les types individualisés"] (like Le Père Grandet) (Demetz 406). As he expressed it on another occasion: "So, everywhere I will have given life – to the type, by individualizing him, to the individual, by typifying him" ["Ainsi, partout j'aurai donné la vie – au type, en l'individualisant, à l'individu en le typisant"] (Lettres 204). Balzac's words go to the heart of Galdós's construction of eccentric figures, for they indicate the close and symbiotic relationship between the individual and the type: all major literary characters are variable mixtures of both elements. The question that this study hopes to answer is: to what extent are these eccentric old men mere types? Or are they more complex individual secondary characters?

THE ECCENTRIC TYPE

When types in literary collections of the nineteenth century were normally designated by their profession or social habits, to establish a group in this study on the basis of a debatable mental disorder may appear somewhat arbitrary, especially as people of other ages and of the opposite sex may be susceptible to the same quirk of behaviour. The adjective itself may also be redundant, as in modern colloquial English and Spanish the word "type," like "character," also contains a certain connotation of eccentricity. What, in fact, does "eccentricity" mean? Is it the same as "madness," particularly in old men prone to senile dementia? A definition of the term is difficult and necessarily subjective on the author's and reader's parts when it largely depends for its initial diagnosis on the external manifestation of abnormal speech, dress, and behaviour. For example, "eccentricity" is defined as behaviour "deviating from what is customary"; it is an "irregularity; oddity, whimsicality" (Onions 581). This accords with the definition of the Spanish term "excentricidad": "rareza o extravagancia de carácter" (Real Academia Española 594). Synonyms for "eccentric" are numerous: "cranky, faddy, erratic, funny, queer, odd, peculiar, crazy, daft," amongst others (Dutch 190). In Spanish, the situation is similar, with Galdós using many of these alternatives: "extravagante, estrafalario, estrambótico, original, raro, absurdo, grotesco, singular, fantástico, insólito, desusado" (Sainz de Robles 484). The temptation to lump together eccentricity and mental disorder under the generic label of "madness" was readily recognized, even in Spain in the second half of the nineteenth century (e.g. Mata Fontanet 216). In his *Responsibility in Mental Disease* (1874), Henry Maudsley, one of the important founders of modern psychiatry, provides a more solidly working definition of the eccentric type, distinguishing between insanity and eccentricity, but underlining their proximity:

Assuredly, it is a fact of experience that there are many persons who, without being insane, exhibit peculiarities of thought, feeling and character which render them unlike ordinary beings and make them objects of remark among their fellows. They may or may not ever become actually insane, but they spring from families in which insanity or other nervous disease exists, and they bear in their temperament the marks of their peculiar heritage: they have in fact a distinct neurotic temperament. (*Responsibility* 40)

What is the evidence for this friendship?

This condition could well cause the eccentric to become insane. And the insane, once he has recovered from his insanity, may well remain an eccentric type. Insanity and eccentricity can even coexist in the conduct of such mentally disturbed people as monomaniacs (*Responsibility* 56). A year later, another English psychiatrist, Andrew Wynter, made similar, if more alarmist, remarks on this closeness of the eccentric and the madman in his aptly entitled *The Borderlands of Insanity,* as quoted by Vieda Skultans (214): the former are incipient lunatics, whose unsoundness of mind, dangerous for both the individual and the public, is mistaken as mere eccentricity. In 1886, in his *Natural Causes and Supernatural Seemings,* Maudsley observed that there were many sorts of eccentricity and eccentrics, although all coincided in the fact that "instead of moving in the common orbit of human thought and feeling, they manifest impulses to start from it – are eccentric." However, he again muddied the waters by saying that "All insane persons are necessarily eccentric, but not all eccentric persons are insane" (Skultans 218). But in all, Maudsley was more disposed than Wynter to accept that the eccentric should be looked on more favourably by society when he is not a danger to it, especially if his eccentricity is allied with intellectual brilliance.[4] The relief from the boredom of normal society that the eccentrics provide is cited as another reason for their tolerance by José María Escuder, one of the important founders of modern Spanish psychiatry and a close friend of Galdós, in his 1895 study on *Madmen and Anomalous* [*Locos y anómalos*].

If for these pioneering psychiatrists eccentricity and madness could be closely related mental conditions, it is also true to say that this theory does not necessarily obtain all the time. Indeed, eccentricity, at one extreme, can take the very mild form of a superficial tic or peculiarity, without having any basis in mental disorder. By the same token, madness can be a generic label covering a wide gamut of mental disorders of diverse origin and therapy, going from the insane to the frenzied. I have chosen to give the main characters examined in this study the general designation of "eccentric," mindful that they display their eccentricity in a number of different ways and that some of them at times do also manifest some form of mental disorder, whose symptoms will be duly noted. But, in all cases, the characters, whether wholly eccentric or marginally mad, do stand out as exceptions, often to be laughed at, within the surrounding society, and thus raise an important question about the accepted definitions of so-called normal human behaviour: are these eccentrics-madmen, in fact, wiser than the normal members of society? If they do discharge such a function, the eccentrics could be associated with other similar types in Western literature: the buffoon, who is a conscious fool (Welsford 3), the wise fool ("Don Simplísimo" in Rodríguez's designation for our Galdosian types), and the holy idiot (McKnight 35). Dwarfing all these potential literary models for Galdós's eccentric old man is, of course, Don Quixote.

THE SPANISH NINETEENTH-CENTURY TYPE TRADITION

Galdós, however, had a more immediate source at hand to guide his first steps in the representation of stock figures, whether eccentric or not: the sketch of customs, the "cuadro de costumbres," which appeared in illustrated cultural journals of the 1830s and 1840s. The most important collection of all, *Spaniards Painted by Themselves* [*Los españoles pintados por sí mismos*] (1843), concentrated exclusively on types, following the lead of the very popular French *Physiologies* of the period (Da Cal 125). No attention was to be given to individualized characters: types embodied the special customs, thoughts, and actions of a particular social group or profession; they were merely seen from the outside, and in a generic way (Montesinos, *Costumbrismo* 109, 129). Name, body, dress, and speech provided a typological shorthand that had some of its popular justification in the theories of Johann Caspar Lavater (1772–1810) on physiognomy and pathognomy and those of Franz Joseph Gall (1820–40) on phrenology. In short, the type a person was could be decoded from the visual signs transmitted by the face and its motions (Lavater) or by the size and shape of the head (Gall). And because, for example, one antiquarian was just like another, a contributor to *Los españoles pintados por sí mismos* argued, it was sufficient to paint one to represent the whole group (1:406). However, another contributor was much more discerning when he said that no two people or things are ever exactly alike and that individuals are not types *(Los españoles* 1:351), thus going to the heart of the question of literary typification that Galdós would later address in his own way in his small group of old male eccentrics.

However, the fundamental challenge faced by these collections of type sketches, not only in Spain but throughout Europe, was to capture contemporary types before they disappeared with the ever-quickening pace of change in society, as both Balzac in the "Avant-propos" to his *Comédie humaine* and Mesonero Romanos in his article "Contrastes" (*Escenas matritenses* 979) noted. The latter believed, however, that people were basically the same from one generation to another and that changes were limited to superficialities of form and appearance, like names. For example, the devout person was now called the humanitarian and the historian the man of history. In time, both labels would become as anachronistic as had their predecessors.

GALDÓS'S IDEAS ON TYPES AND ECCENTRICS: 1865–70

Claims made by critics like Michael Nimetz (31) that these snippet sketches of types persist in the contemporary social novels of Galdós between 1870 and 1897 in such figures as the aristocrat or the Madrilenian, for example, are generally valid, but they do not do full justice to Galdós's awareness from his earliest weekly columns for the Madrid newspaper *The Nation* [*La Nación*], between 1865 and 1868, of the complexities that typification could and should entail. Galdós claims in a 7 January 1866 article that the types and scenes sketched by Mesonero Romanos, his own acknowledged Spanish mentor, are the result of a careful and accurate observation of people, buildings, and objects as he strolls through the streets of Madrid. In this character sketch, Galdós emphasizes Mesonero's very inquisitive staring at all he sees: his eyes are the primary instruments by which he appreciates reality before transcribing it into the words of a sketch. Galdós's own staring at Mesonero standing staring at others in the street reemphasizes the artistic process, except that Galdós is painting Mesonero the individual whereas Mesonero is painting the Madrid people as types. At the same time, however, Galdós shows an important awareness of the inherent limitation of any personal vision of the human scene: even Mesonero Romanos's penetrating vision as an observer may be controlled by a subjective urge to search in what he sees for beauty to admire rather than defects to criticize *(Los artículos* 258). The final link in this process is the reader's response to the literary re-creation: Galdós now recalls, when looking at the figure of Mesonero in the streets, his own personal delight when reading Mesonero's two series of *Escenas matritenses,* published in the 1830s and 1840s. Reality and literature are intimately entwined, both in the compositional stage and the reading of the final literary product.

Two years later, on 8 March 1868, Galdós wrote another portrait of Mesonero Romanos for the same paper. On this occasion he deliberately used the vocabulary of typification to underline the exceptional nature of this apparent "costumbrista" sketch. The bio-pic is part of a series, suitably entitled "Gallery of Figures of Wax." The journalist's false modesty maintains the illusion of a traditionally external type sketch: he apologizes for entering the forbidden world of type painting and for using a coarse brush. His aim, however, is far from that of the type sketcher: he wants to paint the most delicate moral and literary figure of the greatest Madrid "costumbrista" (*Los artículos* 444). Even so, Galdós has to begin with the external body features, principally the face, with the intensely inquisitive eyes behind bluish glasses. But this type is an exceptional individual whose talent for re-creating in literary form the totality of contemporary Madrid life merits a classification that explodes the traditional categories of types and characters and their relation to literature: Mesonero is Madrid incarnate, but when he has to die, his great work on the capital, *Old Madrid* [*El Madrid antiguo*], will preserve his spirit: the guide to the capital is Mesonero Romanos written and printed in folio. Literature will preserve the human artistic genius that captured the complex life of the metropolis. Balzac's category of Romantic types like Hamlet and Don Quixote came from literature and were universalized. In the case of Mesonero Romanos, Galdós has here elevated a unique, historical individual into the representative, not of all capital cities, but one in particular: Madrid. Literature is the medium that ensures the immortality of this exceptional individuality, whose street behaviour might have struck the ordinary passer-by as rather odd or eccentric.

Madness and monomania are given some prominence in another, somewhat more theoretical, study on characterization that appeared in another Madrid journal, the *Review of the Intellectual Movement of Europe* [*Revista del Movimiento Intelectual de Europa*], almost four months earlier, on 11 November 1867. The elaboration of ideas is presented through a dialogue between two unnamed voices (presumably those of the novice writer and his mentor). The former begins by admitting that he is overcome by the magnitude of the task of describing the life of the inhabitants of Madrid. The problem is correctly and understandably presented here as one of size and distance: the capital is home to four hundred thousand souls, whom the mentor categorizes in the tradition of the French physiologistes and Balzac as bees. Madrid is one giant beehive. This downsizing of the human dimension also conveys the abnormal distance from the subject matter at which the would-be novel writer finds himself. The picture is not in focus: the novice can only perceive the general outline of human beings, the uniform type, the collective physiognomy of this restless animal; he can not yet penetrate the individual face (Hoar 233). In order to solve this problem, the novice, according to the mentor, should select one member of the beehive for analysis under the microscope. He will then see that the specimen is as much an individual as he himself or the mentor. The scanning of his inner character (now termed "su interior, su fisonomía moral, su carácter") is the final stage in this ever-narrowing focus that is the literary process of characterization; for this a different kind of microscope will be required, but the views will be rewarding, especially if the figure's past is included. The individual specimens can then be classified into groupings of types – "individuos, en fin, unidades, caracteres, ejemplares" (*Los artículos* 234), or in Balzac's parlance, "les *individualités* typisées" – according to the dominant passion or emotional force that drives them. One such important force is madness in its multiple forms, including monomania and eccentricity: "You would observe the most varied manifestations of madness, passion, whim; the intellectually mad ... scientific, love and business monomaniacs" ["Observaríais las variadísimas manifestaciones de la locura, de la pasión, del capricho; locos de genio ..., monomaniacos de ciencia, de galanteo, de negocios" (234).

One of the most important pieces of literary criticism that the young Galdós wrote before he began publishing novels in 1870 was his article for *La Nación* of 9 March 1868 on Charles Dickens. It is important for a number of reasons: first, it appeared the day after his very perceptive and enthusiastic, second pen-picture of Mesonero Romanos, as if he were taking stock at this time of what he had learnt about literary techniques (including characterization) from his two principal sources of inspiration. Second, it prefaced the first instalment of his translation of *The Pickwick Papers* in the same newspaper.[5] Finally, the review is important for what it says about Galdós's appreciation of Dickens right at the beginning of his career. When most of his contemporaries favoured French melodramatic novelists, he praised Dickens (and other British novelists like Laurence Sterne, Oliver Goldsmith, and William Thackeray) for his characters, which Galdós called types representing the gamut of human passions, often contradictory ones. Again, the figures are types and individual characters at the same time; French melodramatic novelists created mere types. What impressed Galdós most about Dickens's art was his ability to paint the different sides of the human character, especially when criticizing human faults with his use of ridicule and humour. This is the main appeal of *The Pickwick Papers,* in which the unforgettable Mr Pickwick towers above all the other characters, and whom Galdós describes as a kind of wise fool or "Don Simplísimo." The eponymous hero is a strange mixture of the sublime and the ridiculous: on the one hand, there is the gravity of his mission in life, the pompous intonation of his words, and the solemnity he gives to the most trivial things. On the other hand, his understanding is weak, and he cuts a ridiculous figure when driven by his overdeveloped sense of kindness and charity. He looks like a wise man – he is after all the President of a Society of Wise Men – but he is, Galdós says, "what we call a nice guy, a sad little man, although being that is not entirely incompatible with being wise" ["lo que llamamos nosotros un buen señor, un pobre hombre, si bien esto no es enteramente incompatible con la sabiduría"] (*Los artículos* 454).[6] This is a remarkable piece of literary criticism by the young Galdós (Gilman, *Galdós* 192n10; Bonet 99), for it accords with the analysis of such modern critics of Dickens's work as the novelist J.B. Priestley, who reminds us that the transformation of Mr Pickwick from "a half-witted, pompous old ass" into a "very lovable old gentleman, a new kind of hero" was the result of changes of direction as Dickens worked on the novel and improved his novelistic technique (202–3).[7] This appreciation of Mr Pickwick is also noteworthy because it represents Galdós's first identification in literature – as opposed to real life – of the type of comic eccentric/wise old man that he was later to incorporate in his own novels. The only problem is that Mr Pickwick is not a secondary character. However, according to one critic, many of Dickens's funniest eccentrics are to be found amongst the minor characters of this novel, including Mr Jingle with his staccato manner of speech (Davis 231). Alternatively, could the substantial secondary character, Sam Weller, be a more likely model for Galdós's eccentric type, if the latter is, indeed, derived from Dickens's novels? Mr Pickwick's ever-present manservant is described by Dickens as "that eccentric functionary" (10) – "este excéntrico funcionario" in Galdós's translation of the novel (1:145) – and later, by G.K. Chesterton as the poor man's intellectual, "that great wit, philosopher, and diplomatist" (256). But really, Sam Weller is far more than a minor or secondary character. Quite the opposite: he is Mr Pickwick's Sancho Panza (Wright 266), as Galdós would have readily appreciated during his painstaking work on the Spanish translation[8] Could, in fact, another of Dickens's characters have triggered Galdós's interest in this funny but wise eccentric type? In his review article, Galdós does allude to other novels by Dickens, including *The Personal History of David Copperfield*, in which the eccentric Mr Dick has a far from insignificant role despite his infrequent appearances. Galdós did possess an 1866 French translation of this novel, although there is very little evidence of marginal annotations (de la Nuez 127). In future chapters it will be argued that some of Galdós's eccentrics display some of the peculiar mannerisms and tics of Mr Dick.

It is Spanish, not foreign, literature and art to which Galdós refers in his most comprehensive examination of characterization before he published his first novel in 1870: the extensive review of two collections by the short-story writer Ventura Ruiz Aguilera entitled "Observations on the Contemporary Novel in Spain" ["Observaciones sobre la novela contemporánea en España"]. A fundamental feature of the new Spanish novel that Galdós was advocating was the realism of the characters, which would provoke in the reader a response commonly associated with the figures in the novels of Cervantes or in the paintings of Velázquez: they would be so life-like that the reader would feel that (s)he knew them from a previous acquaintance. It is important to remember that Galdós is not saying that characters should have existed in real life, but that they seem so life-like that they must have existed. Human verisimilitude is the distinguishing mark of characters in the new novel. By the same token, if the characters created by the greatest novelists and artists can resemble real people, some people seen in the street can appear like characters from fiction if judged only by their external appearance. This corollary is made all the more significant for our study when Galdós identifies some of these people as very strange or eccentric individuals ["algún individuo extremadamente raro"] (*Ensayos* 126). The viewer's reaction, on meeting them in the street, is to laugh because they appear as strange as they did when (s)he met them in their strange ["extravagantes"] books. Amongst the numerous bourgeois types inhabiting the imaginary society of Ruiz Aguilera's sketches (*Comic Proverbs* [*Proverbios cómicos*] and *Exemplary Proverbs* [*Proverbios ejemplares*]), the eccentric and the foolish are pointedly signalled out: "la jerarquía de los extravagantes, la familia de los tontos" (*Ensayos* 134). The use of "fellow" as a synonym for the Spanish "fulanos" suggests that Galdós is recalling the world of *The Pickwick Papers* that he had translated two years previously. In the stories Galdós selects for this review, it is again worthy of note that he highlights the comic and absurd characters. In fact, the most memorable figure of all is the Barón de la Esperanza in "My Husband is a Drummer" ["Mi marido es tamborilero"], who is the most comically serious character on earth, a type who belongs to the group or "family" of complete idiots (*Ensayos* 137); he is always devising strange ways to alleviate his great hunger. Another laughable eccentric is a certain González in "A Weak Dog is All Fleas" ["Perro flaco todo es pulgas"], because he never learns from his constant exploitation by others to cure his stupidity (*Ensayos* 138). Both of these strange types prove the cardinal point Galdós had made earlier in his article: that the reader immediately relates them to unknown individuals whom (s)he has seen in the street, and who do not realize their value as models for the new novel.[9] But it is Ruiz Aguilera's artistic skill that has caught the physiognomy of these types with the rapidity of photography and the beauty of painting; they are types on the border of becoming characters.

Similar words of praise are found in Galdós's prologue to the verse sketches by his good friend José Alcalá Galiano, *Social Stereoscope* [*Estereoscopio social*] (1872) (*Los prólogos* 45–51). They exposed ills, vices, or eccentricities ["extravagancias"], either inherent in human nature or generated by fashion and routine, that society preferred to ignore. Wise fools and foolish wise men abound in this verse collection, whose types, according to its author (xi), are taken from the living book of contemporary reality. Two sketches are appropriately entitled "madhouse" ["manicomio"] and "stupidhouse" ["tonticomio"], the first recalling a series of satirical articles Galdós himself had penned for *La Nación* four years previously in 1868 and entitled "Manicomio político-social." Both Ruiz Aguilera and Alcalá Galiano, then, reproduce individuals seen in the streets of contemporary Madrid as life-like literary types. At the same time, however, it is significant that Galdós should especially highlight amongst the myriad types in both writers' collections the comic eccentric and the incarcerated madman, clearly differentiating between the two categories.

GALDÓS'S JOURNALISTIC SKETCHES OF ECCENTRIC TYPES

It surely cannot be mere coincidence that the "Manicomio" series began the same day – 8 March 1868 – that Galdós wrote his second bio-pic of Mesonero Romanos and the day before he published the first instalment of his translation of *The Pickwick Papers* and his study of Charles Dickens, all for the same newspaper. It is as if Galdós's thoughts about Dickens and Mesonero Romanos and their respective treatments of types, more specifically, male eccentric ones, had now converged into a desire to see what he himself could create in literary terms. But Galdós goes further and chooses to paint truly insane types: four nameless types – the ultra-Catholic, the Don Juan, the materialist philosopher, and the spiritualist – occupying separate cells in an insane asylum pronounce soliloquies in which, unconsciously and, hence, with dramatic irony (Peñate Rivero 524), they satirize themselves, as well as raise questions about the sanity of the guardians of society who have incarcerated them. It as if Galdós were already anxious to indicate the insights of wisdom imprisoned mad people could reveal about the so-called normal society that lived beyond the walls of the madhouse.

These four short sketches would have fitted well into the collections of type studies that were once more proving popular. In fact, Galdós was a contributor to some of these collections, and again in these sketches he continued his reflections on the nature of the type character, often within the context of abnormal or eccentric behaviour. In two contributions to *Spanish Women Painted by Spanish Men* [*Las españolas pintadas por los españoles*] (1871), the obligatory female perspective provides an indirect means by which to register the strangeness of male types found in the real world, such as the miser, the hypocrite, the liar, and other more or less strange characters. This eccentricity becomes even greater in the female partner, because her personality is moulded by that of the male. This is what happens to the eponymous protoganist of "The Philosopher's Wife" ["La mujer del filósofo"]. She and other wives of eccentrics become incorrect facsimiles, photographic aberrations, caricatures of the original male (Correa Calderón 2:324). The same function, as refractive appendages to their male partners, is ascribed to the women of Galdós's second contribtuion to the same collection, "Four Women" ["Cuatro mujeres"]. More prominent in this sketch, however, is the parodying of the "costumbrista" type sketch as a genre. The narrator begins by saying, rather sententiously, that the subject has to be the representation of a real person, for he cannot deliver the latter to the coordinator of the collection, Roberto Robert. However, this literary platitude only undermines the seriousness of his intentions. Furthermore, he almost admits a lack of originality on his part when he says that even the newest member of the literary profession could assemble a composite picture of female features from what (s)he saw of women in the street. The narrator of "Cuatro mujeres" shows a lack of serious commitment to his task when he has to summon up energy to introduce the next type in the gallery, or when he delegates this responsibility to the collection's coordinator. His distrust of the whole process of type-making is evident at the end of the sketch, when he delivers the samples to the coordinator for final treatment: they are just artistic impressions to be melted down by the latter in the same solution of turquoise from which the types drawn by other contributors have emerged to form a gallery of figures. The coordinator is the one who has the right mould in which to touch up and improve the four figures. The narrator feels only relief at having the sketch completed and his duty done (360).

The same parodying of type sketches, even more strongly connected to the question of strange and eccentric behaviour, occurs in Galdós's most ambitious contribution to this mini genre: "That One" ["Aquél"] published in The Spaniards of Today [Los españoles de ogaño] (1872). Galdós now goes to the opposite extreme: he converts his male type into one who represents all other types, in an absurd deflation of the whole pretentiousness of the genre. This is clearly signalled in the title of the piece: the demonstrative pronoun is an abrupt change in the tradition of providing a professional or social class label as the title. The deliberate confusion of its meaning is only clarified at the end of the article. His universality is stressed: everybody sees him, and he is present at every social function. The disturbing possibility that he is the

optical image of all our hallucinations confers on him the status of an
eccentric or madman (Correa Calderón 2:535). He is, in fact, a most
singular social phenomenon, who defies definition. In his essential typicality, he sums up the problem raised by all types and which Galdós
had noted in his 1870 manifesto: he is seen by all, but nobody really
knows him. This jocular attack on the nineteenth-century type collections now assumes a direct focus, when he wonders aloud about the
value of philosophy, zoology, and Buffon's coming into the world, if
Mr That remains unclassifiable. The author does consider some labels
– the lazy man, a secret policeman, an impoverished count, even a
social writer like himself – but the word that best sums him up is
"eccentric." The Spanish equivalents are repeated in quick succession:
"es persona extravagante," "filósofo extravagante," "un ser extraor-
dinario," "ente singularísimo" (536–7).

A bridging text between Galdós's journalistic thoughts on, and
sketches of, the eccentric type and his novel-length treatments of the
subject is a short story published a year earlier than "Aquél": "The
Novel in the Tramcar" ["La novela en el tranvía"] (1871). The choice
of a first-person narrator-protagonist is particularly apt for this story
of a tramcar journey into the centre of Madrid: the narrator is well able
to comment on other people and incidents, but he lacks any self-analy-
sis or criticism. The mutually silent staring of the passengers is a collective exercise in Lavaterian physiognomics with all its shortcomings,
for, while some passengers seem excellent people whose disembark-
ment from the vehicle the narrator regrets, that of others is greeted
with enthusiasm because they possess a disagreeable appearance (*Cuentos* 76–7). The impression that Galdós is embarking on a narration
that questions the parameters of typification is reinforced by the news
that the protagonist is a voracious reader of very bad novels and that
the reason for this tram ride is to return some books – presumably of
the same sort – to a friend. It is the wrapping around these books – the
newspaper pages containing a "folletín," or an instalment of one of
these serialized "bad" or sentimental novels – that accelerates his
flights of imagination during the rest of the journey after he hears a
bizarre story from a friend and fellow passenger, Dionisio Cascajares,
about a butler blackmailing his aristocratic employer over her adultery.
Eamonn Rodgers (*From Enlightenment* 43) does not question the reliability of this anecdote, which he prefers to view as an example of life
feeding the narrator's fantasies, when really what it illustrates is the latter's lack of consistency. The narrator informs the reader that Cascajares, a doctor, has a great reputation for his inquisitiveness, which he
categorizes as a mania and vice (72), but he then fails to consider
whether this particular piece of gossip has any foundation or not. The

reliability of the narrator-protagonist is further weakened when, after reading the fragments of the "folletín" and dreaming up scenes of his friend's story, he believes that those fellow passengers whose physiognomies had at the beginning of the journey quickly aroused his sympathy or hatred are actors in the same story. He truly believes that, for instance, a passenger who has just boarded the tramcar is the countess's lover, especially after he overhears some of his conversation. The conspiracy of language, spoken or printed, when ingested by a vivid imagination, can lead to a mammoth distortion of the truth. The result is that the narrator-protagonist, with his "extravagancias," becomes a comic, eccentric character for the other passengers on the tramcar, particularly a red-faced Englishwoman whom he had annoyed when he let his books fall on her knees as he was dreaming. Apart from being an obvious reminder of the novelistic world of Dickens in which Galdós had immersed himself three years earlier, the matron is an exaggerated comic type herself, who goes so far as to label the narrator-protagonist a madman: "*¡Ooooh! gentleman, you are a stupid ass*" (92), and "*¡Oooh! A lunatic fellow*" (94), with a finger pointed at her head as she makes the last accusation.[10] Indeed, not only does he look like a madman but he acts like one too, when, in what he terms another "extravagancia," he jumps off the tramcar and chases after the person who he believes is the wicked butler responsible for poisoning the countess.

Yet, if reading sentimental novels led to his madness, writing this short story is the means by which he slowly recovers from his temporary breakdown and reorders the sequence of his traumatic adventure on the tramcar, which, in an inspired metaphor, he characterizes as a symbol of life (77) with all its emotional turmoils. The narrator-protagonist's attempt to make sense of his disparate adventures in logical and literary prose certainly entitles him to our sympathy (Rodgers, *From Enlightenment* 44). Yet, the story ends on an enigmatic, comic note, for he now tells us that he has transferred all his attention from the countess to the irascible English matron (104).[11] Will the narrator's imagination lead him to invent a colourful, melodramatic life story based on her appearance as an international type, or will his newly displayed powers as a literary analyst of human action and impulses enable him to probe beyond the silhouette of the surface shape? No precise answer is possible because the narrator conveniently ends the text at this point. The Dickensian Englishwoman, however, is a semi-useful point of reference: she had typecast the narrator-protagonist as a madman, a lunatic, an eccentric; that is how he had appeared to her in his actions and words. But she had no means of knowing the sequence of events that had led to his strange behaviour in the tramcar.

Nor could she know how prophetic her classification of him as a lunatic was to prove, or how he slowly recovered from his lunacy. "La novela en el tranvía" is Galdós's most subtle and complicated treatment of characterization hitherto. The problems of typecasting people on the basis of outward appearance increase when they exhibit strange or abnormal behaviour, more so when they are the narrator-protagonist of their own life story: this Galdós demonstrated again, in greater depth, in his first novel (and the second he published): *The Shadow* [*La sombra*] (1871) (*Los prólogos* 67). Galdós's fascination with eccentric types, evident from his earliest journalistic ruminations on his craft, now found increasingly concrete expression in his own creative work.

CHAPTER ONE

Initial Experiments

Like the narrator of "La novela en el tranvía," the old male protagonist of *La sombra,* Dr Anselmo, relates his own story, but now from within the fiction to an anonymous narrator, who is responsible for transmitting it to the reader. Dr Anselmo has suffered a serious mental breakdown. According to Karen Austin ("Madness" 29), his case is the most extensive and detailed analysis of mental disorders in Galdós's whole output and is "a textbook case and a psychoanalyst's dream." In fact, the real nature of Dr Anselmo's mental condition is the principal subject of interest and contention right from the opening lines of the short novel.[1] For most of his neighbours and acquaintances, Anselmo, as well as being the typical impoverished nobleman, is the utterly mad type ["un loco rematado"] (1, i) rather than the simpleton or "alma de Dios" that his name almost literally signifies ("protected by God" [Albaigés Olivart 39]). The narrator, on the other hand, is more discriminating, preferring to consider him an incomparable man, with a number of positive qualities that counteract this negative typecasting as a lunatic. He has come to this different appreciation because, in the narration of his life's story, Dr Anselmo has moments of common sense and eloquence and demonstrates a discreet use of his prodigious powers of imagination.

For his presentation of the doctor as a person akin to Maudsley's eccentric, the narrator relies on unspecified oral accounts by other people: they say that, with his "simplezas" and "extravagancias," the doctor has never been seen to do things right and in the same way that normal people do them (1, i). Judging Anselmo properly is no easy task, the narrator agrees, but paradoxically he wants the reader to accept his own account of the doctor's life because those of the oral historians are inadequate and fail to see the singular and extraordinary nature of Anselmo's spirit. Here, the narrator seems disposed to accepting, without question, the truth of Anselmo's own words about his obsession with his wife's lover. Like the oral historians he disparages, the narrator wants to believe that his character assessment is the correct one. In physical appearance, Anselmo seems to conform to the normal type of an old man. But he is really a character from fiction, the narrator says, because he is so eccentric and unlike the rest of ordinary mortals, especially when seen in his chemistry laboratory; nobody would have paid him any attention but for "his famous manias and stupidities, and his absurd conversation" ["a no ser renombrado por sus nunca vistas manías y ridiculeces, y por su disparatada conversación"] (1, ii). So Anselmo's fame comes from his typecasting by the public as an eccentric, not because he is a badly preserved, thin, sickly looking, smallish old man. He also limps for some unknown reason and has difficulties both moving his left hand and speaking, which he does in a very hoarse and cracked voice. His face is the pivotal feature of his anatomy, in the tradition of Lavaterian physiognomics, but it does not seem too different from that of any other old person.[2] Only when scrutinized as he speaks does its distinctiveness emerge. His small, sunken eyes begin to shine, and his mouth assumes an unequalled mobility, with its own system of signs that is even more expressive and varied than the words he speaks. The full secret of this unique character cannot be captured by normal language, nor even by his own exceptional eloquence. But it is the use of normal language in a specific context – the oral narration of his autobiography – that triggers the special language of his mouth signs. He talks continuously to himself, and this defines his whole character: his life is an endless monologue (1, ii), even when he practises his other tic (walking in a straight line, as if driven forward by his obsession about his wife's infidelity). Indeed, words of a literary nature dominate his life: those he reads – he is an avid bookworm – and those he is constantly pronouncing silently to himself or aloud to others. If Mesonero Romanos was Madrid personified, Anselmo is narration personified: "His manner, his temperament, his personality was all narration" ["Su hábito, su temperamento, su personalidad era la narración"] (1, ii). The narrator admires the doctor's narrative techniques: the rhetorical tricks, the erudite references, and the lively, diffuse, picturesque style. If he is ignored by the critics, it is because he has never written down anything. His literary talents are strictly oral: he creates his exceptional, unique character by virtue of this constant monologue. But this oral creation will soon constitute the major part of the novel's text: his life story and its telling, not the usual external features of body or dress, are responsible for highlighting his eccentric character. His clothes do not initially stand out from those worn by the rest of society, which "is a museum of the ridiculous in constant exhibition on the streets" ["un museo de ridiculeces en perpetua exhibición por esas calles"] (1, ii). However, his dress coat is exceptional enough, even in society's museum of the ridiculous: it catches people's attention because of its exceedingly high lapel and its patina of fifteen years of dirty, greasy wear and tear. On the other hand, the enormous size of his waistcoat or the strange shape of his tie, whose knot is often to be found at the back of his neck – common in educated people or those who talked to themselves, as a clear signal of their eccentricity – goes unnoticed. For the reader, though, all of these items are strange features of apparel, and they do serve to visually fix this small, strange old man in the mind, as if he were a "card" or "flat" character – i.e. a minor or secondary character – quickly passing through the text. He is one of those eccentric professors, who, losing even the husk of normal human identity, becomes a laughingstock for the unemployed: "perdiendo poco a poco hasta la vulgar corteza de hombres corrientes y haciéndose unos majaderos que sirven para ... hacer reír a los desocupados" (1, ii). When later he hunts for the fugitive Paris (the figure in the classical painting in his home that he has anthropomorphized as his wife's lover), he is laughed at by people in the street, even those accustomed to his eccentric ways: they "stopped as I went past, pointing me out as a curiosity" ["se paraban a mi paso, señalándome como una curiosidad"] (3, iii).

For the information on Anselmo's dress, the narrator has relied on other (unspecified) chroniclers. The revelation of their existence creates a certain difficulty for the reader, for (s)he can never be sure that the narrator is not using them (and the other oral sources) to doctor or supplement the account of his life that Anselmo relates to him and which, in section three of chapter 1, he begins to transcribe, at times verbatim, at others in summarized form. Trust in the narrator is weakened by this lack of procedural transparency, together with his initial approval of the doctor. Sources – whether they are oral or written is not specified – are again cited when the narrator presents a summary of Anselmo's life that is, at one and the same time, an explanation of the characteristics he had previously highlighted in the old man and a preview of his autobiography before he steps into the text to relate it in his own voice. At this point, Anselmo becomes less of a secondary type and more of a primary character as superficial eccentric tics give way to a more profound account of his mental illness. Again a certain confusion is generated by the narrator: at the beginning of his account, he is quite clear about what happened to Anselmo: as a wild young man, he had had mental problems, extreme mood swings, and a wild imagination. These and other symptoms of madness only became worse when, after being left a rich inheritance by his father, an Andalusian nobleman, he married Elena. But then the narrator contradicts himself: having said that nobody really knows what happened in this marriage, authoritative sources ["personas autorizadas"] (1, ii) are credited with reporting a steep deterioration in Anselmo's mental condition: he would stay away from people, overcome with great anger or submerged in a deep melancholy, like a kind of insomnia that gave him the appearance of a senseless man ["un hombre sin sentido"] (1, ii).[3] The death of his wife completes his disconnection from reality, as he becomes the absurd character with whom all are familiar: his judgment is always clouded and restless, his actions incoherent and extravagant (1, ii). Losing his fortune through lawsuits, Anselmo indulges in continuous, nocturnal reading in his attic, which only reinforces the public's view of him as mad, although a while before some had been inclined to consider him a kind of new philosopher. If a few friends continue to visit him, it is simply to enjoy his fantastic stories, full of symbols – that is his only usefulness to society. Written down and printed, these stories would probably be read with pleasure, but the anonymous narrator of *La sombra* fails to see or, worse, to indicate to us that this is precisely what he is achieving in his own manuscript with the transcribed account of Anselmo's story.

In section three of chapter 1 Anselmo finally appears on stage, speaking in his own voice to the narrator, so that it could be argued that the preceding two sections are a psychoanalytical frame that allows us to compare the mad or completely psychotic Anselmo, when he is actor of his own story (Cardona, "Introduction" xxi–xxii), with the psycho-neurotic or half-eccentric, half-sensible Anselmo, as just previewed by the narrator, and as subsequently seen when he recounts his life (Bosch 30; Turner, "Rhetoric" 7). His first live words make a terrific impact on both the narrator of *La sombra* and the reader: with an astounding lucidity of mind, Anselmo is able to diagnose his own mental condition. His great torment, he confesses, is his imagination. It is not the kind that would make him a great writer, for artistic imagination can be controlled, whilst his, like that of the typical madman, is not controllable, and inflicts visions on him. If the artist's imagination is creative in the sense that it "gives birth to organized and complete intellectual beings" ["da vida a seres intelectuales organizados y completos"] (1, iii), his brand of imagination has converted him into a freak of Nature. Though this is only a figure of speech, the reference to repugnant, deformed, and improbable body parts reminds us of

Anselmo's unusual physical appearance. Anselmo is not totally percip-
ient, however, for he fails to see that in his ability to tell stories, more
specifically to narrate the story of his own life, he uses this deformed
imagination to artistic effect and to create "organized and complete
intellectual beings," for he re-creates himself in all his baffling complexity as a mixture of truth and invention (Austin, "Don Anselmo"
46). The medium of the spoken word becomes the transforming filter
for his wild imagination. In his immediate preface to Anselmo's oral
account, the narrator perceptively acclaimed its artistic merit:

Perhaps, without the doctor himself knowing it, he had created a real fable,
drawn from the bitterest period of his life, and he, without even suspecting it,
by heaping a thousand lies and exaggerations into his story, had produced a little work of art, suitably to amuse and even to teach.
[Tal vez, sin saberlo el mismo doctor, había hecho un regular apólogo sacado
del más amargo trance de su vida y él, sin sospecharlo siquiera, al agregar a su
cuento mil mentiras y exageraciones, había producido una pequeña obra de
arte, propia para distraer y aun enseñar.] (1, iii)

Yet, the narrator is not so perceptive about his own actions: he admits
to considerable intervention in Anselmo's artistic creation but does not
seem to be aware of its implications, for, in transcribing the doctor's
mixture of truth and lies, he will rearrange them so that they appear
sensible and have some interest for the reader. The narrator does not
enlighten the reader on the extent of this re-creation or what elements
of the story it affects. The reader can only wonder which words are
Anselmo's and which are the narrator's. The narrator continues in subsequent sections to praise the "extravagante" quality of Anselmo's narration as its main attraction for him (3, i), but, by the story's end, he
has changed his tune: he now tells Anselmo that his kind of unbridled
imagination is not conducive to good art, for it leads him to create a
world of characters in his own image, "attributing to them acts as
strange, absurd, peculiar as his own" ["atribuyéndoles hechos raros,
disparatados, absurdos, como los suyos"] (3, iv).
   At this point in the novelette, medical reasons are also advanced to
explain Anselmo's mental condition, a feature Rubén Benítez ("Génesis" 354) claims that Galdós has recourse to, along with the citation of
literary analogues, whenever he presents his eccentric-mad types.
Whether this happens in all instances remains to be proved. Likewise,
whether the references to neuropathy are a sign of some solid study of
psychiatry by the young Galdós (Bosch 31) or just of name-dropping
(Casalduero 33), the point of interest here and elsewhere in Galdós's
fiction is surely the manner in which he incorporates this smattering of

psychiatric knowledge and words into the fabric of his narrative.[4] The narrator's medical diagnosis is considerably more rudimentary and less convincing than Anselmo's, although both agree in the first instance that the latter's mental illness may also be hereditary, given the fact that his father also suffered from delusions of being persecuted by a shadow; his extraordinary horror of lawsuits constituted his mania or madness (3, iv). Anselmo's diagnosis is really not his own, but that of a famous wise man, who said that it was only a physical illness, explicable in totally organic terms: an encephalic dislocation, a polarization of the axes of some brain cells that affected the optical nerves, causing them to superimpose images on external reality, contrary to normal experience. This pathological state was treatable with arsenate. The narrator's diagnosis is equally second-hand, being derived from a study on neuropathy. Even leaving aside the narrator's credibility, which is problematic throughout the entire narrative, his citation is less convincing than Anselmo's because it is taken from the prologue to the study, which fell only by accident into his hands. The extent to which the narrator understood what he happened to read so briefly is suspect, especially when he prefaced this source reference with a completely oxymoronic statement: "I don't know anything about medicine ... but there's no doubt that we are dealing here with a disease" ["Yo no entiendo de medicina ...; pero que se trata aquí de un estado morboso, no puede dudarse"] (3, iv). The diagnosis that he regurgitates is more psychological than medical, for it stresses the power of an "idée fixe" to change the body and, even more, the spirit, or so he believes, citing – unpersuasively – the example of St. Francis's famous ulcers. He sets out the order of Anselmo's progression to madness: the doctor had become jealous of the attentions paid to his wife by a young friend, Alejandro. Because the doctor thought so much about that relationship, it became an "idée fixe" that affected his sanity. Anselmo agrees, but says that his account of that sequence was inverted because, when he suffered his first hallucinations, he had forgotten their cause. Because this was the order of experiences for him, he wanted to make his account even more truthful. Anselmo the storyteller has had time to recover somewhat from his insanity and to realize the advantages of manipulating the sequence of events for artistic purposes, just as the narrator himself has taken time to assemble and mesh all the material from his different sources into his definitive text that is now that of the published novelette. This is a double object lesson on how to approach the reality of the literary text itself (Rodgers, From Enlightenment 45–8). Anselmo the madman would have been incapable of such an achievement, but Anselmo the eccentric (so close to the former, in Wynter's opinion) is more skilful and able to mix genius and madness, fact and fiction, in his stories. Yet, the full text of *La sombra* would not have been possible but for the overseeing and organizing pen of the narrator.[5] That the latter, however, is not superior to his oral-source-cum-character-of-fiction and, by inference, that he is equally eccentric when it comes to confusing imagination and truth becomes clear when he has to control an urge to return to Anselmo's house to inquire if Paris did reappear in his former place in the canvas. The power of Anselmo's storytelling is such that the belief in this supernatural event has infected the narrator's imagination, despite his dismissal of such a possibility. The closing address to the reader, mirroring that of the initial sentence of the novelette, is a tacit admission on the narrator's part that he cannot control the interpretation of Anselmo's story nor of his own. The reader has the last, unknown word: perhaps that will also be eccentric.

La sombra is a remarkable first novel for many reasons, but especially so for our study. In the character of Dr Anselmo Galdós succeeds in establishing the outlines of both the comic eccentric type and the complex mad character that will appear frequently in his later fiction. By combining both identities in one person, he necessarily provokes a questioning of the respective definitions of eccentricity and madness and their relation to accepted normal human behaviour. In sketching the type, he had recourse to major external features: Anselmo's age, physical appearance, clothes, and speech. Indeed, the latter allows Galdós to transform the doctor into a character of considerable complexity as he narrates his bizarre life story to the narrator. Because this relation and its subsequent redaction by the narrator form the text of the novel, the question of the eccentric-madman's reconnection with literature (oral and written) assumes great importance, particularly when he (and the narrator) can from time to time – consciously or unconsciously – confuse the listener/reader. Anselmo, however, is no secondary character. On the contrary, he is the principal, nay the only character of his own story.

In *Rosalía*, a full-length novel composed in 1872, a year after the publication of *La sombra* (A.E. Smith, "Introducción" 12), but never published, Galdós experiments with his eccentric-mad type in another direction: he moves away from the single figure to create a number who exhibit eccentric features – clinically certifiable madness is now not touched upon. The seventy-year-old Don Juan Crisóstomo de Gibralfaro, the father of the eponymous heroine, is something of a Mr Pickwick figure: naïve, touchy about his honour, and bumbling. He too has embarrassing nocturnal encounters with females: two women who are staying in his house with other English passengers of a ship wrecked off the nearby Cantabrian coast. These guests also make him

the butt of unconscious comic address: "*Don Shibralfar*: Ud *very*
importuno" (9). But when confronted by the more complex society of
Madrid, Juan Crisóstomo does not develop like Pickwick into a sensitive and generous individual. He fails completely to understand the
behaviour of people in the capital and longs to return to his rural
home. His life has a simple routine and his reading material is suitably
conservative: an ultra-Catholic newspaper and *The Children's Ency-
clopaedia*. He is rather similar in physique to that other country squire,
Don Quixote: he is tall, walks upright, and has dried-up skin, although
he has a strong complexion. He is also a great walker and a better
hunter (1, ii). His one obsession seems to be protecting his savings box,
which is sufficient to label him an eccentric in the narrator's view, but
his fifty-year-old misanthropic brother, Hipólito, is even more eccentric. More avaricious than Juan Crisóstomo, Hipólito spends his days
in a room in a tower counting his money. He also has more antiquated views of life (1, iv).[6]

The number of male and female eccentrics amongst the English party
is an all too obvious nod of debt to *The Pickwick Papers*, but could
these figures also be intended as contrasts for the equally eccentric host
and his brother? This certainly foreshadows a technique Galdós will
use with greater sophistication in his presentation of the secondary
eccentrics in his later novels of "La Serie Contemporánea." The ridiculous archaeologist, Míster Trifles, and Miss Sherrywine are very obviously "tipos dickensianos" in name, description, and antics (Pattison,
Benito Pérez Galdós 5). Galdós's narrator explicitly says of the latter
that she is an irascible woman – just like her compatriot in "La novela
en el tranvía" – and deserves to be immortalized by Charles Dickens
because of her eccentricities (7, i). Míster Trifles, whose Spanish form,
"Baratijas," Galdós inserted as a footnote to the folio, is, like Juan
Crisóstomo, clearly modelled on Mr Pickwick: he has the same interest in collecting antiquities of all kinds for the Archaeological Society
in Britain, of which he is an emissary. If in chapter 11 of *The Pickwick
Papers* Mr Pickwick is ridiculed for his discovery of a stone whose puz-
zling inscription turns out to be a fake, Míster Trifles arouses the ire of
Don Juan Crisóstomo when one night he starts demolishing an old
wall of his host's mansion because he thinks an Arabic tomb is underneath it. Trifles is sixty years old, myopic, and has difficulties in speaking, especially in Spanish, which he has not mastered in ten years of
travel in Spain. He is also a "bon vivant," as he shows when helping
himself to his host's best wine with Miss Sherrywine (7, i). For Linda
M. Willem ("Dickensian" 241–2), Trifles also resembles Mr Pickwick
in his enthusiasm and readiness to jump to unfounded conclusions.
Clearly, Galdós took great delight in sketching these eccentric English

types.[7] He was rather reluctant to let go of Míster Trifles, for, when the plot moves to Madrid, the archaeologist is reintroduced to provide information on the whereabouts of Horacio Reynolds (41) and later to rescue Rosalía from an attempted abduction (47).

Rosalía was the culmination of six years of experimentation by Galdós with eccentric figures: he had theorized about typification and characterization in various journalistic pieces, sketched type figures for "costumbrista" collections of portraits, and sensitively probed their more complex possibilities in the study of the erstwhile madman, now eccentric, Anselmo in *La sombra*. That seminal work for this process of learning narrative techniques, *The Pickwick Papers*, prompted Galdós in *Rosalía* to create his own little group of eccentrics orbiting around a Pickwick-type character. He was now ready to move on to a more fixed and precise form and function of this type in his first published full-length contemporary social novel, *Doña Perfecta* (1876).

CHAPTER TWO

Establishing the Eccentric Mould:
Cayetano Polentinos

In *Doña Perfecta* (1876), Cayetano Polentinos, brother-in-law of the eponymous protagonist, is an eccentric pedantic type, very much like Míster Trifles in *Rosalía,* for he shares the Englishman's passion for archaeology and manuscripts, albeit in inverse proportions: he seems more of a bibliophile than an archaeologist.[1]

For a character who seems at first a very minor character, hardly even a secondary one, Polentinos has elicited a surprising amount of critical attention, most of it negative. J.E. Varey (*Pérez Galdós* 44) dismisses him as a mere caricature whose opinions lack importance. Austin has expanded on this point: "his character is too minor and his mental balance too extraneous to the development of the action for it really to grip the reader and give him pause" ("Madness" 34). Rodgers (*From Enlightenment* 60) is more cutting, referring to him as "Doña Perfecta's absurd amateur historian brother." Montesinos calls him simple (*Galdós* 2:181) and always very crackpottish (*Galdós* 2:186). Though Germán Gullón lists him as one of his favourite minor characters ("'Sustituyendo'" 138), he eventually dismisses him as an egotist and moral coward, the typical ostrich who puts his head in the sand when there is a problem ("La obra" 160). Lee Fontanella (60) regards him as the perfect type, whose behaviour is characteristic and responses predictable. Those critics – fewer in number – who have a more favourable opinion of him include Wifredo de Ràfols ("The House" 46) and Marie-France Buard (71), who believe him to be hapless and inoffensive, respectively. Stephen Gilman (*Galdós* 384) thinks that he is well-intentioned, but lacking historical insight. It is

Rodríguez ("Génesis" 14) who, more than anyone else hitherto, has found in Cayetano Polentinos a source of great interest: his name, Rodríguez speculates, could well be a satirical echo of the literary review *El Tío Cayetano*, published between 1868 and 1875 in Santander by a group of writers linked to Pereda and proud, like Galdós's fictional character, of local glories. Second, in his obsession for old books and antiques, Cayetano Polentinos could also be a caricature of the portentous, young Marcelino Menéndez y Pelayo, another native of Santander ("Génesis" 26). Cayetano's patronymic also has appropriate archaeological or antiquarian overtones, assimilable, with the slip of one letter, to palentinos, the name for the inhabitants of the Old Castile city of Palencia, founded by the Romans.

Cayetano's name is introduced early in a casual but natural manner: as Pepe Rey makes his way on horseback to his aunt's house in Orbajosa, he asks his guide, the servant Licurgo, about his relatives. The information supplied immediately creates the impression that Cayetano is some sort of eccentric recluse or loner, like Dr Anselmo in *La Sombra*: he is always buried in his books. When, in a humorous but surprisingly thought-provoking comparison, Licurgo claims that the man's library is bigger than the town's cathedral, the family servant is not only suggesting the exaggerated extent of Cayetano's bibliophilism but also – unwittingly – linking it with what will emerge as the cornerstone of Doña Perfecta's opposition to her nephew's love for her daughter: her fanatical catholicism. Simultaneously, the surprise linkage of cathedral and library hints at the sort of highly religious and orthodox works Cayetano himself reads and writes. So, before he even sets foot on stage, Cayetano has been typecast as an eccentric bibliophile, like Don Quixote and Anselmo, always busy with books, although the precise activity is not specified yet. And this somewhat pejorative description comes from a family servant who, presumably, has no grudge to bear against the innocent old bachelor. More ridicule is unwittingly poured on Cayetano when Licurgo mentions his other passion or mania – archaeology – in humorous peasant terms: "he also pokes about in the earth looking for stones with devilish scratch marks on them which are supposed to be Moorish writing" ["y también escarba la tierra para buscar piedras llenas de unos demonches de garabatos que dicen escribieron los moros"] (2).[2] The probability that Galdós had before him, or in his mind, what he had written of Míster Trifles's activities and interests in *Rosalía* some four years earlier is reinforced by the fact that in a rejected first draft of this paragraph (f. 7½ on the back of f. 265) in the *Doña Perfecta* manuscript, Galdós had included the following sentence immediately after the phrase "Moorish writing" ["escribieron los moros"]: "A lot of English people have been here, and you should just have heard them. I could not understand them, of course, but [illegible] the fact of the matter is that they praised Don Cayetano to the skies, saying that he was the wisest man in the whole wide world. – Yes, we all well know that" ["Aquí han venido muchos ingleses y había que oírles. Yo no les entendía; pero [illegible] ello es que ponían a D. Cayetano por esas nubes, diciendo que es el hombre más sabio del mundo. – Sí, bien lo conocemos todos"]. Could Galdós have also been thinking of Mr Dick in *The Personal History of David Copperfield* as the source model for Cayetano Polentinos? As we shall see shortly, a number of similarities of personality and activities exist between these two (and between Mr Dick and other Galdosian eccentrics).

Cayetano's archaeological collecting, it should also be noted, is connected with his bibliographical activity, for he is interested in the Arabic inscriptions on the pieces of brick, that is, a written text, although his ability to decipher this foreign language is open to question. However, given that the narrator will shortly refer to the bloody battles between Christians and Moors that over the centuries have ravaged these lands, Cayetano's interest in things Arabic is curious when his library has just been colourfully identified with that summit of Christian power that is the Cathedral of Orbajosa. The difficulty in decoding words, even in contemporary Spanish, is put into sharp relief moments later when Pepe expresses his surprise to Licurgo at what he calls the horrible irony of the poetic names (e.g. the Hill of the Lilies) given to the ugly area through which the two are riding. These brief, initial references to the involvement of both Cayetano and Pepe in the decoding of language not only anticipate the friendship of the two men but also, more importantly, alert readers to the deceit of language in any text, oral or written, paper or earthenware, but especially that of the novel that they are currently reading. Consequently, Cayetano may well be more than a laughable eccentric; he may be the reader's (and Pepe's) best guide to the mysteries of Orbajosa and the surrounding area.

Cayetano's full appearance in the novel occurs briskly and suddenly at the beginning of chapter 6, in Doña Perfecta's house. The allusion to his being her brother-in-law is important, especially when his greeting of the newly arrived Pepe is most cordial, almost paternal: he goes up to Pepe with arms outstretched, declaring, "Come here, my dear Don José" ["Venga acá, señor don José de mi alma"]. The warmth of the greeting is explained: Cayetano would often go to Madrid to attend the auctions of book collections; presumably he met Pepe at such an event or visited him in Madrid, although nothing precise to that effect is stated, just as no mention is made of Cayetano's views on the social life of the capital, a subject of bitter debate that is shortly to erupt between Pepe and his aunt.

The anonymous narrator appears to have more respect for Cayetano and his occupation than Licurgo, calling him a distinguished scholar and bibliophile and then describing him as tall, thin, and middle-aged (like Don Juan Crisóstomo and, of course, Don Quixote), but showing all the ill effects of his constant studying. As a man familiar with words, Cayetano's style of speaking is correct and somewhat precious, just as his friendliness can at times be somewhat exaggerated, a judgment that would seem to qualify his effusive greeting of Pepe Rey a minute earlier and to discourage the reader from accepting at face value his statements and actions. The narrator's assessment of Cayetano's obsession with arcane scholarship is couched in words of exaggerated praise: what more could be said of this veritable prodigy of learning, whose name is never pronounced without respect in Madrid, where, if he were a permanent resident, he would have had to belong to all the academies that existed then and in the future? This paean of praise is then ominously punctured by a severe indictment from the narrator: Cayetano's passion for books and his delight in researching alone in his study is comparable to the sin of vanity in the hearts of others, for it has no ulterior purpose. In other words, this mania, or eccentricity, is a human failing. The extent of its power is detailed, with touches of humour once more: Cayetano's library is one of the richest collection of books in the whole of Spain. Moreover, the nature of his scholarly work, which often extends into the night hours, seems pedantically trivial: he is forever jotting down notes and pieces of information, or penning some monograph that the narrator describes hyperbolically as an original study, worthy of such a great brain. In *The Personal History of David Copperfield* Mr Dick is also associated with an upstairs study: David sees him leaning out of its window when he arrives at the Dover home of his great-aunt, Miss Betsey Trotwood. Surrounded by all sorts of writing materials, Mr Dick has been engaged for the past ten years in writing a *Memorial* of his life that he can never finish, because his monomania about the date of King Charles I's execution keeps interrupting his work (14). This period of English history coincides with the century of local Spanish history in which Cayetano is most interested.

Cayetano eats little and drinks even less, the only deviation – suitably termed a madcap escapade ["calaverada"] – from this spartan régime being the occasional picnic in the country area of Los Alamillos, or daily walks to his archaeological dig, the hilariously named

BigWorld [Mundogrande], where, like Míster Trifles in *Rosalía,* he experiences the pleasures of discovering Roman coins, Greek amphorae, or architectural fragments. No mention is made of the Moorish objects to which Licurgo had alluded. These solitary indulgences of his mania or passion are not incidental pieces of information, proper for an eccentric collector, but are integrated into the fabric of the novel's plot: they allow him a certain independence of movement that takes him away, at important junctures, from the oppressive interior of Doña Perfecta's house and also identify him with the surrounding countryside, presented during Pepe's ride into Orbajosa as the scene of conflicts in the past and continuing in the present with the shooting of convicts by Civil Guards.

Widow and brother-in-law have never argued and live in perfect harmony, because each respects the other's sphere of activity: Cayetano does not meddle in the affairs of the house, and Perfecta does not go into his library, except to have it swept and cleaned once a week. The harmony of this cohabitation surpasses that to be found in Paradise, with Perfecta's veneration for Cayetano's papers and books being described as truly "religious," an adjective that was substituted for "scrupulous" in the original manuscript (f. 72, crossed out on the reverse side of f. 321) and which sounds deliberately exaggerated, rounding out nicely the overall ironic tone of the sentence. Mr Dick's veneration for his distant relation and benefactress, Miss Betsey Trotwood, is also excessive, but most sincere (36). The friendship of Cayetano and Pepe, it is now revealed, revolves around books, largely historical: Pepe has brought a crate of them from Madrid. Cayetano's great pleasure at having Pepe as a house guest is genuine enough, even discounting his tendency to exaggeration, but it is not primarily, here, to do with Pepe as a human being: he regards the young engineer as a man of great talent who will be able to help him tidy up some of his library and compose an author index. As befits a "flat" character, Cayetano is given a number of verbal tags or "muletillas": "Isn't it true...?" ["¿No es verdad...?"], "only I" ["sólo yo"]. He can also play with words, the basic substance that fills the objects of his passion (books): he makes a pun on the title of the sullen and devious canon from the cathedral and Perfecta's close spiritual adviser, Don Inocencio, the Penitenciario, when he observes that the latter will be staying to pot-luck dinner ("hacer penitencia," which literally means "to do penance"). At the end of the novel, and then in writing, Cayetano will expose the tragically ironic aptness of the cleric's title.

In a subsequent meal that marks the opening round in what will be a long, drawn-out ideological battle between the scientific, liberal

Pepe and the traditionalist, Catholic Inocencio and Perfecta, Cayetano's basically timid character emerges. He is the only friend and acquaintance that Pepe has, initially, in Orbajosa; he has warmly welcomed the young man and identified a shared interest in books; but he is ineffectual in supporting Pepe against the insidious attacks of Don Inocencio when he denounces modern science. The bibliophile summons up courage on one occasion to sententiously opine that there are always two sides to every question, but thereafter remains silent, content to play around with a small piece of bread, pressing it into all sorts of mathematical shapes, and then, after his customary postprandial snooze, to offer toothpicks to the others at the dinner table. Both are trivial, rather comic, physical mannerisms of the kind that usually fixes a "flat" character or "card" in the reader's mind, but they do contrast with the gravity of his failure to support his friend, more so when Perfecta and Inocencio mischievously use the news of his latest archaeological discovery to goad Pepe into declaring that he is not interested in ruins. Pepe immediately has to correct his error and mollify the offended Cayetano by recognizing the value of archaeological studies (7). If Cayetano's work on this and his historical studies had not been so intense, he would not have then fallen asleep in the armchair and failed to overhear the first declaration of love between Pepe and Rosario or later Perfecta's simmering resentment against her nephew. More comic physical touches, such as a soft grunt and a big yawn, shielded by the palm of his hand, suitably signal Cayetano's forced arousal from his dozing at the same time as they reinforce his essentially vacuous nature and mind at this stage. His initial, torpid semi-awake reply to Perfecta shows how he can associate Pepe only with his own archaeological activities. Fully aroused, he does engage in a long conversation with his sister-in-law about Pepe, but the narrator conveniently hides behind the silence of his sources to withhold all information about it and the reader is left to wonder what Cayetano did say to his sister-in-law. Naturally timid and reticent, like Mr Dick before the imperious Miss Betsey Trotwood, he probably concurred with her increasingly negative impressions. On the evidence of his appearances up to that point in the novel, it is difficult to see Cayetano openly defending Pepe's integrity. On the other hand, the absence of any information about the conversation is a pertinent warning to the reader about the occasional inability of the narrator and even his sources, oral or written, to give a full record of events and conversations, let alone penetrate the characters' motives. The text of the novel can be, deliberately or unavoidably, unhelpful at times.

The first occasion that Cayetano finds himself alone with his young friend from Madrid occurs in chapter 10 after another tense family gathering in the drawing room, in which Jacinto, the lawyer nephew of Inocencio, has succeeded in riling Pepe. Cayetano seizes the moment to go on at length about the current state of his historical research, which he is now going to work on in his library. But this self-congratulatory spiel of boring detail is punctuated on four occasions by concerned questions to Pepe about his state of health. Cayetano is not such a static, eccentric figure after all: here, for the first time, he shows that he can forget – however briefly – his mania for history books and archaeology and observe the external appearance of others correctly enough to be worried by what he sees: he wonders whether the supper has upset Pepe. He has missed the verbal duelling between Pepe and Jacinto, so can be forgiven for not grasping the deeper reasons for the young engineer's disquiet. This is only a small beginning, of course, but it shows that Cayetano has potential for future development.

The account of his research, despite the welter of details and facts, is important in its own right, as it amplifies the role of Cayetano at another level of the novel's meaning: it reveals an absurdly exaggerated appraisal of the virtues of the town's past heroes and of the place of garlic-producing Orbajosa in Christendom. More seriously, as the local historian, Cayetano is responsible for giving a degree of official, intellectual approval to his fellow citizens' pride in their noble past, which is totally at variance with present reality (Penuel 286). His writings are a dangerous mix of conjecture or pseudo local history and real national history (Cardwell 40), capable of disorienting the reader as well as his listeners in Orbajosa.

Cayetano delivers an even more extensive monologue to Pepe in chapter 16, now in his library, and again at night, when the rest of the house is asleep. The scholar cuts a comic figure, sitting in his armchair before a desk strewn with his scholarly jottings. However, his boring catalogue of dates and names is contrasted with the preceding part of the conversation in which recent events are addressed and in which Cayetano shows a developing awareness of surrounding reality. His attitude is again one of friendliness towards Pepe: whilst seeing no wrong in Pepe's visit, with the local, liberal-minded Don Juan Tafetán, to Las Troyas, three orphaned young women who are ostracized by the rest of the town, he does try to excuse Perfecta's anger at this incident. If he has a blind spot about his sister-in-law's excellent character, he also reveals a very clear sense of reality when he generalizes about the high price of moral slips in small provincial towns (presumably, an allusion to the family history of Las Troyas) and when he notes Don Inocencio's tendency to stir up trouble beneath his virtuous exterior.

Cayetano is gradually revealing himself to be more perceptive and in tune with contemporary reality than we had given him credit for hitherto.

Cayetano is forced further out of his world of books and manuscripts by Pepe's astounding news that Rosario has been locked up. Here again, the bibliophile reveals that he has been paying some attention to the real world around him, for he recalls Rosario's sickly appearance, especially the stupor in her beautiful eyes in recent days. He deduces from these symptoms that she must be suffering an attack of the family sickness: at first he calls it "madness" ["locura"], only to immediately qualify it as "manias" ["manías"]. This revelation is a vitally new piece of information that not only surprises Pepe but puts past and future actions of Perfecta, Rosario, and Cayetano into a completely different light. The irony of the latter's claim that he is the only one in the family not to have been afflicted by the hereditary disease becomes apparent when he indulges his "mania" for local history before Pepe as his audience. This happens after he has again disconcerted the reader with his surprisingly informed remarks (not as scientifically formulated, however, as those of Anselmo in *La sombra*) about therapies for mental breakdown: the peace and quietness of total isolation is the only hygienic cure that has been successful with all the other members of his family. Equally sensible is his opinion that Pepe's proposed visit to see her will be the one most likely to upset Rosario's delicate nervous system. Again, as in *La sombra*, there is a fine irony in the fact that it is an eccentric who raises the topic of madness, thereby suggesting the proximity of the two general conditions and the possibility of moving from one to the other. Cayetano, or as the narrator calls him, "the good Polentinos" ["el buen Polentinos"] (16), continues to appear more clever and less eccentric than he had earlier: he now conveniently looks over his papers as he excuses himself from persuading Perfecta to let Pepe see Rosario. He knows full well that such an attempt would be futile, and it seems that he does not want to incur his sister-in-law's wrath. However, once he has launched himself on a recitation of recent research findings about local heroes of the past, he loses this balance, and, carried away by his love for Orbajosa, makes some absurd claims, for example, that it is the famous birthplace of Spanish genius. Other claims, even now debatable, will be proven tragically untrue at the end of the novel:

Here everything is peace, mutual respect and Christian humility. Charity is practised here as in Biblical times; here envy is unknown as are criminal passions; and if you hear talk of robbers or murderers you can rest assured that they will not be sons of this noble land.

[Aquí todo es paz, mutuo respeto, humildad cristiana. La caridad se practica aquí como en los tiempos evangélicos; aquí no se conoce la envidia; aquí no se conocen las pasiones criminales, y si oye usted hablar de ladrones y asesinos, tenga por seguro que no son hijos de esta noble tierra.] (16)

Orbajosa's idyllic atmosphere was enough reason for Cayetano to refuse the invitations of his many friends in Madrid to move to the capital. This same atmosphere had also prevented him from suffering the family curse of madness, or more properly speaking, had cured him completely of it, for in his youth, like his father and brothers (he now suddenly confesses), he tended to experience the most absurd manias, but what they were is not specified. In another ironic twist, Pepe predicts, ghoulishly but accurately, that this same atmosphere will soon make him maniacal if he stays in the town much longer.[3]

As an "off-stage" actor spending most of his time in his ivory tower of a library or at his archaeological dig, Cayetano cannot be expected to chronicle the history of events happening in Perfecta's house. His interest is manifestly the history of Orbajosa's distant past. But could he also be the secret, unnamed, local correspondent who sends daily reports to the Madrid newspapers about the clashes between the government troops who come to occupy the town and the local insurgents captained by Perfecta's henchman, the centaur-like Caballuco? This seems highly improbable at this stage in the novel, but in retrospect may not be so far-fetched. Extracts from the reports are listed without attribution or date at the beginning of chapter 21 by the narrator, whose silence is surprising given his subsequent substantial reflections on the difficulties faced by the impartial historian trying to discover the motives and thoughts of the actors of history, whether international, national, or local. This psychological brand of historiography seems beyond Cayetano's ken at the moment, as he collects and collates snippets of information from old documents or books, or assembles fragments of archaeological finds. But, the narrator too has to admit the obvious limitations of his own role as historian of the events in Orbajosa when he remarks familiarly: "One does not know what to believe, and the lack of reliable information can give rise to terrible mistakes" ["No sabe uno a qué atenerse, y la falta de datos ciertos da origen a lamentables equivocaciones"]. He concedes that a partial solution is to cite a few words by the great leaders (here Caballuco) and let the reader draw his or her own conclusions as to their motives. It as if the omniscient narrator, now posing temporarily as a historian, is abdicating total control of his study. On the other hand, this statement is a suitable justification for the type of war reporting in which Cayetano engages in this chapter, if he is, indeed, the unnamed local correspondent.

The narrator of *Doña Perfecta* and Cayetano are once more closely associated, indeed definitively so, in the penultimate chapter, whose title, with its somewhat archaic use of the possessive adjective, could well have been penned by Cayetano himself: "Finale. – From Don Cayetano Polentinos to a Friend of His in Madrid" ["Final. De don Cayetano Polentinos a un su amigo de Madrid"]. It also suggests the form of the contents: five letters all written by Cayetano.[4] This is the longest and most substantial appearance in the novel by an eccentric, secondary character who has been more conspicuous by his absence than by his presence so far. That he should be given an entire chapter to himself and at this climactic point in the narration indicates the sudden and startling importance that he is now accorded by the author, if not by the narrator, although the latter had given earlier a couple of hints about a deeper side to him. We now see for the first time evidence of what before he had only talked of doing: writing down words in coherent texts, here a series of letters to a friend living in Madrid. As narrator of this chapter, he is responsible for the whole of it: all the words are his own. Why should the anonymous narrator – suddenly and without any explanation of any kind about how he found the letters, how he ordered them as he did, or indeed, if he has cut or censored them – allow one of his characters to take over the narrative completely at such an important juncture, when previously he had permitted only the partial disruption of the narrative discourse with epistolary intertexts, as we saw, in chapter 21? After all, turning over his responsibility of informing the reader about the tragic, nocturnal death of Pepe at the hands of Caballuco in Doña Perfecta's garden at the end of chapter 31 is no small matter.[5] Cayetano has now become the de facto narrator, tying up all the loose ends of the narrative before it comes to a sudden halt in the epilogue-like final chapter.

Cayetano's letters have generally provoked negative criticism from commentators: his lack of a sense of proportion in reporting the events of Pepe's death alongside details of his historical research or praise of traditionalist Orbajosa makes him unsympathetic (Varey, *Pérez Galdós* 44; Cardona, "Introducción" 28, 54). Furthermore, his version of the murder is false (R. Gullón 413). The letters become a parodic intertext (G. Gullón, "'Sustituyendo'" 139) of the main text. Or, at an elementary level, the letters are just an epilogue, clearing up the loose ends left by the preceding narrative (Lerner 213). More positive and more complex interpretations of these letters have emerged in some recent studies: Peter Standish (230) argues for a less simplistic conception of Cayetano's character, whilst Mario Santana (298) maintains that the letters are not a mere epilogue and that the sudden change of narrative voice that they represent raises important questions about the intentionality of the work. In his reassessment of these letters – the most balanced to date – Ribbans (*"Doña Perfecta"* 218) believes that the change of narrative voice can be explained by Galdós's desire for a "necessarily ambiguous, indeterminate conclusion." This epistolary chapter is, then, far from being a conveniently quick change of technique to end the novel; rather, it contributes greatly to converting the hitherto largely eccentric, bibliophile-cum-archaeologist, stock type into a complex character, as well as underlining the ways in which Galdós perhaps intended the novel to be read. It merits some detailed analysis.

Cayetano's five letters, composed in an appropriately archaic style and sent to an unnamed and unidentified friend in Madrid, are arranged in chronological order through a calendar year: the first two are in quick succession (21 April, 22 April) and are written from Orbajosa; the third is dated almost six weeks later, 1 June, and written from Barcelona; the last two, again from Orbajosa, are composed on 12 December and 23 December, after almost six months. The total nine-month period covered would lead the reader to expect a possible variation in the tone and content of Cayetano's letters.

In the first part of the first letter, Cayetano appears in his usual role as eccentric bibliophile: his friend in Madrid is to buy at any price an old book he has long wanted and which has come onto the market. Its authenticity is to be confirmed by return mail, after he suddenly remembers that the telegraph service has been disrupted by the civil war in the Orbajosa area. The correspondent is duplicating the service that Pepe had previously rendered Cayetano, perhaps with more professional expertise, for he seems to have read Cayetano's manuscript on the famous families of Orbajosa. In praising its great merit – modestly rejected by Cayetano – the friend seems prone to unjustified hyperbole. So, Cayetano, here seen to be an effective letter-writer, has at last completed his oft-mentioned manuscript and is now going to Madrid to arrange its publication in book form. He is more than a mere note-taker; he can put words together in a coherent whole, however arcane and boring the subject.[6]

If Cayetano is clear-headed enough to see through his friend's exaggerated praise of the manuscript, he shows some discretion in mercifully avoiding lengthy references to its contents, as was his wont when talking about it with Pepe Rey. Furthermore, he can articulate the book's aim with a surprising use of the vocabulary of eccentricity and madness: he hopes that, by reading it, modern youth will come to admire the moral and cultural values of their ancestors, forsaking "this mad desire for change and the ridiculous mania for absorbing foreign ideas" ["este loco afán de mudanzas y esta ridícula manía de apropiarnos ideas extrañas"]. Readers could object, with some reason, that such an aim is equally mad, and unattainable, as Cayetano himself fears, but he is no longer just the chronicler of historical minutiae or the voice of patriotic rhetoric. Here he shows some sense of a philosophy of history, even forecasting that the new Spain will hardly recognize itself in the mirror of the past.

These gloomy remarks about mad youth and its search for vain utopias and barbarous novelties provide an appropriate preface for the news about the death of Pepe Rey in Perfecta's garden at night. Cayetano, however, prefers a more circumlocutory route, saying that he does not want to put his pen down without mentioning an event: the death of Pepe. The disclosure of the name, very formally expressed as D. José de Rey, comes at the end of a longish set of phrases relating first the dead man's character, his reputation in Madrid, his profession, and his relationship to Doña Perfecta. The impression given is that the correspondent has not heard of Pepe, which is somewhat at variance with the previous observation about the latter's reputation in the capital. Cayetano continues to be very factual in his account of events, citing the location, time, and manner of death (suicide: gunshot to the right temple). For these facts, he has to rely on the information given to him by Perfecta, for he had spent the night at Mundogrande. She is gradually recovering from the shock. *Pace* Fontanella (63), the extent of Cayetano's feelings emerges clearly through the facts of his report: it is a sad event, a disastrous death of a highly esteemed, unfortunate young man. At the same time, Cayetano reveals a new side to his character: although he seems to have accepted his sister-in-law's version of events, he still has not made up his mind about the reasons that led Pepe to "this horrible and sinful act" ["esta horrible y criminal determinación"] (The first version of this phrase was more indicative, if somewhat tautological, of Cayetano's feelings of sympathy for Pepe's fate: "disastrous catastrophe" ["funesta catástrofe"] [f. 478]). Cayetano's concern for his sister-in-law and confidence in her Christian fortitude in the face of adversity are to be expected in this open document to a distant friend. What is not expected is the sudden, confidential aside giving his own thoughts on Pepe's motives. Ribbans's advice to readers ("*Doña Perfecta*" 218) to make a sharp division between the facts Cayetano reports and his interpretation of them is sensible enough, but fails to underline the relevance of Cayetano's new-found ability to focus a great deal of attention on the reality of events that have just taken place in his own house, instead of escaping into the world of the past with its minutiae of dates and names. The antiquarian now proves that he can also be a modern amateur detective, delivering a number of potential motives for Pepe's sinister act: thwarted passion, remorse for his conduct, and a bitter, spiritual hypochondria. The speculation appears, at first sight, gratuitous, for, unlike Cayetano, the reader had been privileged at the end of chapter 31 to see some of the action in the garden, action that would not suggest Pepe killed himself. On the other hand, because the whole picture was not painted in the closing lines of that chapter, suicide cannot be ruled out entirely, and Cayetano's listing of motives cannot be dismissed out of hand either.

The rest of this first letter consists of a presentation of the conflicting opinions about Pepe. For his part, Cayetano is sincere and genuine about his own regard for Pepe: he truly liked him and thought he had excellent qualities. On the other hand, nobody in Orbajosa, from what he has heard, had a good word to say of him: he was a modern, scientific atheist, disrespectful to the church, with "extravagant ideas and opinions" ["ideas y opiniones extravagantes"]. Cayetano is at a loss to understand the discrepancy, because Pepe always concealed such heretical views from him. Here the bibliophile is trying to present the truth of his experience: "In honour of the truth, I must say that ..." ["En honor de la verdad debo decir que ..."]. As well, he is attempting to reconcile conflicting opinions about the victim, in order to help his Madrid friend understand the crime. Cayetano is both amateur detective and surrogate/alternative narrator, who summarizes previous events and analyses character behaviour. On the other hand, Cayetano still makes some absurd statements: he thinks that the reason Pepe did not reveal his atheistic beliefs was his fear of Cayetano demolishing them with the machine-gun fire of his arguments! Real gunfire in the vicinity frightens him enough to drop his pen at that moment.

In his second letter, dated the following day, Cayetano fulfills his promise at the end of the first to give his friend some news of the ongoing civil war. Again we see Cayetano in a new light: as an amateur war correspondent, so to speak, he gives a fair, general impression of what had happened, but without giving precise detail about where the clash between guerrillas and government troops took place, or what the precise number of casualties were on both sides. This reporting lends some substance to the claim that he could have penned the extracts on events in Orbajosa in chapter 21. The reporting is not totally unbiased: he recognizes that both sides fought bravely in bloody skirmishes, but he openly praises the local rebels, especially their egregious leader, Caballuco. The inclusion of a minor detail – the strange wound on the latter's arm – was made as a correction to the manuscript (f. 481) and then refined at the proof stage. Cayetano may remember this mark, but he fails to explain the reason for it or even wonder about it. For the reader, on the other hand, the detail only creates more suspense about what really happened in Doña Perfecta's garden, for the last words of chapter 31 had suggested that Caballuco had fired a shot at Pepe, as ordered to by the latter's aunt. A couple of sentences later, Cayetano has swung to the opposite extreme, impressing us with his prophetic wisdom about how the civil war will end with a nice little arrangement between the two sides, with Caballuco becoming a general in the national army. Cayetano is a perplexing mixture of the sublime and the ridiculous: he deplores the war, but believes that the local rebels cannot be blamed at all for it. He is absurdly naïve to believe that if the government were to read his forthcoming book, there would be no more civil wars. Yet, a minute before, he had shown himself to be no fool at all (Mazzara 54) when expressing some wise words of political realism: any people whose way of life, ideas, and values are threatened with change will inevitably resort to armed resistance.

At this point, Cayetano picks up the thread of what had been his major topic in the first letter: Pepe's death. Again he is a helpful and informative correspondent, covering new developments, like the refusal of the local clergy to bury the engineer in consecrated ground. This absurd decision, which he had tried – unsuccessfully – to get the bishop to overturn, still rankles with him. To his further credit, Cayetano had provided the land for Pepe's final resting place: a hole on his dig at Mundogrande. The action is not without its tragic irony, for Pepe had expressed earlier a total lack of interest in archaeology, as we have seen, but his bones are now destined to become objects of curiosity for a Cayetano of another century. Cayetano, if we are to believe his words, and there is no reason to doubt a single one of them in this passage in the letter, even carried out the interment himself: the use of the word "to package, parcel up" ["empaquetar"], in reference to covering the corpse in a shroud, inevitably recalls the package of books that Pepe had brought Cayetano from Madrid at the novel's beginning, except that Cayetano's repayment of that favour now takes on a more noble form. Moreover, the bibliophile's great act of Christian charity in seeing to the burial of Pepe is no cause for self-praise, far from it: Cayetano includes others (unnamed) in the act of interment, notes the presence of the only other person – Don Juan Tafetán – at the funeral, and mentions that a little later the three Troyas girls prayed a long time over the young man's rustic grave, an action that had greatly moved

him, despite it seeming an act of ridiculous officiousness.[7] Rather than
being Cayetano's "single convivial gesture" (Ràfols, "Lies" 479), the
arrangement of Pepe's burial elevates the eccentric bookworm into a
sublimely Christian character of genuine charity, akin somewhat to
Joseph of Arimathaea, who secured from Pilate the body of Christ after
his crucifixion and wrapped it in clean linen cloth before laying it in
his own tomb hewn out of a rock (Matthew 27: 57–60). In this regard,
J.B. Hall (98) has plausibly suggested that the Troyases's visit to Pepe's
grave is meant to recall the visit of the three women (Mary Magdalene,
Mary the Mother of Christ, and Salome) to Christ's tomb on the first
Easter Sunday.

The subject of Pepe's burial leads the letter-writer back to the cause
of his death, but without any reference to his previous letter in which,
quoting Perfecta, he had listed suicide as the sole possibility. He now
reports the rumours circulating around the town to the effect that Pepe
had been murdered by persons unknown, for Pepe had survived long
enough – an hour and a half – to reveal that fact, if not the identity of
his murderer. Here Cayetano has returned to his role as sleuth, laying
out all the facts he has gathered, keeping his sources confidential, and
without making any personal judgment at this point. Despite Perfecta's
distress every time the topic is raised, Cayetano, who feels genuinely
sorry for her, seems unable to drop it, as if it is a nagging question for
him.

His final piece of news is Rosario's nervous breakdown. Here again
he can speak with some authority, for, as we know – but probably not
the friend in Madrid – he has seen plenty of similar cases of this family disease, and Rosario's, by far the worst, reminds him of his mother's
and sister's. His enumeration of Rosario's symptoms – incoherent
speech, atrocious delirium, and deathly paleness – which he labels as
those of true madness and not just mania, would probably sound more
authoritative to his friend after his declaration that he is the only family member to have escaped this plague and to have preserved his full
sanity. The reader knows, however, that by his own admission he had
suffered bouts of mania before the good air of Orbajosa saved him
from complete madness, and that his bibliophilism and historical
scholarship are, perhaps, a lingering mania. Consequently, his autocer-
tification of sanity is not to be accepted without demur, nor is it to be
accepted as proof that he alone can see the total truth about recent
events. His contradictory personality is then illustrated in miniature in
the letter's closing paragraph: in the same breath in which he informs
his correspondent of Inocencio's sudden illness and refusal to see even
his friends, Cayetano assures his friend that the Penitenciario will soon
be translating for him the Latin epigrams the former had sent through

him to the cleric. Then he reports live, as it were, the sound of gunshots and troops leaving town as he writes. Amidst the factual reporting of serious developments, both on the collective and individual fronts familiar to the reader, Cayetano has once more allowed his passion for books to intervene, as is his wont, but at the same time, without realizing it and therefore without addressing it, he raises an important new question in the reader's mind: what is the relation of this good friend in Madrid to Inocencio and perhaps Perfecta? Hitherto nothing in Cayetano's correspondence has intimated any close connection between them.

In many ways, the third letter, dated 1 June, is the pivotal one in this mini collection. The passage of forty-one days has, as expected, produced significant new developments. Cayetano is now writing from Barcelona, after leaving the now incurable Rosario at the insane asylum at San Baudilio de Llobregat. Its friendly and spacious grounds are where he would like to be taken if he finally succumbs to the family disease. This whimsical aside, reminding us of Cayetano's fragile mental state and susceptibility to more serious illnesses, now leads into a longer digression about the historical details he is going to add to his manuscript when he corrects the proofs that he expects to be waiting for him on his return to Orbajosa. Once more, Cayetano reveals his propensity to lurch from the serious to the irrelevant and trivial. But perhaps this is more realistic, especially in personal letters, than the ordered development of a novel's story. In addition, the historical data that seems to bother him here – the correct lineage of a certain local hero of the past – is not without application to the story of his own dysfunctional family. The only problem is that Cayetano does not realize this connection, as the reader does. But that is precisely what the anonymous narrator of *Doña Perfecta* had declared the latter would do, when discussing in chapter 21 the difficulties of penetrating the motives of the heroes of history.

Then once more Cayetano the letter-writer astounds us: he shows us that he can prioritize the contents of his letters. He now reveals the principal reason for this letter, and he goes directly and clearly to the point, pulling no punches, leaving no doubt that he is being deadly serious with his friend in Madrid. The main reason for this letter is nothing less than to issue a warning to his friend. Curiously, the letter has no traditional epistolary greeting whatsoever, which is in stark contrast to the effusive headings of his previous two letters: "Dear friend" ["Querido amigo"] and "My unforgettable friend" ["Mi inolvidable amigo"], respectively. Having jolted both the friend and the reader out of their complacency with this thunderbolt, Cayetano, showing considerable epistolary tact, immediately seems to move to another subject without elucidating what his warning is. He prefers to contextualize it first. In a very precise and factual style, he reports that he has heard many people in Barcelona talking about Pepe Rey's death, and their version is the correct one: "telling it as it really happened" ["refiriéndola tal como sucedió"]. For the readers of the novel and letters this is a perplexing statement, for in Cayetano's last two letters two different versions (those of Perfecta and certain townsfolk respectively) had been presented without prejudice by the impartial reporter, Cayetano. He now reminds the friend that he had revealed to him the correct version (i.e. the third one) when they had met in Madrid. Lack of precision about its content, as well as the time and place of their meeting, creates suspense for the readers, but is perfectly acceptable between the two correspondents. Furthermore, Cayetano is imprecise about when he learnt of this accurate account, just saying that it was sometime after the event, presumably, some time after 22 April, but certainly well before 1 June. However, the true version, or what Cayetano is convinced is the true version, of Pepe's death, really takes second place to his anger with his friend (the only person to whom he had told it) for having repeated all the details to others in Barcelona. These feelings are masked by a choice of polite words and sentence structure, as well as by an opportune insertion of the normal epistolary salutation that he had omitted at the beginning of the letter: "my dear friend" ["mi querido amigo"]. His indignation is expressed as surprise, his accusation as a hypothesis ("in case you have inadvertently talked about this to someone" [my translation] ["por si inadvertidamente ha hablado de esto con alguien"]), and his warning as a reminder that the account is a family secret. A final declaration that these words are sufficient to such a prudent and discreet person as his friend forms the climax of this near explicit rebuke, with its mixture of praise and understatement.[8] The abrupt end of the letter, when he briefly exults over Caballuco's defeat of the government troops' commander – a report he himself could not have written for the Barcelona newspaper in which he reads the notice, although it is very similar to those he had included in letters one and two and those unattributed reports that had been sent to Madrid newspapers in chapter 21 – also strengthens the tartness of the criticism. Cayetano must be pleased with himself for having successfully constructed and executed a reprimand to his friend for breaking confidentiality: his friend has been put firmly in his place. Unfortunately, however, Cayetano does not realize that such an admonishment is totally useless, given that the true account of Pepe's murder is now common knowledge in Barcelona and Madrid, if not in Orbajosa. Furthermore, why should Cayetano be concerned that the account remain a family secret? In view of his military success, Caballuco is not likely to be brought to trial in Orbajosa or anywhere else. If it were a family secret in the first place, why did Cayetano himself reveal it by telling it to this friend in Madrid? Was it because his friend was the unspecified publisher of his book? If so, then, their relationship will, probably, never be the same again. Perhaps this is why, at the end of the novel, his book remains unpublished, just as in *The Personal History of David Copperfield,* Mr Dick's *Memorial* is never completed. The final irony in this interplay of rival narratorial authorities is that the friend in Madrid does not heed the second warning from his friend in Orbajosa: he has handed Cayetano's letters over to the narrator, who may well be this unnamed friend himself. If that identification is possible, then these letters of Cayetano show a narrator that cannot be totally trusted when it comes to secrets and even to other people's letters, let alone telling the reader the full truth.

At another level, has time now changed Cayetano's feelings for Pepe Rey, feelings that had been of genuine distress and true Christian charity in the previous letter, written just over five weeks earlier? Certainly, he is more occupied and preoccupied with his friend's breach of confidentiality than with the significance of the sequence of events that fateful night in Perfecta's garden. If the reasons for this inversion of values are really only petty and personal – and there is no suggestion of other more sinister motives – then Cayetano offers another example of how human feelings can affect any text that attempts to transmit factual information.

For readers of the novel, the account of the details of the murder takes precedence over Cayetano's display of controlled anger simply because it offers a new version of Pepe's death that accords better than the first two, and in more precise detail, with what the readers had only half seen at the end of chapter 31: first, Pepe entered the garden, then he fired at Caballuco when he saw him ready to attack with a knife. Caballuco then fired a shot at Pepe from his own revolver; this shot killed Pepe instantly. The report is brief, precise, and speedy. But it lacks any reflection whatsoever on Cayetano's part about why those events happened the way they did and in the order they did. Cayetano cannot bother with these questions, because he is more preoccupied with his friend's betrayal of a secret. This would reasonably explain his failure to correct the unexplained fact of Caballuco's wounded arm in his previous letter. But, at the same time, he fails to relate Caballuco's killing of Pepe with his recent defeat of the government troops. His mind conveniently compartmentalizes and separates facts that are inherently connected and can be analysed together. Inevitably and unwittingly, however, he invites his letter reader and the novel's readers to raise those questions in their own minds, as if Galdós were using him as a surrogate teacher giving a lesson to all his readers on how to read the new contemporary Spanish novel that he had envisaged six years earlier in his "Observaciones" manifesto. The eccentric bibliophile, Cayetano, is like the eccentric storyteller, Dr Anselmo, in *La sombra:* he believes that he is master of his own text – in Cayetano's case, the five letters, in Anselmo's, his oral story to the narrator. Cayetano's confidence in his own handwritten words and in those printed in the local newspaper reporting Caballuco's recent military success seems to brook no self-doubt. What is crucial in this epistolary lesson on reading methodologies is the failure of the correspondent (here Cayetano) to realize the wider implications of his narrative: that he is challenging the reader to re-construct the reality that lies behind the jigsaw of the text. The final question then becomes: if the reader realizes that he or she cannot rely entirely on the transparency of the narrator, can (s)he really trust her or his own abilities to interpret correctly the text?

Cayetano's last two letters, written over six months later, contain no more allusions to Pepe Rey's murder.[9] Instead, Cayetano reports on the respective deterioration in the mental state and physical condition of both Inocencio (letter 4) and Perfecta (letter 5), but without for one moment thinking that there could be a connection between these two alarming developments or any involvement with the murder of Pepe Rey. Or, if he has seen the link, he has carefully refrained from voicing it to his Madrid friend, probably for fear that he might spread abroad these private thoughts, as he had earlier divulged the family's secret about Pepe's death.

The revelation in the final letter that this friend in Madrid has a law practice is another example of Cayetano's masterful control of his texts. It is surprising that he has not made any reference to this fact in his earlier letters, even in a nonchalant, passing sort of way. If he mentions it here, it is for a precise reason: to recommend Jacinto as an apprentice lawyer. At least, that is the stated reason, but the reader can easily surmise that this move by Cayetano has deeper intentions: to buy the silence of María Remedios, who knows exactly what happened in Perfecta's garden that fateful night and could very easily incriminate Perfecta and ruin the family's reputation, or, alternatively, blackmail the family. Furthermore, Cayetano could well be trying to mend bridges with his Madrid friend after his temper tantrum in letter three. Cayetano is really a much more astute and wily letter-writer than Ribbans ("*Doña Perfecta*" 220) and others allow. The fact that he does not cite his various sources for the details of the murder, when the opposite is true in the rambling conversations on his own historical detective work, shows that he knows what to conceal, to whom, and when. Likewise, he knows very well what to exaggerate in the character of Jacinto and his mother: the driving ambition of both to succeed, and very possibly in politics, with Jacinto a good bet to become a conservative minister. There is an intimation that this friend in Madrid is a right-wing traditionalist, a fact that is compatible with the interest he shares with Cayetano in old books and classical literature.

The bibliophile's confidence in making this recommendation also raises interesting questions that he is hardly likely to voice openly. Is he taking for granted that his conservative friend in Madrid would not dare refuse him this favour, after his earlier revelation of the secret of the Polentinos family, whose matriarch, Cayetano slyly inserts, sends the friend her best wishes? Her daily church attendance and funding of religious events in Orbajosa are, it is also reported, a great cause of relief at a time when Spanish patriotism is in decline. Are these remarks that Cayetano assume will go down well with his letter-reader in Madrid? Cayetano's letters are, indeed, a successful cover-up of a family and political murder (Zahareas 320), but they also reveal a far more complex side to his character than could have been imagined from his previous appearances in the novel. Cayetano uses language to supreme effect, knowing when it can be a smokescreen (all the historical and book talk), a very effective instrument of pressure (his warning to his friend), or a means of expressing deep emotion (his feelings on the burial of Pepe Rey). Consequently, Cayetano can be said to be in control of his own text, that is, of what he writes in these letters. The interpretation of its meaning, of course, is the responsibility of others. But is Cayetano fully in charge of his own text? In his fifth letter, there is an interestingly perceptive comment about María Remedios's excessive maternal love for Jacinto: "Maternal love in her takes the rather colourful form of worldly ambition" ["El amor materno toma en ella la forma algo extravagante de la ambición mundana"]. Whilst echoing those comments on the same topic and person made by the narrator himself in chapter 26 ("Sacred and noble as it is, maternal feeling is the only sentiment which is allowed exaggeration" ["El sentimiento materno es el único que, por lo muy santo y noble, admite la exageración"], Cayetano's sentence is far more critical. Has the narrator of the novel, who, after all, has been given Cayetano's letters by the friend in Madrid and included them in his full text, deliberately left intact this more focused comment by his replacement narrator?

The last paragraph of Cayetano's fifth letter – his last words in the novel – seem to sum up in miniature his contradictory character as revealed in this chapter. On the surface, it seems that Cayetano is up to his old, eccentric tricks: he has just finished correcting the proofs of his book and they will be sent off the following day, but not before he has added, presumably overnight, as per his usual custom, two more pages on a new local hero he has discovered – it is to be assumed that he has already added the six additional pages he had envisaged in letter three written in Barcelona.[10] Consonant with other examples of vagueness and imprecision in these five letters is his failure to say if he is sending the proofs to Madrid (presumably) and to his friend (possibly, but less certainly). At a deeper level, however, as in other sections of these letters, the apparently boring historical trivia do offer an ironic reverberation of the main outline of Pepe Rey's story. Cayetano's newly discovered local hero, Bernardo Amador de Soto, was stableboy to the Duke of Osuna in the seventeenth century. Pepe Rey had made his entry into the novel and Orbajosa riding a horse, like Christ entering Jerusalem on a donkey; and in this town, like Christ in Jerusalem, he will finally meet his death. His murderer will be Ramos – Christ had entered Jerusalem on Palm Sunday, "Domingo de Ramos" in Spanish – so the parallels with Christ's crucifixion and burial that Cayetano had unwittingly forged in his second letter are echoed here. Furthermore, Ramos is more often called Caballuco ("Horsey") in the novel, very appropriately so, because of his centaur-like appearance. This particular horse has indeed killed the stableboy walking in front of it in Perfecta's garden. Cayetano's concluding comment about this newly discovered local hero is extremely curious: he has evidence that proves the stableboy took no part at all in the "plot" ["complot"] against Venice, an allusion to the Duke of Osuna's manoeuvres as viceroy in Naples. Why would Cayetano make an issue of such a trivial point? Why would he allude to this particular incident in the Duke of Osuna's career? Well, there has been a plot in Orbajosa to get rid of Pepe Rey – a plot hatched primarily by María Remedios, but with the connivance, to varying degrees, of Perfecta and Inocencio, and executed by Caballuco. On the other hand, Pepe Rey has had no part whatsoever in what the people of Orbajosa would term a "plot" by the central government in Madrid to destroy their way of life and customs. That such complicated connections and resonances between the two contexts – the dead past and the dead present – can be derived from this historical chit-chat is a tribute to Cayetano's intelligence, moral purpose, and subtlety as a writer, since the conclusion that he cannot utter is that the man he buried in his excavation site nearly nine months before is a new "local" hero worthy to be included in a book similar to his soon-to-be published study.

But the novel does not end with Cayetano's letters. The omniscient, anonymous narrator feels honour-bound to discharge that function, but he does so in a way that immediately provokes thought. The last chapter is really a parody of a chapter, for it consists of barely two sentences and is the only one in the novel not to have a title. It fully deserves the disparaging label Fontanella attaches to it (64): chapterette. Its terseness suggests that it is not so much an epilogue as an afterthought. The tone is familiar, unliterary, and hasty: "Now it is finished. For the time being, there is no more we can say about people who appear to be good but are not" ["Esto se acabó. Es cuanto por ahora podemos decir de las personas que parecen buenas y no lo son"]. To what does "esto" refer? Certainly not to the novel or the plot. About whom is the narrator thinking when he refers to the good people: Perfecta, Inocencio, Pepe, even Cayetano? The chapterette also has the ring about it of a peeved retort to the preceding collection of letters by Cayetano. Fontanella (64) believes that its purpose is to rubbish Cayetano as a historiographer; Santana (301) proposes that the narrator's little moral could also apply to good and bad writing. But its ill-humoured terseness could also be a tacit admission by the narrator of the novel that his replacement narrator for the penultimate chapter has taught him a lesson or two in narration: that Cayetano's rambling, diffuse mixture of fact, conjectures, strong feelings, as well as pregnant silences, is a masterful achievement; that Cayetano is far more clever, subtle, and capable of insights than he had given him credit for in his main narrative. In other words, that the eccentric oldish researcher is as good a, if not a better, creator of mystifying language as he is. And the anonymous narrator has no other choice but to consider Cayetano as an equal who straddles both the real world and that of the fictional text, because he himself had elevated the bibliophile to that equal status by temporarily ceding the control of the text to him. If the narrator is also including himself in the group of people who appear good but are really not, then he is showing that he has learnt the lesson of indirect suggestion and implication that suffuses all of Cayetano's letters, but especially that seemingly irrelevant last paragraph of letter five. The grumpy, off-handed brevity of chapter 33 also constitutes an admission that, whilst, as overall narrator, he could so easily have destroyed Cayetano's good work by making changes and alterations in it before sending the manuscript to the printers, he has chosen not to do so, and, thus, quickly signs off the text, in this vague, Cayetanoesque way.

Galdós has transformed Cayetano, through his own words, into a complex and baffling character, forcing the reader to revise her or his previous judgment of a person who had merely seemed a funny background figure given to out-of-the-ordinary pastimes. This penultimate chapter would have been a mild diversion with which to round off the novel had the climactic event of the preceding narrative – Pepe's murder in his aunt's garden – already been presented with full clarity. Cayetano's rambling letters could then have been enjoyed as a collection of whimsical afterthoughts by a crackpot. But because the details of Pepe's murder were not presented with full clarity in chapter 31, Cayetano's letters become vitally important for the reader's better understanding of the events. Although that is achieved, almost by accident and in a perfunctory sort of way, Cayetano's letters raise more questions than they answer and sow more confusion than they clear up. Furthermore, they raise important methodological questions about how the preceding novel and any new novel of the 1870s that Galdós wanted to write are to be read and interpreted by the reader, as well as about the narrator's part and purpose in this process. No greater role could have been found for such an innocuous, seemingly irrelevant type. Galdós has, in Cayetano's final and dramatic takeover of the narrative, hit on a perfect formula with which to upgrade a comic type who flits briefly in and out of a novel. He has finally settled on the basic outline of his new template: the type with a number of external peculiarities can easily be amplified into a secondary character of more depth, and, pertinently, play a pivotal role in the final elaboration of the novel's meaning. The details of the components will vary in subsequent novels, but the main frame has been established. One detail, however, is still missing: a love interest. In *Doña Perfecta,* this element is transferred to another character acting as a sort of mirror to Cayetano, as the English matron in "La novela en el tranvía" and the English characters in *Rosalía* had done.

DON JUAN TAFETÁN

Cayetano had associated himself with Don Juan Tafetán in letter two, when he had reported that he was the only other person at Pepe Rey's burial. Tafetán had been the latter's only other male friend amongst the people of Orbajosa. Pepe and Tafetán had first met in chapter 12 in the town's casino. His typecasting as a dirty old man ["viejo verde"] is suggested by his first words to Pepe ("you old rogue!" ["picarón!"]) when he assumes that Pepe is making faces at the three Troyas girls, who live in a house opposite. Like Cayetano, he shows Pepe cordial friendship and true admiration. The omniscient narrator approves of Tafetán, calling him "a likeable man" ["un sujeto amabilísimo"], a phrase altered at the proof-correction stage from the original "a very nice little old man" ["un vejete amabilísimo"] in f. 185 of the manuscript. Tafetán is in the habit of improving his aging appearance by putting rouge on his face, dying his moustache black, and combing his hair carefully to hide his bald spot. Lively eyes and an unprepossessing build complete a portrait that is quite the reverse of such models of classical Greek male beauty as Antinoüs. If Tafetán is given a memorable portrait, typical for a "flat" or "card" character, it is because physical appearances define his obsession: an interest in young girls, like the three Troyas sisters. He is a faded Don Juan.[11] Tafetán complements Cayetano in another way: like Anselmo in *La sombra,* he has a gift for telling funny, but not slanderous, stories that everybody likes. If Cayetano's erudite disquisitions can be soporific for Pepe, Tafetán's frequently humorous and friendly style gives him many moments of pleasure. Tafetán also tends to laugh a lot, causing grotesque wrinkles to appear over his entire face. The narrator, an endless source for tidbits of information about Pepe's second eccentric friend in Orbajosa, who only spends a very limited time on stage, informs us that "poor Tafetán" is not financially well off: having once been a civil servant at the provincial level, he now has to supplement his current job in the welfare office by playing the clarinet on important religious occasions and in the local theatre, when a touring company comes to town. If Cayetano is associated with the world of books and archaeology, Tafetán is clearly identified with that of the theatre, especially when he is described as having been a formidable Don Juan in his youth. Recounting his past conquests makes the listeners die with laughter, because he was such an original example of this type. In this respect, his patronymic, which means "taffeta" or a thin, silk fibre that is used to make women's dresses, is an apt choice. For Thomas R. Franz ("*Doña Perfecta*" 127–8), the description of his physical appearance recalls portraits of Rossini, who was also a Don Juan in his youth and whose father had to eke out a living by playing in orchestras and bands. Such a literary resonance would reinforce Tafetán's connections with the theatre. What is striking about Tafetán, though, is not so much his ridiculous acting of the Don Juan part as his genuine pity for the impoverished condition of the three Troyas girls, as well as his enjoyment of their natural liveliness and impish humour. The healthiness of such an attitude is underlined by Pepe's similar reaction to the girls when Tafetán takes him to their apartment. Tafetán and Las Troyas form an oasis of natural affection and friendship in the middle of the emotional desert that is Orbajosa. By frequenting the company of these socially ostracized individuals, Pepe inevitably invites censure from his aunt and others, who now oppose his romance with Rosario with even greater force. In turn, Pepe realizes as a result of this visit that the only way he can enjoy a normal, affectionate relationship with Rosario is by abducting her from her mother's house, as he vainly tries to do in chapter 31. Given even less space than Cayetano, Tafetán is still important enough, for two reasons: he serves to point a way forward to Pepe at a critical juncture in the plot, and, more significantly, his surface persona as a decadent ladies' man conceals more admirable human feelings. His fantasies, like Cayetano's obsession with antiquities of stone and print, can give way to more noble concerns.[12]

CHAPTER THREE

Loyal Go-Between:
José Mundideo

Since *Gloria* (1877) was published a year after *Doña Perfecta* and had obvious roots in the first section of the unpublished *Rosalía*, it is perhaps not surprising that its eccentric type, José Mundideo (more frequently called *Caifás*), should have some initial affinities with Míster Trifles and Cayetano Polentinos. As the sexton of the abbey in Ficóbriga, an imaginary town on the Cantabrian coast, he dabbles with art objects – church statues and ornaments – which he is constantly repairing. But *Caifás* represents a further advance in the development of the role of the eccentric type, now a secondary character, in Galdós's contemporary social novels. Putting aside for the most part any involvement with the transmission of a fictional text (although he is presented as intuitively foreseeing the novel's storyline), Galdós now extends the eccentric's interest in the opposite sex from within a more traditional, albeit still dysfunctional, family environment. In addition, Galdós integrates the sexton into the plot through a more consistent interaction with the principal characters (intermittent in *Rosalía* and *Doña Perfecta*), for whom he will serve not only as an important plot intermediary but also as a spiritual mirror.

Caifás makes his first appearance early in the novel, when he is seen by the eponymous heroine in the belfry of the abbey with his three young children, waiting to announce the arrival of her uncle, the bishop, with a peal of bells (1, 3).[1] This early introduction, like that of Cayetano in *Doña Perfecta*, is not without significance: the humanity of this family seems to contrast with the grotesque features of the tower (and, by extension, of the institution of the Catholic Church itself) that, dominating the Ficóbriga skyline, pries oppressively into the houses and lives of the parishioners living below. The significance of the fact that it is Gloria who is responsible for introducing this family into the novel is signalled slightly in part I, chapter 7, when it is reported that the sexton had performed the task of burying the two infant brothers that Gloria had cared for after their mother's own premature death. In part I, chapter 15, the closeness of this relationship emerges much more fully when Gloria visits the family and they appear on stage in their own right.

The spiritual ennobling of *Caifás* and his family is immediately conveyed in the description of the small, chaotic structure, with a tri-level roof, that they inhabit behind the sacristy: currently serving four functions for the family (warehouse, carpentry store, workshop, and bedroom), it was built on the former site of the abbot's palace. The narrator has much laughter at the expense of the outward manifestations of religion that appear in a big jumble in this cramped space: for example, a statue of St Peter, which has no hands, and therefore no keys, pokes its nimbus-circled, bald pate above a pile of broken pieces of wood, whilst the painted backdrops for a theatre production or a Holy Week parade serve as the headboard for the children's bed. This is the absurd artistic backdrop against which *Caifás*'s obsession in the novel is noted: his extreme devotion to his benefactress, Gloria. Unable to offer his lady a better seat than the base of a statue of the Virgin Mary, he exclaims that God would not be angered if she were placed on an altar (I, 15). This obsession is given an appropriate plastic comparison when the sexton's pose before her is described as the exact image – but for the clothes – of the greatest paintings that have depicted a worldly figure ["una figura mundana"] praying on its knees to the Virgin. In the manuscript the adjective used was "grotesque" (f. 1:132), which obviously anticipated the detailed portrait of the sexton that followed. With the eyes of a mole, an angular face, and bow legs, he makes a more grotesque sight than Cayetano and Don Juan Tafetán and forms a complete contrast to the seductive beauty of Gloria. On the other hand, given the young age of his children, he is probably not as old as the other eccentrics studied so far, although his age is not given. The adjective "worldly" used in the art reference is also pertinent to *Caifás*'s proper name, Mundideo, which is now given for the first time. The unusual surname could be literally parsed as a compound Latin form meaning "God of the World." Whether this has some symbolic meaning for the novel, as is common with the names of Dickens's eccentrics, will only be determined later, as will the relevance of the nickname – another frequent characteristic bestowed on types or "flat" characters – he is given by the townsfolk of Ficóbriga. The reason for his nickname is not specified, yet the nomenclature lends an air of age and authority to the sexton, when, with his physical appearance, he could easily have been classified as the town idiot rather than an eccentric. The aesthetic contrast between the beauty and the beast also reflects a more essential difference between their attitudes to life's misfortunes: *Caifás* is always given to bemoaning his lot in melodramatic terms that will, by the novel's end, sound tragically ironic: "I cannot think how anyone can care to live; a pretty business life is! It is true that we were not given our choice" ["No sé cómo hay quien quiera vivir. ¡Bonito oficio es este de la vida!...Verdad es que como no nos lo dieron a escoger"] (I, 15). He is prone to such maudlin comments, in spite of the generous cash presents he receives every week from Gloria. She, on the other hand, points out that there are people worse off. *Caifás*'s self-pity now turns to tearful self-abasement as he recognizes the justness of his forthcoming dismissal from his sexton's job by the hard-hearted priest, Don Silvestre, for his debts to the money-lender, Juan Amarillo. His tendency to assemble phrases in rhetorical groups of three – more a stylistic than a verbal tag – is another quick characterological device for establishing types and "flat" characters in the reader's mind. But here it also suggests that the sexton's self-pity, like his praise of the heavenly Gloria a little later, is over-done. The effect is hilarious when he repeats the town's epithets that define him as the local idiot, fool, or eccentric: "I am nothing more than stupid, ugly Caifás – Caifás the idiot, as they call me – Caifás the unfortunate, as I call myself" ["Yo no soy más que *Caifás* el estúpido, *Caifás* el feo, *Caifás* el idiota, como me llaman en Ficóbriga, y *Caifás* el desgraciado, como me llamo yo"] (I, 15).

By always presenting José Mundideo in the company of his children, Galdós has been able to emphasize the family as a unit, but never once has he alluded to its one permanent absentee: the mother, who, we are now told in part I, chapter 15, is a domineering woman and steals money from her husband for drinking sessions with her fellow miners. *Caifás*'s marital problems are much more complexly drawn than those of Anselmo in *La sombra*: essentially a single parent, he drowns his sorrows in drink and self-pity. This development in the eccentric type's relationship with women will be re-used by Galdós. *Caifás*'s present wish to drown himself in the stormy sea outside, whilst being another example of his extreme self-pity, is also an ironic anticipation of the important events that will set the course of the plot: the Jew, Daniel Morton, nearly drowns when his ship breaks up in the storm, and his subsequent convalescence in Gloria's house will lead to the impossible romance between the couple that will end in Gloria's own death. So, an idiot/eccentric secondary character is given an important role in forecasting the novel's future direction.

More particularly, *Caifás* had also dreamed the previous night about the relationship between the two lovers and its origin in a storm. His gift of prophecy extends to the details of the lover's face (as beautiful as Christ's) and the dénouement: his Divine Shepherdess will be taken far, far away by her lover, that is, she will die, which is what Gloria had first assumed when José had announced that his dream was a sad one. *Caifás*, in short, gives an intuitive outline of the rest of the novel's story. Like Cayetano, he is as much a creator of the text – albeit on a very minor scale – as the narrator. His forecast of the plot is a mini-work of art far superior to the bits of religious objects that clutter the room; his assurance of its details is likened to that of "a narrator fully possessed by his subject" ["de un artista muy poseído de su asunto"] (I, 15).

When, nine chapters later, José finds himself out of work, he becomes the object of the competing charity of Gloria and Morton and the means by which the two lovers come together: the former is able to persuade her father to lodge him in an old shack out in the country and Morton redeems all the possessions he has had to pawn. For Gloria, *Caifás* is, despite his reputation for being dissolute and evil, a kind soul ["alma de Dios"] whom she has to help (I, 24), although she thinks that he has gone mad when, telling her the news of his recovered possessions, he jumps around and laughs for joy at his good fortune (I, 25). Mundideo is beside himself with joy, believing it is all a miracle. His elevation of Morton to a divine status (the Divine Redeemer) on a par with Gloria's (the Divine Shepherdess) is underlined by his kneeling and kissing Morton's feet on being handed the money from the pawnbroker, an action that the ex-sexton himself recognizes afterwards as perhaps mad. Certainly, the sacristan's use of Biblical language – he had sung psalms in the abbey choir – is misplaced in this context of monetary favours. The effect of such exalted religious language is, paradoxically, to undermine the future lovers' status as paragons of virtue. *Caifás*'s intrinsic emotionalism is now being exploited by each one to find out information about the other and to enhance their mutual standing. In the words of Pattison ("The Manuscript" 58), *Caifás* is the lovers' favourite charity, their altruism now tinged with self-interest. Both patronizingly advise him to be of good behaviour as they embrace him on departing, yet, ironically, they should have heeded their own advice, for, at the end of part I, their lovemaking is discovered by Gloria's father. The cause of the lovers' downfall is precisely Morton's generous impulse to return to Ficóbriga to defend *Caifás* against charges of robbery.

Part II opens with more scandalous news: Morton is revealed as a Jew and is, accordingly, shunned by the townspeople, including *Caifás*.

Now the appropriateness of the former sexton's nickname becomes clear: he may not be as condemnatory as the high priest at Christ's trial before the crucifixion, but, as the title of part II, chapter 10 ("Hospitalidad a medias") intimates, *Caifás* is torn between gratitude to his former benefactor and guilt in helping the person responsible for bringing so much misery to the Lantigua family. *Caifás* does lodge him for the night in his new hovel in the cemetery, for he is now the town's gravedigger, a job that links him to Cayetano and Tafetán in *Doña Perfecta*. Just as he had prophesied Morton's arrival in Ficóbriga to Gloria in part I, in part II he now indicates to Morton, when taking him through the cemetery, the pantheon being constructed for the Lantigua family, which is where Gloria will be laid to rest at the end, or as the gravedigger says in general terms: "This is the great bed where we must all lie down to rest" ["Esta es la alcoba grande donde todos hemos de dormir"] (II, 10). In the ensuing conversation in the shack, it is Morton who initially behaves more like the high priest of the New Testament when he shakes José and calls him an idiot for falsely judging his behaviour. José's dilemma is very real, as his tears and emotional language make clear; unlike any other character in the town, he had genuinely idolized Morton and still does, passing along information about Gloria's condition. But his conscience is now confronted with a problem: his gratitude towards his benefactor has to be weighed against the harm Morton has done, as well as against his Jewish faith. In his verbalization of this difficult inner conflict, *Caifás* could be said to be acting as the narrator's mouthpiece at this important juncture in the novel. He has spent sleepless nights trying to sort out the mystery of Morton's ambiguous character, and the mental anguish makes him look twice as horrible as he normally looks. The genuineness of his bewilderment prompts a poetic turn of phrase when he describes Morton as a mixture of the good and the bad: he is the morning dew and the fire of the sky in one (II, 10).

The narrator contextualizes *Caifás*'s meditations within the parameters of religious problems that other, more learned characters would have resolved one way or the other. But *Caifás*, unlike his New Testament namesake, can only find confusion, chaos, and bewilderment: "that lurid half light of the human soul when its faith is deeply rooted but reason, like an incubus called up by some magic art, comes wantoning in, to disturb and upset everything" ["el claroscuro incierto del alma humana cuando la fe vive arraigada en ella, y la razón, como diablillo inquieto evocado por la magia, entra haciendo cabriolas, enredando y hurgando aquí y allí"] (II, 10). The final playful image notwithstanding, *Caifás*'s genuine perplexity is far more admirable and fair than the demonization of Morton carried out by others in

Ficóbriga.² The possibility that this intense meditation may in some way be connected with his new job as a gravedigger, just as Cayetano's involvement with Pepe Rey's interment may have led to his greater emotional identification with the murdered engineer, is increased by Morton and the bishop watching José's burial of a pauper and by the narrator's moving comments on the corpse: it is entering "the vast mystery of subterranean decomposition – without a friend, unsung, unblest, unwept – without a wreath or even a winding-sheet. For them all is bare realism and cold clay – they indeed are dust to dust" ["en la inmensidad misteriosa de la descomposición subterránea sin amigos, sin cánticos religiosos, sin lágrimas, sin flores, sin mortaja. Para ésos todo es materia y verdadero polvo"] (II, 11).³ Gloria will soon meet the same fate as the pauper, Morton two years after her. *Caifás's* role, rather comic, in part I, as forecaster or vehicle of important plot developments that affect both lovers, is given more gravity in part II when he becomes a spiritual guide figure, pointing out in words and actions the problems the two created for themselves at the end of part I. But Morton fails, like Gloria, to appreciate fully this sensibleness on *Caifás's* part: as in part I, the Jew continues to rely on him as an intermediary with Gloria, especially after he discovers the truth about their love child. When Gloria dies of ill health at the end of the novel, it is *Caifás* who cuts the saddest figure at the burial, in sharp contrast to most of the townsfolk, who attend out of curiosity. Like Cayetano and Tafetán, he has to bury his great friend and protectress, the Divine Shepherdess. Galdós's choice of words is again moving: "Mundideo looked like a corpse himself, risen to bury someone alive" ["*Caifás* parecía un muerto que salía del hoyo para enterrar un vivo"] (II, 33).

Caifás is, perhaps, more of a middle-aged village idiot or fool to be pitied than an old eccentric to be laughed at, but he can be included at the edge of our group, since he does utter words of wisdom about the behaviour of the two main characters as well as prophetic insights about the principal plot developments. His affection for the pair of lovers is much more pronounced and effective than that of either Cayetano or Tafetán for Pepe Rey and Rosario. His entry into the novel is also more prominently signposted. The result is that greater attention is focused on his activities in the novel. He is as necessary as the couple he serves for the unfolding of the story. A card type becomes a vital intermediary or secondary character.⁴

CHAPTER FOUR

A *Principal*:
José de Relimpio y Sastre

In his famous 4 April 1882 letter to Francisco Giner de los Ríos, Galdós declared that *The Disinherited* [*La desheredada*] (1881) marked the beginning of a new "manner" in his writing, but without explaining what that meant in terms of his technique of characterization (Cossío 257). The omission is perhaps not all that surprising, given the criticism of de los Ríos, another of Galdós's mentors, in his review of *La familia de León Roch*: de los Ríos had written that Galdós's principal male characters were too symbolic and superficial, compared with those of Dickens and Thackeray, whilst the secondary ones were far superior ("Sobre *La familia*" 70). The creation of José de Relimpio y Sastre in *La desheredada* might be viewed, then, as Galdós's indirect, but brilliantly formulated, acknowledgment of the criticism, for Relimpio is more than one of these highly praised secondary male characters; he is a sort of principal, in what is a remarkably rapid, but logical, progression in the development of the initial firm eccentric type portrayed in Cayetano Polentinos.[1]

Relimpio is introduced into the text in stages, each carefully planned. He appears first as a name only, at the beginning of chapter 2 of part I, where he is identified as a relation and a godfather of Isidora Rufete. The narrator teases the reader by deliberately deferring more information until a more convenient time. Two chapters later, he mentions that José with his talk of past exploits is one of the means by which the daydreaming Isidora is brought back to reality. This role elicits words of praise from the narrator: Isidora's godfather is "the extremely kind Don José de Relimpio" ["[e]l bondadosísimo don José de Relimpio"]. After another suitable interval, it is Isidora who sings his praises, calling him "such a marvellous character" ["el tipo más célebre del mundo"] (I, 4, i). He is one of a kind, so to speak: the best type, a real individual, then.[2] She is assigned the task of providing his first pen-picture, appropriately so, not only because of their family connection but especially because of Isidora's great talent for oral portraiture. Don José is another old Don Juan: "galán viejo" are Isidora's words. His facial features (for Smith and Varey [202] a mask incapable of expressing normal human emotions) instantly corroborate Isidora's typecasting of him: his cheeks are rosy; he has a little blond moustache, which seems like angel's hair; he purses his lips; and the colour of his eyes is like that of syrup or overripe grapes. For the first time, one of our eccentrics is given a striking item of dress to wear: Relimpio's cap has a gold tassle. His manner is affectedly polite. Isidora provides more precise information about what he does for a living: he helps his two daughters with their sewing jobs by operating the Raymond's "Canadiense" machine, an activity that contributes to the impression that he is a somewhat effeminate character. Isidora's growing closeness to her godfather, manifest in the luxury presents (fittingly, sweetmeats and a cigar) that she buys him on her shopping sprees, provokes resentment from Relimpio's stern wife, Doña Laura, who thinks that, instead of puffing on a cigar and looking at himself in mirrors, he should be working (I, 7). These are small pointers of tension existing already within the traditional family unit in which Relimpio is initially situated.

The narrator finally decides that it is time to stop teasing the reader and to bring his character on stage for the first time, but he does so in a way that instantly confounds normal expectations for a secondary character. First, the title declares that Don José is to have a chapter all to himself and his family. Next, he is shown as a character who seems to enjoy some autonomy; he is, according to the narrator, one of the principal figures of this true story who is now claiming his place in it and demanding the proper attention from the author and the reader ["A la mano se viene ahora, reclamando su puesto una de las principales figuras de esta historia de verdad y análisis"], in the same way that some of the characters in Mesonero Romanos's sketches did. The "costumbrista" connections were even more obvious in the La desheredada manuscript, where a phrase, subsequently rejected, described him as a characteristic type and good person ["qué característico tipo y qué buena persona" (f. 1:270)]. It is almost as if we see in action, through the manuscript changes, the progression Galdós is making in his mind from Relimpio the type to Relimpio the character, as if Galdós has made the final step in his long meditation on eccentric types and is now prepared to convert the type into a major character, without losing his essential typicality. Moreover, this is not the text of a novel, the narrator declares, but rather a history of truth and analysis.

The reader is then invited to verify Isidora's earlier portrait as a faithful copy of the live model, for the narrator more or less repeats the same words she had used to describe his physical appearance: if the detail of the hat is omitted, it is now clarified that the old Don Juan does, in fact, use rouge on his cheeks. But the narrator is more explicit than Isidora ever could be about Relimpio's character, which is the logical extension of his soft, effeminate physical features.[3] Relimpio is a type in terms of human character, albeit one not often created anymore by God: he is the incarnation, in looks and attitude, of satisfaction ["complacencia"], the representative of uselessness and sweetness, born in the aptly named town of Much Honey [Muchamiel] in the province of Alicante. As a representative type of these qualities, he is accordingly dehumanized when he is compared to a bouquet of confectionery on display in a shop window, with a sign indicating his full name (I, 8, i). His matronymic, Tailor [Sastre], now revealed for the first time and taking second place to his status as a representative type of physical taste, is a suitable choice, given his occasional work with the sewing machine, as well as his likeness to a shop window exhibit.[4] Following the brief and confessional style of "costumbrista" penpictures, the narrator concludes with two dabs of his brush: Don José was the best man in the world and, at the same time, the most useless. But this representative, dehumanized type is also one of the principal figures of the novel. He is, perhaps, to be viewed as one of Balzac's individualized types.

Certainly, a number of the details of his past life that the narrator now furnishes link him with one or two of the other eccentric types previously studied: he is sixty years old and had once worked in the civil service (the Office of Income ["Rentas"]) as well as in the theatre. But, whereas in the novels of the "Primera Epoca" such details were presented as interesting facts from the type's past, here, in Galdós's new, contemporary, social novel, they are more integrated into the fabric of the story and, in particular, related more directly to qualities possessed by the character in question. Galdós continues to underline Relimpio's uselessness: in both the ministry and the theatre, where he had been employed as an accountant, he was such a disaster that he was fired, as he had earlier been from the militia.[5] This shortcoming also extends to his marriage, where his disgruntled wife calls him a dummy of a man, perhaps with overtones of sexual inadequacy. Don José's automatic line of defence is that he is an accounting expert, a claim that the narrator proceeds to ridicule through hyperbolic comparisons to the discoveries of Isaac Newton and Christopher Columbus. Furthermore, Don José's failure to keep his own domestic accounts questions the relevance of the many abstract treatises on accounting he had written but not published.

Don José's other mania or obsession is pretty young girls, as the narrator now illustrates with examples: he still cannot resist his natural impulse to chase after them, even with a shaky step and torn cape, or to take advantage of being near them in parades and religious processions by muttering cloyingly sweet words to them. He would always try to steer conversations with his friends to the topic of romantic adventures, drolling over small feet and pretty ankles he had seen as a woman got into a carriage, or a glance or gesture directed his way. This catalogue of minor erotic escapades inevitably prompts laughter, tinged with pity, at the old roué, and serves as a salutary warning about possibly similar intentions behind his effusive welcome of his beautiful goddaughter: "How happy he was to see her again, now fully grown, how much he sympathized with her misfortunes, and with what pure concern he offered himself to her service in whatever manner might prove necessary!" ["¡Cuánto se alegró de volver a verla ya crecida y cuánto compadeció sus desgracias, y con qué puro interés se ofreció a ella para servirla en todo lo que hubiese menester!"]. José is delighted to give her a lesson on how to operate the sewing machine because this means standing close to her, which gives him a sexual thrill. Yet, his words of welcome could also be interpreted as a genuine desire to help her. The lesson is a waste of time, but the fault is not Relimpio's: Isidora is simply too engrossed in other thoughts. His potential for productive work is seen a while later when he helps the hardworking daughters with the sewing. He may not have a permanent job, and he may play at doing the family bookkeeping, but he is not totally useless. The mania for pretty girls, now localized in Isidora, is perhaps slowly turning into something more complicated: sexual fantasies can be accompanied by a genuine desire to help the individual object of attention. Relimpio is becoming an ever more complicated character. This fact, together with his more frequent and substantial appearances as the novel progresses, due precisely to his increasingly intimate relationship with the protagonist, will justify, in retrospect, the status of a principal character that the narartor had been so ready to confer on him on his first full appearance in the novel.

Nor is Don José a figure of fun all the time now: this is evident in his indulgence of another pastime that could have been left undeveloped as just another example of his eccentricities: every night before going to bed, he must roll a cigarette and read the political reports in the newspapers. To be sure, some of the ideas of this patriotic arm-chair politician are ludicrously simplistic and unrealizable: for example, he believes that if political parties were abolished and Spaniards united for the good of the country, that would be the end of political strife and revolutions. Equally unrealistic are his three pet peeves, which could be classified as sub-obsessions: the British should return Gibraltar to Spain; ex-ministers should not continue to receive high salaries; and a statue should be erected to the hero of the Pacific War of 1865–66, Admiral Méndez Núñez. The latest addition to this string of political pet topics is, however, of a different kind and more perceptive, even though it is not appreciated at all by his semi-sleeping wife: King Amadeo is a decent person who is being unjustly harassed by the politicians of the day – this is early 1873. The tight interweaving in this bedtime conversation of these comments and the personal events in Isidora's life, as reported by the indignant Doña Laura, add weight to the developing parallelism of the two topics (Bly, *Galdós's Novel* 2–23), as well as reminding us that, for Doña Laura, her husband, in his obsessive fascination with Isidora, is merely "a sight, a fool, a soft soul, a simpleton" ["esperpento, bobo, alma de Dios, un simple"] (I, 8, ii), all synonyms for our generic term "eccentric."

This more serious side to Relimpio y Sastre's character resurfaces with greater intensity in the climactic penultimate chapter (17) of part I, when, distraught at the rejection of her claim by the Marquesa de Aransis, Isidora wanders dazed around the crowd-filled streets of Madrid the day of King Amadeo's abdication, 11 February 1873. Relimpio had not complied with her earlier order to return home and is waiting for her when she leaves the Marquesa's palace. Gone now is the old Don Juan's frothy, sensual delight in being close to her; it has been replaced by a new note of seriousness as he confesses to her his inability to live without seeing her; he addresses her as his daughter (I, 16). This Relimpio is completely different from the laughable old dandy, a new state of affairs suggested by the insistence with which he has stared earlier at the balconies of the Aransis Palace and now, in chapter 17, at those of the Royal Palace on this fateful day. It is extremely significant that in an early version of chapter 17 in the manuscript, Isidora meanders through the capital's streets alone (Entenza de Solare 153). It is as if, by adding the figure of Relimpio in the final version, Galdós already had in mind the great transformation his bumbling eccentric was to undergo in part II. Understandably, but unfortunately, Isidora is totally oblivious to her god-father's affectionate concern as well as to his pertinent and accurate remarks about the king's abdication, the urban landscape, and the sky scene. Don José now shows the same concern for Isidora, and in the same words, as Cayetano Polentinos had for Pepe Rey during a nocturnal conversation: "There's something the matter with you. What is it?" ["A ti te pasa algo...¿Qué tienes?"]. It is a measure of his common sense that this formerly ridiculous old fool can now call Isidora mad for wanting to be left alone in the middle of the crowd. Relimpio argues from his own experience as a street chaser of girls that she is in danger of being propositioned or attacked by passionate males. Of course, the old Relimpio still wants to enjoy the pleasure of walking close to her, but the resolute abandonment of her godfather for the arms of her lover leaves him doubly distraught, for it happens in the place that another political hero of Relimpio's (and of Galdós's), the charismatic prime minister and leader of the 1868 revolution, General Juan Prim, had been assassinated barely two years before. His distress is complete when Isidora sends for her possessions a day later: he is overcome by a general depression, more pronounced and pathetic in the printed text than in the manuscript (Schnepf, "Galdós's *La desheredada*" 8).

This serious side to José's character stands out in the climactic penultimate chapter of part I, then (chapter 18 is a kind of epilogue). But, equally important, it dominates the next structurally important juncture: the first chapter of part II, where the narrator gratefully acknowledges him as a source of information about Isidora's family, José's own family, and the nation at large during the tumultuous thirty-four months between March 1873 and December 1875. The narrator is noticeably silent about how and why he received this information from Relimpio (rather than from someone else, for instance), limiting himself to the polite, but rather cryptic, statement that Don José's kindness in supplying the information was inexhaustible. Nor is it made clear if the diary of events that then follows is Relimpio's own or the narrator's. If the former, has it been transcribed with total fidelity or has the narrator altered it? Furthermore, the phrase "efemérides verbales" could refer to a written as well as to an oral account.[6] If it is the latter case, then clearly the text is by the narrator. Relimpio would be quite capable of writing such a diary of historical and personal events, given his composition of accounting treatises (albeit unpublished) in part I, but it would represent a considerable achievement and expression of serious interest by someone who is not seen engaged in this activity elsewhere in the novel. The reader is forced to conclude that the narrator himself is the scribe of the text, although, through the occasional use of the free indirect style to report José's thoughts and feelings, as well as his three pet political peeves, he clearly intends to convey the impression that he is writing from a position very close to the bookkeeper. For example, he notes with considerable emotion the old rake's genuine anguish at the tragic developments in the civil war taking place in the Basque Country, at his wife's death, and at his daughters' unimpressive marital unions. In one sense, the narrator partially surrenders the text to the voice (adulterated) of this eccentric old dandy, but, unlike Cayetano Polentinos in *Doña Perfecta*, Relimpio does not gain control of it, in whole or in part. What is the point of this ghostwriting by the narrator? Principally, the diary is used as a contrast with Miquis's more festive talk in the first part of the chapter about the birth of Isidora's deformed child and the need for a social revolution in Spain. Relimpio's gravity and emotional anguish also contrast with the narrator's own boredom with the political events, which he had rapidly dispatched in the opening sentence of the chapter. This second part is Relimpio's own work in the sense that he provides all the information that the narrator regurgitates, whether with alterations or not. This is not an insignificant advance in prominence; he is being accorded more deference by the narrator.[7]

As if he then regretted having given Relimpio this prominence, the narrator reverts in the next chapter to his original tone, festively greeting him as the "Great Don José." He is, we are assured, the same old incarnation of honeyed sweetness that we knew before (II, 2, ii). Indeed, in an earlier draft of these lines in the manuscript, the narrator categorically affirms that nothing had changed in the good Relimpio since we last saw him, the years passing without leaving any sign of decay (f. 2:41 on the back of f. 2:48). Doth not the narrator protest too much? The inescapable truth is that that Don José has grown in stature through his political observations that firmly straddle the novel's structural epicentre. But the narrator, preferring to forget this nobility of mind, persists in reminding us of the more trivial Relimpio y Sastre. His old habits and attitudes are recalled: his sensual thrills when he takes off Isidora's earrings, his childish delight in romping on the floor with Riquín. His unbecoming facial appearance is rendered even more grotesque by Encarnación's comparison to that of a half-dead sheep. His expertise with the account book and the sewing machine are deliberately mentioned here as a means with which to help Isidora control her expenditures and to suggest a way in which she can earn some money. But both avenues of action are even more improbable now. Relimpio, for all his good intentions and economic rhetoric, cannot see through the character of Isidora or offer a good example of thriftiness or industry himself. His vain boast of being one of Madrid's leading accountants and his fanciful enumeration of all the minor domestic tasks he can do for her, now (it is true) more possible since the death of his wife and the dispersion of his children, underline instead the absurdity of any plans to reform old habits by either of them. Such pretensions are clearly ridiculed by the dream that this failed office-worker (Ràfols, "From Institution" 74) has the night after this exchange with Isidora: sleeping like a seraph, he sees himself as the head of the accounting department of a wealthy mansion, directing the book entries as if he were conducting an orchestra. His promises to creditors of the imminent arrival of funds are as illusory and empty as Mr Micawber's famous phrase that "Something will turn up."[8] Ironically, when something does turn up, in the shape of Isidora's new lover, the wealthy member of Parliament Sánchez Botín, Relimpio is booted out of the house with his books and told never to see Isidora again. The narrator's concluding comment is one of ironic pity: "My poor little Don José! Now you really are the most unhappy of men. ... What unparalleled cruelty! There are men who are more like savage beasts ... José, you are a martyr" ["¡Pobrecito don José! Ahora sí que eres el más infeliz de los hombres. ... ¡Crueldad sin ejemplo! Hay hombres que parecen fieras ... José, eres un mártir"] (II, 3).

The narrator maintains this tone of playful pity towards the godfather when he describes José's forlorn physical state during this period of separation from Isidora: his cheeks lose their rosiness and become wrinkled. This aging accelerates even more when he is reduced to acting as go-between – like *Caifás* – from Isidora to her string of lovers in order to secure funds to finance her lavish and dissolute ways. Consequently, his idyllic, pastoral dreams of a happy cohabitation with his goddaughter and her child turn into terrible nightmares in which he sees himself defeating her repugnant lovers. Relimpio has now entered the final phase of his life, in which his former practical uselessness will be replaced by a far more valuable spiritual usefulness that elevates him to unexpected heights of noble altruism. That such a transformation is occurring is evident in a scene that reprises that of his family's Christmas Eve party in part I, in which, after getting drunk, he had to be carried off to bed. The printer Bou's party to celebrate a lottery win, his inheritance, and a big business contract is attended by, amongst others, Relimpio, who has put on his old frock coat and blue tie. His taciturn composure during most of the evening suddenly disappears after he has tasted some champagne, and he challenges Bou to a duel for having sullied the reputation of his peerless Isidora. His solemn, if somewhat slurred, speech only makes the other guests laugh, more so when he breaks a plate by banging his hand on the table and falls onto a divan after claiming victory over his opponent, who, equally inebriated, had fallen to the ground after trying to embrace Relimpio as a friend. Notwithstanding this slapstick comedy, Relimpio cuts a sympathetic figure as he tries to match words with actions in support of his heroine. The theatrical overtones are more clear in the next chapter (12), where the text is arranged in the dialogue format of a play with corresponding stage directions: again Relimpio is the go-between for Isidora as he delivers money to the destitute Pez. The stage directions at first seem to form a parodic comment on Relimpio's strong emotions towards the former lovers (hatred for Pez, deepest compassion for Isidora), with allusions to Shakespeare. However, when Pez plies him with champagne, his behaviour becomes less absurd; if he drinks, it is only in order to forget his mental pain, he says. The stage directions, now more succinct, convey the full extent of the feeling hiding behind the old man's words: for example, the expression on his face changes from a sweet gaze to a horrible contortion when he is asked by Pez if he has any pain. After one sip of the champagne, Relimpio drops his head and closes his eyes, cursing the wretched world, only to jump up the next moment and hurl well-deserved insults – hitherto, confined to asides – at Pez and at Isidora's other lovers. His attempts to engage in a duel with all four figures, who, he believes, are in the room, end in the same fashion as those of the previous party scene: he collapses onto the sofa. Alcohol liberates, for a moment, the new man struggling to break out from within the shell of comic eccentricity. Once the effects of the champagne have worn off, however, Relimpio reverts to his usual pusillanimous self. In part I revelations of a different character had been confined to his anguished interest in the contemporary political scene. Here, in part II, the new Relimpio that is emerging is not only a more assertive individual but also, more importantly, one who is more ready to confront the inner truth about himself. This can be clearly seen when, on a visit to the imprisoned Isidora, he explains his earlier drunken state as a need to kill his inner pain. He, like everybody else, has his own weaknesses: getting drunk allows him, however briefly, to be another person, ready to commit all sorts of sublime deeds on her behalf, before returning, when sober, to his normal self and all the miserable reality of decrepit old age. The weak, faltering voice in which he relates this change of character, the great clarity of mind with which he can now recall the various stages of the process, and the sheer, honest enjoyment he feels when he, an old, fragile nobody, lives this other life endow him with spiritual nobility more unmistakeably than the narrator's semi-burlesque words of sympathy had done in the previous drunken scenes:

I had an internal revolution, my "dizzy spell" swept over me and I became a totally different man, I mean I was another man, I was a knight, a young man, a hero and I don't know what else ... It's good, isn't it, to be something special for ten minutes? ... To be something special for ten minutes! We who are nothing are prey to these dangers. ... We're all weak ... At my age.
[Hubo en mí una revolución, me entró el mareo y con el mareo pasé a ser otro ser distinto, quiero decirte que fui otro hombre, fui un caballero, un joven héroe, qué sé yo ... ¿No es cosa buena ser algo por espacio de diez minutos? ... ¡Ser algo durante diez minutos! Los que no somos nada, caemos en estos peligros ... Somos frágiles ... A mi edad.] (II, 17, i)

His desperation when Isidora begins another relationship is so extreme that, in an echo of the penultimate chapter of part I, when he had wept in the spot where Prime Minister General Prim had been assassinated, "the good old man" ["el buen viejo"] (II, 17, ii) wants to kill himself by banging his head against the wall of a church. Only drink, to be obtained from a nearby tavern, might give him Dutch courage to complete the task. He is totally powerless to prevent Isidora's final escape to the underworld of prostitution. Her parting words of scorn for his constant attention wound him to the quick. Close to tears, Relimpio confesses that she is the most precious thing in his life, the person he loves most: "My dearest girl, I love you more than anything I've ever held dear. I'm concerned for you, for your welfare, and I don't want you doing anything foolish or that you should come to any harm" ["Hija mía, yo te quiero más que a las niñas de mis ojos. Me intereso por ti, por tu bien y no quiero que hagas disparates, ni que te pase mal alguno"] (II, 18). These words, his subsequent kneeling before her, and his offer to marry her and to work in order to support her border on the sentimentally ridiculous, given his condition and her material needs. Yet if pathos is held in check and Relimpio takes on the airs of a tragic hero (Hafter, "Galdós' Presentation" 28), it is because he means every word he says, and, faced by a crisis, does his best to deal with it. In what the narrator terms a providential moment of philosophical insight, he tries to convince her not to erase the shame of the past by doing something even worse. For all his constant idealization of Isidora, Relimpio shows here that he can see clearly her moral faults and what she now intends to become. The narrator may say that his tone is priestly and solemn when, after recognizing the stupidity of his offer to marry her, he urges her to return to her first and only true love, the detested Pez, but the advice is surely very wise, as it is the lesser of two evils. These words of realism, when separated from the correspondingly dramatic gestures and the comments of the narrator, make Relimpio's attempts to save her all the more admirable and noble, as when he tries to prevent her from seizing the key from him: she will only get out of the room over his dead body. But the narrator chooses to emphasize the comic side of this dramatic action by observing that Relimpio's voice sounded cavernous and that he felt like he was a hero in a play, whereas moments earlier the same narrator had struck the completely opposite note of admiration and approval: "becoming greater than himself and revealing the strength that sometimes surges from the feeble spirit of the weak, as in certain moments of crisis sublime wisdom bursts from the mind of an idiot" ["haciéndose superior a sí mismo y mostrando la energía que a veces surge del flaco ánimo de los débiles, como en ciertos momentos de crisis las sublimidades brotan del cerebro de los tontos"] (II, 18). The narrator seems to be ambivalent again about the change in his old rake's character: one minute he thinks that José is grotesquely theatrical, the next, full of admirably passionate sincerity. And finally, in a third comment – when Relimpio declares that Isidora would not dare outrage and offend her father – he swings back to clear approval, noting that these words, accompanied by tears, were very eloquent.

Don José is a long way from being the laughable Don Juan of part I; he has become a wise old fool, a saintly idiot – at least intermittently.[9] His response to Isidora's exit from his life is another drinking session that leads him, after being stretched out on the floor all night, to his death the next day, but not before he has professed his service and love for his lady, whom he enjoins her other "vassals" to rescue from the streets. Relimpio's death takes the form of one of his drunken, dizzy spells, which give him "an apocryphal life, composed of a strange simulation of youth, passion and strength" ["una vida apócrifa, compuesta con extraños fingimientos de juventud, pasión y energía"] (II, 18). The narrator again switches to his bantering, condescending tone of voice: after wondering philosophically if the old madcap has become Isidora's champion in eternity, he addresses him familiarly as a martyr, an angel, almost in the same manner in which Sam Weller intoned his praise of Mr Pickwick as an angel towards the end of *The Pickwick Papers*.[10] In Relimpio's case, this change in status had been directly envisaged from his first major appearance in part I. The seeming incongruity of that accolade of principalship has been gradually eroded through the novel until, in the final section, it disappears completely.

Relimpio's final words before dying peacefully are extremely relevant, as they summarize the moral of Isidora's story for those gathered around his bedside as well as for the reader: she fell into the mud of the street because she rashly wanted to climb too high with false wings. Incredibly, these words are categorized as stupidities by the narrator, but they are exactly the same words he himself then uses – without attribution to his erstwhile diarist – in the first sentence of the moral that he directs to the readers in the final chapter, or "chapterette," which is so similar to that in *Doña Perfecta*: "If you feel the urge to reach difficult, craggy heights, do not put your trust in artificial wings" ["Si sentís anhelo de llegar a una difícil y escabrosa altura, no os fiéis de las alas postizas"] (II, 19).[11] Because the narrator is piqued at the way in which his former eccentric and now mad old fool has dominated the novel's ending with his words of wisdom, he cannot refrain from reasserting his authority: a terse chapterette, a visible parody of the normal chapter size, is his abrupt retort. But it cannot destroy the fact that Relimpio has indeed fulfilled the billing he received when he first entered the novel. Unlike the prominence of Cayetano Polentinos at the end of his novel, that of Relimpio has nothing really to do with the plot and everything to do with inner development of character. Admittedly, this transformation is induced by physical causes (alcohol, lack of eating, and emotional stress) leading to some mental breakdown, but the result is one of spiritual value: he comes to see his own weaknesses and those of Isidora, and he confesses them openly. It is in this act of public introspection that the principalness of his character really lies. Sixteen years later, in *Misericordia* (1897), Frasquito Ponte will perfect this act of sublime humility.

TOMÁS RUFETE

To set in relief Don José's spiritual prominence, Galdós resorts to the technique he had used in previous novels, but now on a much more extensive scale: he arranges a group of minor characters (equally eccentric or even madder) around this principal eccentric with which to compare and contrast him. This happens primarily in part I. The first figure is Relimpio's relative and Isidora's father, Tomás Rufete, who opens the novel; he does so with a volley of disconnected phrases, in a violent and almost unintelligible succession of questions and exclamations. He is patently mad, rather than eccentric, when he compares the elusive sum of money that he claims the country owes him to a ball of mercury sliding around his head, or when he believes that he is the prime minister of a country that he calls Envidiópolis and he has to defend himself against the envy of others. If read as a collection of separate sentences, as the truncated formatting of the paragraph invites, rather than as a coherent whole, Tomás's soliloquy contains, as well as utter nonsense, some remarkable insights into the country's moral condition – akin to those at the end from Relimpio about his daughter – that, in retrospect, compare favourably to the vacuous oratory of, for example, innumerable committees set up to examine the social problem of child delinquency (I, 6, iv), or of that race of bureaucratic types, the Pezs (O'Byrne Curtis 201). Rufete even anticipates the ladder simile that José and the narrator use in delivering the moral of Isidora's life. Tomás's greater interest in the welfare of the country also anticipates that displayed by Relimpio, who had also once worked as a civil servant. His commitment to the job was more impressive, however: he was secretary in three provincial governments and would have been a provincial governor but for political intrigues. Above all, Tomás was a financial expert on income and budget matters, composing at night all sorts of reports, laws, and decrees in what was, like the bookkeeping of Relimpio, an unconscious parody of typical bureaucratic practices (Ràfols, "From Institution" 72).

Tomás is clearly more than eccentric – he is mad. The narrator says that he has the most unhinged head in the whole world (I, 2).[12] (According to his daughter, his father was even madder, so obviously insanity runs in the family.) Tomás does not use cosmetics like Relimpio, but his facial appearance, with sparkling eyes and mobile features, is another confusing, abnormal physiognomic surface, not easily identifiable according to Lavaterian principles: he could be middle aged or old, a genius or an imbecile. The problem is serious, because those who look at him and listen to him do not know whether to pity him or laugh. But then the narrator immediately contradicts himself by launching into a precise anatomical description of the old man, with the head and facial features especially highlighted. A bald head, a thin, greying beard (half-shaven, just like a half-cut meadow), a drooping, upper lip (with a constant shake that makes him look like a rabbit gnawing at cabbages), a pallid face, a papyrus-like skin, thin legs, a short build, and a slightly bent back, all give the impression that he is another example of a funny old man, albeit opposite in complexion to the sweet fleshiness of Relimpio. If the only item of the latter's clothing that had been signalled out was his cap with the gold tassle, Tomás's tie stands out amongst the rags that are the rest of his. As Relimpio preens himself in mirrors around the house, so Tomás Rufete uses the wall of the insane asylum as a mirror by which to knot his tie.

If Isidora's father foreshadows some of the physical features and activities of Relimpio, why has he, and not Don José, been removed to an institution for the mentally insane? Rufete's presence in Leganés inevitably raises the question of what differentiates the madman from the eccentric.[13] Rufete, with his voice covering all possible registers of laughter, insult, and sermonizing, is also a type, an individual representing many other kindred minds in the asylum, some of whom enter the text briefly with one peculiar action, facial expression, or monologue.[14] The staff on duty in the paupers' section of the asylum to which Rufete has been transferred are no longer the psychiatrists in the fee-paying section, but strong, bored, male nurses, more like policemen, "the inquisitors of nonsense" ["los inquisidores del disparate"] (I, 1, ii), devoid of all compassion, charity, or gentleness. The living conditions in this section are much more inhuman, and the narrator's condemnation of this social institution, an asylum-cum-hospital-cum-prison, becomes very bitter and almost apocalyptic.[15] There is no doubt about their identity: Tomás Rufete and companions are all totally mad, the only human feature they have is their body; the word "imbecile" is repeated often. The sane person looking at these inmates would feel his blood freeze and his spirit overwhelmed.[16] Eschewing medical descriptions of the respective manias of the inmates, Galdós concentrates on their strange, hurried poses or movements of body and voice, their strange requests for materials like writing paper, or their speeches to invisible interlocutors. They all serve to contextualize and explain the antics and verbal incoherence of Tomás Rufete that we had read at the novel's beginning, as well as to colour our interpretation of Relimpio's words and behaviour both in the remainder of part I and, especially, in part II.[17]

Sandwiched between these terrifying pictures of Rufete and the other madmen is a most curious passage of commentary by the narrator that goes beyond the assimilation of Isidora's father and eccentrics like Relimpio. In this startling passage the narrator reaches out beyond the confines of the fiction to involve not only his readers but all those who live outside the walls of Leganés in Madrid, Spain, and the rest of world, because he is anxious to explode the normal concepts of the differences between the sane and the insane. Indeed, the manias of the mad are only exaggerations of the moral and intellectual ideas that all humans have:

And to consider that that miserable colony represents nothing more than the exaggeration or irritated extreme of our many moral or intellectual personal peculiarities ... that all of us, in varying degrees, have the inspiration or muse of absurdity within us, and soon after we relax our control we enter completely into the shadowy realm of psychiatric science! For no, the differences are not so great. The thoughts those poor wretches have are the same as ours, but dislodged, loosened, freed from the thread of sense that orders them so neatly. These poor madmen are our very selves, as if we went to sleep last night with the mind capable of the splendid variety of all possible thoughts, and awoke this morning in the aridity of a single obsession.

[¡Y considerar que aquella triste colonia no representa otra cosa que la exageración o el extremo irritativo de nuestras múltiples particularidades morales o intelectuales ... que todos, cuál más, cuál menos, tenemos la inspiración, el estro de los disparates, y a poco que nos descuidemos entramos de lleno en los sombríos dominios de la ciencia alienista! Porque no, no son tan grandes las diferencias. Las ideas de estos desgraciados son nuestras ideas, pero desengarzadas, sueltas, sacadas de la misteriosa hebra que gallardamente las enfila. Estos pobres orates somos nosotros mismos que dormimos anoche nuestro pensamiento en la variedad esplendente de todas las ideas posibles, y hoy por la mañana lo despertamos en la aridez de una sola.] (I, 1, ii)[18]

The narrator is at pains to blur, not to demarcate, the dividing lines between the mad and the sane – in part I, chapter 14, the whole of Madrid at Christmas time will be likened to an open madhouse. The narrator proceeds to represent this idea visually in terms of a theoretical map or plan of the colony's location within Madrid, which, through a comparison to those drawn by philosophers and saints of the past, implies that madness has something in common with saintliness and wisdom and is not to be despised out of hand, and, indeed, that it is something perhaps positive and beneficial. Then, without any contextualization whatsoever, the narrator suddenly cites a maxim by Tomás Rufete, no less, which, as well as being appropriate from the representative of all the other sub-types in Leganés and the maddest character in the novel, summarizes and illustrates the point just made by the narrator: that the line between madness and sanity is invisible: "There are many sane men who are reasonable lunatics" ["Hay muchos cuerdos que son locos razonables"]. This pithy expression of encapsulated wisdom, standing in marked contrast to the collection of inchoate ideas that he had blurted out in the initial paragraph of the novel, could well constitute Galdós's own definition of his old eccentrics like Relimpio.

To some extent Rufete's death seems, in retrospect, an inverted parallel to that of Relimpio: whereas Don José dies apparently mad (in the opinion of others), muttering praise of Isidora as a celestial creature, Tomás Rufete, his second cousin, dies apparently sane, believing that he is in Leganés, despite the attempts of the medical staff to deny that truth. This clear echo of Don Quixote's deathbed return to sanity could also have been prompted by the almost completely negative answer Alhama Montes received from the director of Leganés about the insane recovering their reason before death (Robin 95). The two cousins die with much more sanity and clear-sightedness than those around them: Relimpio knows that Isidora has left him to become a street prostitute; Tomás, in retrospect, tries in his last, enigmatic, and disjointed words – "My children ... the Marquesa" ["Mis hijos ... la Marquesa"] (I, 1, iv) – to reveal the truth about their identity.

Isidora has many young male lovers, but she also has a number of old male advisers: before the novel starts, her father, and as it progresses, her godfather. Both may be useless by the standards of normal society (Kirsner 92), but both propel and support Isidora on her life's quest, Tomás deluding her with the idea of a noble origin, Relimpio solidifying it with his unbridled praise of her charms. Yet coexisting with their respective madness and eccentricity is a sharp and realistic appreciation of the corruption of the political and social system in which they live and of those who exploit them.

CANENCIA

Another old inmate of Leganés, Canencia, also anticipates the future elaboration of Relimpio's role as a guide for Isidora. When she meets him in the asylum office, he seems to be doing the accounts of the institution. Like Relimpio, he is a pensman of figures, a bookkeeper. His bookkeeping could be regarded as more effective than Don José's in that, if payments are not made, as in the case of Tomás Rufete, they are noted in his books and the inmate is downgraded to the paupers' section. His calligraphy is perhaps more noteworthy than Relimpio's. He is identified immediately as a type, but for the moment just a social one, a relic of the civil service of the past (I, 1, iii).[19] The physical appearance of Canencia is given some attention, even though he is not to reappear in the novel, but this is the usual procedure for fixing a colourful "flat" type in the reader's mind. Unlike Tomás Rufete, he has a totally shaven face, which looks like a priest's; he is old, small, wrinkled, and fairly dark-skinned, with a sweet, melodious voice, somewhat like Relimpio's. Some articles of dress are highlighted: like Relimpio, he wears a hat (a small, oldish beret on his head), and he also has small green elbow pads. He also possesses a peculiar physical tic: from time to time, he stretches open his mouth and sucks in a big breath of air, a humorous trait that along with the twirling of his pen, injects a comic note into his homily on life's pains in this vale of tears, where Christian resignation is a

prerequisite. Like Relimpio in part I, Canencia rolls his own cigarettes, another trivial action that deflates his religious sermon on the
advantages of the afterlife. Like Relimpio in part II, the little old
man looks at the admiring and grateful Isidora with eyes full of
sweet looks. His verbal tic is more lexical than stylistic: "complying
with the sovereign will" ["el cumplimiento de la voluntad sober-
ana"]. Canencia is also credited with perspicacity, as when he can
see that Isidora is trying to say that the lineage of her true family,
Aransis, is socially higher than that of the Rufetes. Again Galdós
uses the old man's mannerisms to deflate the whole idea: he takes off
his beret most respectfully before absurdly comparing Tomás Rufete
to another putative father, St Joseph. Isidora, far from seeing the
inappropriateness of the simile, is overwhelmed with pride and
emboldened enough to snobbishly criticize Tomás's social ambition,
whereupon the venerable penman launches into a spirited denunciation of this motivating force, pertinently using the same metaphor of
the ladder that Rufete, Relimpio, and the narrator all had used or
will use to categorize what he really considers is a disease of the soul
["enfermedad del alma"]. In citing, rightly or wrongly, the spiritual
defect of ambition, rather than real mental disorders, as the reason
for many inmates being in the asylum, he helps to reinforce the narrator's earlier-stated belief that the dividing line between it and the
outside world is non-existent. Canencia is living proof of this truth,
for it is the lawsuits of his children (presumably over money, that is,
social ambition or greed) that have kept him in Leganés for thirty-
two years. The ultimate irony, of course, is that social ambition is
the principal cause of Isidora's misfortune in the novel. The words of
wisdom from the eccentric Canencia will go unheeded; normal society does not want to learn the lessons given by the madmen of
Leganés.

We then see the eccentric Canencia attacked by a fit of insanity: he
becomes agitated, the disturbance being signalled by external body
movements: trembling lips, shaky hands, lit-up eyes, and slurred
speech. He now frightens Isidora with the accusation that she has
insulted his paternal feelings as well as his white hairs, an indirect association with his name, which is now finally revealed.[20] His accusation,
theatrically expressed to the director, is like that of Rufete's that had
opened the novel: one of ingratitude. His mania or mental derangement, which surfaces every couple of years, is the belief that he has an
electric machine in his head and that people are insulting him, and then
he runs around until he calms down. The director recognizes that, otherwise, he is a most judicious and helpful person, a simple soul, a saint
and a philosopher, with comforting solace for relatives. On the scale of

eccentricity-madness in the novel, Canencia occupies a half-way spot between Relimpio and Tomás Rufete.

There has been some discussion in recent years as to whether Rufete and Canencia are the same as, or relatives of, characters of the same name who had appeared in the second series of *Episodios nacionales,* which Galdós had completed in 1879 (Gilman *Galdós*; Rodríguez and Carstens; Ribbans, "Unas apostillas"). In the last words of that series, Galdós had declared that they would be used as family models for contemporary types, hinting that these would soon appear. Tomás Rufete and Canencia in *La desheredada* are both mad to varying degrees. They serve as a reference point for the eccentric type, Relimpio, who becomes, not a madman, but a sublime eccentric.

EL CANÓNIGO

At the crucial narrative juncture in the novel, the final chapter of part I, another old eccentric-cum-madman appears suddenly to offer Isidora one last lesson of worldly wisdom before she embarks upon her affair with Joaquín Pez, as well as to put into relief the guidance she has so far received from Relimpio y Sastre in the climactic previous chapter. His name is Santiago Quijano-Quijada, her uncle and guardian, who lives in El Tomelloso, La Mancha. The obvious connections with Don Quixote continue with the details of his life in the country: a bachelor for more than thirty years and living with cousins and nephews, he hunts, eats well, and reads novels. He is nicknamed the Canon – an ironic echo of the cleric in part I of *Don Quixote* – because of his comfortable, sybaritic lifestyle. In part II, we are also told that that, like Cayetano Polentinos in *Doña Perfecta*, the Canon is fascinated by the question of Spain's past greatness. An amateur historian, he knows by heart the history of the great aristocratic families of Spain. And like Cayetano, he intrudes prominently in the important closing stages of a narrative, in the guise of the writer of some mystifying correspondence. No physical description of the Canon is provided, nor is it really necessary.

The Canon is the fourth old male eccentric-madman to serve as a guide figure for Isidora in part I. His appearance is by proxy – through a letter, which contains reams of advice on how to live in Madrid. It is concentrated in one long sermon that Isidora is forced to read rather than listen to intermittently, as she often does with Relimpio's conversations, and it is certainly meant to be taken seriously, for the Canon is close to death – confirmed in a second letter received at the same time. The narrator explicitly categorizes this counsel as very solid. Yet the letter also contains the one element Isidora needs in order to press her claims to the Aransis estate, as well as live in the high style she has longed for: the money of her inheritance. Against such a formidable tool, how realistic is it to expect that the good advice of the Canon will have any effect? The narrator does not show any awareness of this obvious contradiction. Nor does he bother to comment on some similarities with Relimpio, although he authoritatively enumerates the facts of the Canon's life. Both are cousins of Rufete: the Canon, a first cousin, Relimpio a second cousin. Unlike Relimpio, however, who had dreamt of being a steward in a big Madrid mansion, the Canon has occupied such a position, as well as that of administrator in a number of others in the capital. Both like the lazy, good life, and the Canon is described, like Relimpio, as an extravagant, very eccentric person: "extravagante," "muy sumamente excéntrico," and "[de] no comprendidas chifladuras" are the terms the narrator uses. Furthermore, although he lives in deepest La Mancha, his way of speaking and writing, another characteristic he shares with Relimpio, makes him appear to belong to the upper crust of Madrid society. Divergences of opinion abound in the region over his meanness or generosity, his wisdom or eccentricity. Consequently, how can the reader be sure of the narrator's initial categorization of this letter as full of wisdom, especially when it was the secretary of the town hall, and not the Canon, who had written it?

Confusion is generated even by the Canon's opening to the letter: after the precision of the place and date of writing, he calls Isidora "My dear niece (or something akin) " ["Mi querida sobrina (o cosa tal)"], only to say in the next line that it was Isidora who called him – a mere sinner – uncle, but he has acted more like a father to her. The same confusion occurs when the Canon signs the letter as "your very loving uncle (or something akin)" ["amantísimo tío (o cosa tal)"] (I, 18). The Canon is quite convinced that Isidora is the true granddaughter of the Marquesa de Aransis; he even suggests that, if the lawsuit is going badly, she should search her body for some telltale mark, as so often happens in sentimental and chivalresque novels. The Canon's level of judgment is not very profound, as is evident from his belief that Joaquín Pez is chivalry personified. He is very much responsible, then, for rescuing Isidora's self-esteem and morale after her humiliating dismissal by the marquesa on the day of King Amadeo's abdication. Moreover, he provides her with the wherewithal to press forward, legally and socially, with her claim. What the narrator has called good practical wisdom is really predicated on the belief that she is a noble woman by birth, and, therefore, his counsel is dovetailed to fit the life of an aristocrat. The virtues he preaches, reminiscent of those professed by the Knight of the Green Cloak in

Don Quixote, are eminently noble and ideal in principle: moderation in dress, expenses, and meals; avoidance of vanity; charity to the poor; modesty and virtue in everything; and being a good Christian. But these are virtues that Isidora has hardly exhibited in the novel to this point, and will be totally ignored hereafter, thanks precisely to the Canon's shipment of money. After thirty or more years in the country away from the capital, the Canon's view of the social behaviour of aristocrats, and of political changes in Madrid, is outdated and wildly ludicrous (Nimetz 120), especially in view of what Isidora had experienced on the streets of the capital in the previous chapter. The purpose of the Canon's letter is to indicate the difficulty Don José will have in changing her course of conduct in the chapters to come, a difficulty to which he, like the Canon, has already contributed with his own countervailing compliance with, and encouragement of, her whims. The proximity of the roles and characters of the Canon and Relimpio in part I is recollected in part II (15, i) by the lawyer, Muñoz y Nones, who calls the former one of the simplest or stupidest men that ever lived, "completely daffy" (Nimetz 119), echoing words of the narrator about Relimpio in part I and subsequently by Isidora herself, who will finally blame both guide-figures for fomenting her obsession with the inheritance. But Don José, the only old eccentric of the first part of the novel to survive into the second, is afforded the chance to redeem himself, if not to save his goddaughter from her own weaknesses of character.

As if to underscore for his readers the importance of what he had set out to achieve with Relimpio – converting a stock, superficially comic type into a significant plot facilitator as well as a human being with some depth of feeling and insight – Galdós introduces a typical "flat" character to whom he devotes a surprising amount of space, rather disporportionate to his role: Muñoz y Nones, lawyer for the Aransis family. Galdós deliberately focuses on his physical appearance, for it subverts the central notion of "costumbrista" type sketches. The fifty-year-old Muñoz is not what he looks like: in contravention of good Lavaterian principles of physiognomics, he does not look like your typical lawyer, all ugly, thin, and lanky. His handsome appearance and affable, generous manner would suggest that he was a diplomat, a sportsman, or even a nobleman. In this confusion of identity, he is like other professional types in contemporary society: sailors look like judges, philosophers like church canons – an ironic example, in view of what we have seen of El Canónigo's intellectual powers at the end of part I. Relimpio, though, is the exception in this picture gallery: at the beginning he looks what he is: a soft,

mushy, useless old man obsessed with pretty young women. His physical appearance subsequently deteriorates somewhat, but not to
transform him into some other recognizable type. His transformation
is of a far more important, internal kind, as he becomes increasingly
upset by Isidora's slide into immorality. Outer appearances are now
meaningless in Relimpio's case, as they are, in a different and totally
hollow way, for Muñoz and other contemporary types. Galdós is, as
it were, debunking the traditional habit of interpreting the social and
professional identity of types solely from external appearances.[21]
Muñoz is given a number of external identifiers that turn him into
another Mr Pickwick, except that he lacks the latter's (and
Relimpio's) inner development of character: he insists on wearing a
white waistcoat all year, even in winter, so as to hide his protruding
stomach. Behind his shiny bald pate lies a constant obsession to
found a penitentiary for young delinquents, and his intense staring at
those to whom he is talking is extraordinary. Although he appears on
one occasion only in the novel, he is also given his own set of dupli-
cate verbal tags: "Very well, very well" ["Mucho, mucho"] when
agreeing with anything, and "There is no such thing, nor is that the
right road" ["No hay tal cosa, ni ése es el camino"] when disagreeing. His stock phrase for every comparison is "As clear as the noon-
day sun" ["como la luz del mediodía']. The climax to Galdós's ridiculing of this new "costumbrista" type occurs when the lawyer has to
explain to Isidora the baseless nature of her legal claim: his convoluted and absurd account of the way in which Tomás Rufete tricked
his children into believing they were born into a noble family is preceded by an even more absurd account of the most extraordinary
practical jokes he and colleagues practised on the mad Canon, like
loading the pistols for a duel with salt, another echo of the duels that
the nobly inspired José de Relimpio was prepared to engage in in
order to defend Isidora's honour.

Relimpio is, in fact, Galdós's real "new" type, whose inner developments are far more important than the colourful externals of face,
clothes, and speech. This was the kind of evolution in typification that
Alas had also strongly urged in the same year that *La desheredada*
appeared. In his essay "Del teatro," Galdós's friend argued that the fictional character was not the embodiment of single qualities: nobody
was just a miser, or liar, or hypocrite, for example. If they were symbols, they could not be real, or, as he phrased it: "there is no *type* who
is dramatic" ["no hay *tipo* que sea dramático"] (*Solos* 60). Two years
later, he could welcome the demise of the novel of types and local customs ("Crónica literaria"). Don José de Relimpio y Sastre represents

Galdós's contribution to this evolution with secondary types. There was still some room left, naturally, for the perfection of Relimpio's mould, turning his sensitive, spiritual pre-eminence into a more undeniably principal status, but that would only be achieved in 1897, in *Misericordia*. In the meanwhile, in other novels Galdós was to advance towards this goal by expanding the range of roles he entrusted to his secondary eccentrics.

CHAPTER FIVE

Armchair Politician and Educator: Florencio Morales y Temprado

Florencio Morales y Temprado, along with Relimpio (but none of our other eccentrics so far examined) was included in the group of Galdosian characters whom Alas, in his review of the 1883 *Dr Centeno* [*El doctor Centeno*] in which Florencio appears, labelled "this race of peaceable madmen" ["esta raza de locos pacíficos"] that Galdós could paint so well. Alas astutely pointed to their commonality by referring to them as a race, in other words, as a collectivity. Most significantly, he also called them peaceful madmen, a mixture of opposing qualities: the comic and the honourable, the high-sounding and the grotesque ["lo cómico y lo honrado, lo altisonante y lo grotesco"] (*Galdós* 115), a designation and explanation that sound like a close approximation of my term of "eccentric."

Florencio is another member of our group who appears very early in the text: the middle of the first chapter, and with a purpose similar to those of his fellows: to establish a relationship with the main character, Felipe Centeno, or Celipín, a provincial lad recently arrived in the capital. Morales, the caretaker of the Madrid Observatory, is a tall, affable, oldish man whose clothes reflect his transitional social status: his well-kept overcoat and black silk tie with its gold-capped tie-pin indicate affluence, whereas his cloth cap – something he shares with Canencia and Relimpio – betokens a certain lack of economic resources. He may be a caretaker, but he looks like a "serving knight" ["caballero sirviente"], more real and less metaphorical in the aid he now offers to the sick Celipín, than the knight Relimpio had believed himself to be at the end of *La desheredada*. His names are given a peculiar mode of presentation that immediately sticks in the reader's mind: the poet Cienfuegos intones his name on greeting him with a certain cadenced syllabification, as if it were a hendecasyllable line of verse: "Don Floren...cio Mora...les y Temprado" (I, 1, ii), transcribed accordingly by the narrator.[1] The appropriateness of the Christian name becomes apparent when Morales is next seen standing in the vestibule of the Observatory, with its Grecian-style architecture: he is compared to a decorative statue guarding the entrance to the temple of learning. However, the seriousness of that metaphor is immediately deflated when Don Florencio has to stifle a yawn of hunger as he awaits the start of his wife's birthday party: he is as hungry as Celipín, who, recuperated from his bout of cigar-puffing outside the building, thinks that the respectable old man is the owner of the observatory, now grandly called the Florentine domicile ["domicilio florentino"] (I, 1, iii). Conveniently, but again appropriately because of the growing association of the old man and the boy, the physical portrait of Florencio is given by the narrator through the eyes, if not always through the mind, of Celipín, as he watches what is going on at the table from his restricted angle sitting in the hallway. This perspective enables the narrator to move from one register to another and create an amusing mixture of contrasting characteristics: Morales's tall figure is solemn, paternal, and polite, but then, on a lower level, his dark, bushy eyebrows are like two strips of tapestry and, finally, his black and white moustache is short and bristly like a scrub brush (very visible in the sketch Galdós penned of a male face on the back of f. 1:43 of the manuscript). He wears a silk cap (originally it had [back of f. 1:42] a gold braid, like that worn by Relimpio) for indoors, as well as big shiny boots, in which his measured gait up and down the room relates him to the pendulums in the observatory's machinery. His sublime voice is the only echo of the harmony of the spheres studied by the telescopes; otherwise, the building looks like a tenement house. He is a confusing amalgam of pompousness and fun, like Mr Pickwick. He appears stern and solemn, but is very kind too, especially to Celipín, at whom he constantly smiles from the table and to whom he then brings some food. He is really the incarnation of his matronymic: he is a moderate in all things, neither fully one thing or another. Here he criticizes alcohol (apart from Valdepeñas wine), preferring to drink the water of Madrid, which, as a connoisseur, he rates as the best in the world. The caretaker also likes moderate-tasting cigars. But the additional purpose of this sequence is to slowly bring into focus the presence at the table of the priest, Polo, and the two Sánchez Emperador sisters. The priest is the polar opposite of the middle-of-the-road Florencio, as his patronymic also suggests: his boisterous behaviour reflects his enjoyment of food and drink, as well as of pretty female company. Florencio, like other eccentrics discussed, is the conduit of information for the other characters and for the readers. He may be the butt of jokes from the young students who visit the observatory, but he is also presented as kind and thoughtful, bringing them sherry and cakes to celebrate his wife's birthday. He now supports Polo taking Celipín as a student helper in his primary school. His vigorous reconciliation of the priest's religious vocation and worldly habits – one of the novel's major threads – is generous and warm-hearted, but its advisability or effectiveness is already put into doubt by the high-sounding oratory he tries to use, imitating his political idol, Salustiano Olózaga: he is always losing himself in his own grammatical structures (in triplicate form, like those of *Caifás*) and has to come to an abrupt halt (I, 1, iv). His very attentive listening to political and religious speeches has only left him with a jumble of cliché phrases, which become his own amusing tags, often repeated in quick succession: "by the way," "I am old," "I have the great satisfaction," "stop, stop," "order, order," "if I weren't convinced" ["entre paréntesis," "yo soy viejo," "cábeme la satisfacción," "alto, alto," "orden, orden," "si no tuviera el convencimiento"] (I, 1, iv). Despite all these verbal crutches, he is unable to complete full sentences, except on one occasion, when the narrator confers on him the accolade of unwitting orator.

These customary external appurtenances of the "card" type succeed, then, in fixing him largely as a figure of fun. This effect is reinforced by the lengthy review of his major pastime: the close following of political events and figures. First, he appears ridiculous (less so in an earlier version: f.1:51, on the the back of f.1:71) when, in front of the jesting students, he carries an empty sherry bottle in one hand and with the other makes slow, pompous circles. His cheeks are a little red, and the cap pushed back a bit, as he tries unsuccessfully to make some profound statement, regurgitating the vacuous political phrases that he has read in the evening newspapers. He is mocked by the narrator with a comparison to Solomonic gravity. He seems to have actively participated in national events, such as the First Carlist War, although he is vague about details. The comic ambivalence of his dress extends to his political ideas. He believes, naïvely, like a number of members of the moderate Progresista Party of the period 1863–68, that democratic ideals of individual freedom could be reconciled with the absolute authority of the Church in social matters, and he repeats the cliché of the conservatives of the Unión Liberal government of the 1860s: "there are no traditional obstacles" ["no hay obstáculos tradicionales"].[2] If Relimpio was always mentioning his three pet grumbles about recent Spanish history, Morales has three similarly fossilized ideas about the Progresista party: imprudence will kill the party; exaggeration is the cause of all its troubles; and its electoral triumph is compatible with the continuation of traditional Catholicism. True to his matronymic, he only likes those politicians who are temperate and judicious, so he becomes disturbed and upset when people make sly remarks about the Church. The announcement to the students of his three contemporary European idols – Emperor Napoleon III; Cardenal Antonelli, the champion of papal power, and Salustiano Olózaga, an old-fashioned Progresista (an incongruously eclectic selection, in Ribbans's view [*History* 117], because they all failed in what they wanted to achieve) – is delivered in a grand, dramatic style: he half turns on his way out of the room, and then exits with military precision before his listeners can make any more interruptions or sardonic comments. Similarly ostentatious is his boasting of being friends with important political figures, like Fermín Caballero and Pedro Calvo Asensio. Galdós continues to deflate these out-of-date ideas by mock praise, addressing the lowly caretaker as "the most majestic Don Florencio Mora...les y Temprado" ["el majestuosísimo don Florencio Mora...les y Temprado"] when he pontificates at a party to celebrate a sermon by Pedro Polo (I, 2, x). By the time the meal ends, he cuts as comic a figure as Relimpio did at the Christmas Eve supper: still vehemently opposed to wine-drinking, he ends up drunk, nevertheless, after drinking too much of his beloved Madrid water.

7

   Yet, for all of Don Florencio's funny exaltation of past heroes and embracing of old-fashioned ideals, the depth of his feelings in these matters, like those of Relimpio, commands respect: the old man is right, for example, to be upset at the death of Calvo Asensio, because, as the narrator comments in an aside, it did mark an important watershed in contemporary politics, leading to the September 1868 revolution (I, 3, ii). Morales's opinion that his compatriot would have done better to remain a pharmacist instead of going into politics may be simplistic, but it contains some grain of common sense and truth. He is to be admired, then, for joining the funeral procession to the cemetery and for wanting to throw his handful of earth onto the coffin as a mark of respect to this political giant. It is at this juncture that his other role – as the dispenser of words of wisdom to guide Celipín – emerges. The boy, who had been listening most respectfully to this eulogy of Calvo Asensio, is given advice about the future course of his own life, which will be the main subject of the rest of the novel: in words of Socratic wisdom, Don Florencio tells the boy to behave himself if he wants to prosper. So, the old caretaker is a bewildering mixture of the ridiculous and the sublime in physical appearance, manner, political ideas, and approach to life.

   Morales disappears after this lesson, only to resurface in the novel's penultimate chapter, where, again like his fellow eccentrics, he is to discharge an important role, and, pertinently, face to face with the same Celipín, who has now accepted his offer of help. However, though Morales is willing to give Celipín some sweetmeats and to feed him when he is hungry, just as he had at the beginning of the novel, he cannot supply him and his destitute second master, Alejandro Miquis, with money. The observatory caretaker, glowingly addressed as the "Great Morales," takes advantage of the occasion to give the boy another lesson on what to do in life. As if to underline how much he has failed in this task since the boy first made his way up to the observatory, Morales delivers his homily after climbing the slope to the building and wiping away the sweat from his face. There is some considerable irony in this eccentric calling Celipín's master a madman for his wasteful and lazy lifestyle. The accusation is not inaccurate, true, but Morales then loses his direction when he makes a sweeping generalization, attributing the decadence of modern youth to the importation of foreign ideas. The lesson soon turns to his other obsession, thus joining both together: commenting on the political scene in Spain. Morales's view is certainly alarmist and exaggerated when he foresees rivers of blood flowing in the imminent revolution, yet he shows a deep concern for the stability and well-being of his country that surpasses the narrow, petty egotism of others. Furthermore, he correctly reads the drift of the current political crisis; he is also eager to offer a solution. Unfortunately, if it sounds perfectly idealistic and noble in theory, in the reality of the contemporary context, it is highly naïve and simplistic:

Give us the Militia, the 1812 Constitution, and that's enough. The clergy, in their place; the Militia, to keep order; the Army, for if there is a war; Parliament, all year, good seminaries, lots of discussion, lots of liberty, lots of Religion, and let's have peace. This is so clear and simple!
[Póngannos la Milicia, la Constitución del 12, y basta. El clero, en su puesto; la Milicia, para defender el orden; el Ejército, para caso de guerra; Cortes todo el año, buenos seminarios, mucha discusión, mucha libertad, mucha Religión, y venga paz. ¡Si esto es claro y sencillo!] (II, 3, ii)

The longer Florencio rambles on, the more absurd his political ideas become, especially when he claims that Castile is the breadbasket of the world; that the English should vacate, not Gibraltar, but the sherry town of Jérez de la Frontera; and that Spanish generals, lawyers, and politicians (with precise examples) are the best in the world. This ludicrous chauvinism reaches its climax when he claims that Spain has the best actresses in the world. Clearly, the reader is not being asked to subscribe to these opinions; indeed, quite the opposite: they are plainly absurd and probably were a contributing factor in the eventual failure of the 1868 revolution, when such extremes of freedom of religion and the rights of the Catholic Church could not be reconciled (Caudet, *El doctor Centeno* 65n72). Morales appears incredible when insisting that they are viable solutions. What, however, is not so laughable, quite the contrary, is his concern for his country's welfare. Accordingly, he is the character in the novel most responsible for painting the larger picture of national events, which do affect all the characters, including those who stand to gain most personally in a material or financial sense and who have contributed most to the national crisis (e.g. Celipín's master, Miquis). Morales, like the previous eccentric misfits in Spanish society, has a goodness of heart that is not displayed by other more "normal" characters. Morales had really launched Celipín's career in Madrid when he took him into the observatory at the beginning and gave him food and found him a job with Pedro Polo. Now at the novel's close, he repeats his gestures of personal charity and political instruction, only to have both totally unappreciated by life's pupil.

JESÚS DELGADO

As in *La desheredada*, Galdós positions around his master type a number of cognate figures in order to set in relief the mixture of concern and naïveté in Morales's idealistic belief that individual Spaniards can learn to change their ways. His political concerns are refracted through the gossiping and essay-writing of the unemployed civil servant Basilio Andrés de la Caña, who displays slight touches of eccentricity.[3] It is Jesús Delgado, however, a lodger at Doña Virginia's boarding house in Madrid, who, at the beginning of part II, provides the intellectual arguments for Morales's pious wishes about the need for Spain's youth to learn more about life. He is more than eccentric, he is mad in a number of ways: he is delusional and paranoiac. The old man spends most of his time in his room writing letters that he posts to himself, a variant of the kind-faced old priest inmate of Leganés in *La desheredada* who sent letters every day to the pope and looked like a Christian Diogenes, as he paced around with a copy of Kempis's prayer book in his hand (I, 1, i). The appropriately named Jesús Delgado is a polite, urbane person who keeps to himself, only speaking to ask if the mail has been delivered − more of a mysterious person than the sick, weepy figure in Galdós's first draft.[4] His obsessional letter-writing, amounting to about fifteen replies per day, is carried out in his room until the morning hours. This monomania has earned him the nickname of the corresponding Greek word ("eautepistológrafos") from one of the student lodgers. Both Morales and Delgado are, thus, elevated to the spheres of Greek antiquity in keeping with the aim and history of the science practised in the observatory. Delgado's letters have nothing to do with fictional characters or even a lady love, as the students imagine, and everything to do with a philosophical plan for national education reform

grafomanía

based on the revolutionary theories of the foreign educators Friedrich
Froebel and Johann Pestalozzi, whose books he is always consulting.
This burning obsession had led earlier to his dismissal from the Ministry of Education after twenty years of service, his progressive ideas
being considered "very strange ... and outlandish peculiarities"
["rarezas ... extrañísimas ... estrambóticas"] (II, 1, vii). Delgado is shy,
sensitive, and modest, regarded by his relatives as a peaceful madman
to be left alone: a member of the family peeks at him in his room when
he pays the monthly rent to the landlady, who thinks that he is an angel
in the same way that the narrator had addressed the dying Relimpio.
The physiological symptoms of his mental disorder include constant
facial grimaces and exclamations like "oh! ah!," which become his written and spoken tag. In his review of the novel, José Ortega Munilla,
another close friend of Galdós, saw some affinity between Delgado and
Dickens's Mr Dick (2). If this comparison derived from some private
conversation with the author, it would strengthen our earlier proposal
that Dickens's eccentric kite-flyer had influenced Galdós's development
of his eccentric-mad types in *Doña Perfecta* and subsequent novels.

Delgado's letters are the outpouring of his obsessional ideas on how
to educate modern youth. If Morales looks back to a past for guidance
for Alejandro Miquis and Celipín, Delgado sees the solution lying in the
future, when the country's drugged and dark mind sees the light of truth.
At the heart of Delgado's reforms lies the belief that the most important
thing in life "is not to appear, but to be" ["no es parecer, sino ser"] (II,
1, viii), a concept that is not so far removed, really, apart from its verbal
formulation, from Morales's recommendation at the end of the novel to
Celipín that Alejandro Miquis change his lifestyle. As with the observatory caretaker, there is something sadly ironic in the failure of Delgado
to communicate this advice directly to Alejandro Miquis and his friends:
his ideals are sound and laudable, but they are useless if contained in letters to himself, when around him he has a captive audience for their dis-
semination. This situation, however, changes totally when Delgado is the
recipient of a hoax letter from the students dated twenty years into the
future and reporting that his educational reforms have now been imple-
mented. This practical joke has an instantaneous and traumatic effect on
his mind that is relayed to external parts of his body: his face almost
comes apart under the force of his grimaces, his hair stands on end, and
he has an attack of St Vitus's dance, pacing up and down the room in
great agitation before going out into the corridor, like Canencia at the
end of his conversation with Isidora in *La desheredada*. The severity of
Delgado's nervous attack is signalled by the unusual barking of his dog,
called "Julián de Capadocia." In trying to comfort him, the animal
behaves more humanely than the animal-like students, in the tradition of

Cervantes's talking dogs, Cipión and Berganza, in his short story, "El coloquio de los perros" (1603–04), or of Orfeo, the dog owned by Augusto Pérez in Miguel de Unamuno's *Niebla* (1914). When the dog is made the recipient of the next letter, Jesús Delgado seizes the opportunity to write some home truths to the students and to provide them with a true lesson in Complete Education that has more to do with character formation than classroom syllabi.

Delgado the madman pens a sermon of common sense, and through the same medium: a letter to his dog, a letter that leaves no room for the students to doubt that he has seen through their pranks. The letter contains damning criticism of their lack of courtesy, their ignorance of the principles of education that he is discussing, and their empty lifestyle. If they had thought him mad, Delgado now calls them "poor fools" as they eagerly read the letter, because they do not realize that the acquisition of knowledge requires two qualities, neither of which they have: learning and discipline. Significantly, he considers Alejandro Miquis the sickest of the students, in much the same way that Morales will later call him a madman. Delgado perceptively foresees Alejandro's end: he is a triple suicide, because he is neglecting his health, conscience, and intelligence. Delgado's obsession with abstract educational programs does not prevent him, any more than Morales's passion for political talk, from being concerned with a fellow individual, here the co-protagonist of the novel. The forces against which these intuitive and sensitive wise fools are fighting can be measured by the reaction of the students to Delgado's bombshell of a letter: some think that he is an eccentric ["extraviado"], others that he is just regurgitating ideas found in foreign books. The real truth and purpose of his letter eludes them completely.

JOSÉ IDO DEL SAGRARIO

Complementing Delgado's role as educational theorist and offering another layer of reflection on Don Florencio as an instructor of youth is José Ido del Sagrario, Polo's assistant, who is the incarnation of the long-suffering classroom teacher. He appears very early in *El doctor Centeno*: in part I, chapter 2, entitled "Pedagogy" ["Pedagogía"], after a brief introduction of Pedro Polo and his school. His presentation (absent in a first draft of this chapter) so soon after that of Morales in chapter 1 (aptly entitled "Introduction to Pedagogy" ["Introducción a la pedagogía"]) suggests that Galdós, on reflection, could see the possibility of contrasting the roles of both characters in the education of Celipín: Morales, through his hospitality to the destitute boy, had provided the opportunity to obtain a job in Madrid and would later instruct him about the problems of the country; Ido would prove to be his companion, mentor, and protector as his career progressed.

Three points are established about Ido in quick succession: he is, by profession, a teaching assistant; he has a comic surname that, in its initial, abbreviated form, unequivocally suggests madness (Shoemaker, "Galdós' Literary Creativity" 117), and he is very conscientious about his duties. But the narrator seems more eager to describe Ido's strange physical appearance that, given the portrait's length – also expanded at the proof-correction stage – would have been more suitable for a major character. Ido's figure is certainly Dickensian, caricaturesque, almost grotesque (Ribbans, *History* 57). But what is important about this portrait is that the features selected are described in such a way as to form an ironic anticipation of Ido's main claim to fame, with which the paragraph ends: his calligraphy. For the narrator emphasizes the elongation of his features: he has a thin, bloodless figure, like that of a ghost. The elongation and whiteness are accentuated in his face: he is as pale as a candle, and the warts spotting his face are likened to drops of wax running down its side. A lock of black, spooky hairs on his forehead looks like a smoking candlewick, and his moist eyes, with their flickering eyelashes, always seem spluttering with weepy elegies – Mr Dick also possessed prominent, watery eyes, but he had a more robust build than Ido (*David Copperfield* 13). In conformity with good Lavaterian physiognomics, Ido's whole appearance presents a symbolic message that the narrator can easily read: he has spent a lifetime of suffering devoted to the service of children. The ecclesiastical connotations of the candle imagery applied to his face, as well as its mystical mien, elevate this life to one of religious martyrdom, for as the high priest of the religion of writing, he has provided society's rulers with their baptismal certificate as writers. The narrator's assertion that Ido is the cornerstone of many family fortunes, the father of generations, and the foundation of infinite glories is hilariously hyperbolic, implying that the opposite is true. The same inference is to be drawn from his direct summons to a long list of these alumni (now, in 1883, when Galdós is writing the novel, ministers, politicians, businessmen, notaries, poets, lawyers, doctors, journalists, and lovers, but not, it is to be noted, novelists) to remember Ido. This invocation, an obvious example of prolepsis, suggests that originally, in Galdós's mind, Ido was to be viewed as a somewhat oldish character.[5] The portrait ends with a kaleidoscopic sampling of some of Ido's calligraphy: the letters, humorously compared to military accoutrements of the past, stand out with their bold, florid lines, which contrast so markedly with the unidimensional elongation of the writer's own body. If Delgado and de la Caña are eccentric writers because of what they write, Ido is an eccentric writer because of the way he writes

– Mr Dick is also an excellent penman, who willingly earns money to support his revered Betsey Trotwood by copying out legal documents (*David Copperfield* 36). The climax of Ido's sample piece is the announcement of his full name, duly italicized, in the signature at the bottom. The religious connotations of the matronymic ("sacrarium" ["sagrario"]) now extend the series of religious allusions noted earlier.[6]

Ido not only helps Polo's students with their reading, he also writes letters for the schoolmaster. One of his physical features comprises the need to take breaths just to articulate each syllable: Polo tells him at times to shut his mouth so that his soul does not escape. Just as Don Florencio had been the butt of the university students' jokes, Don José is the target of the infant schoolchildren in the pictures they draw on the walls of buildings, which add further anatomical features: Ido is so thin that his clothes, from his tie to his trousers, are lower down than they should be; his Adam's apple is also huge. If the narrator stretches credulity with his initial litany of epithets of angel and seraph for Ido (which Relimpio had only earned at the end of his tale), Polo's descriptors are taken from the opposite end of the verbal scale: he is "stupider than simple cerate" ["más tonto que el cerato simple"] (I, 2, iii), an appropriate substance, given his candle-like figure. Even the narrator now tones down his compliments: Ido is not really a human being, but a plant – a mimosa – because he is so sensitive and always ready to cry when upset (I, 2, x). Ido has even more difficulty in keeping classroom order than his fellow teacher and madman of an earlier age, Patricio Sarmiento, and even less respect from the students, who endow him with a few nicknames: "Simple cerate, Calamity, Dido" ["Cerato simple, Calamidad, Dido"] (II, 2, vi).

When Celipín re-encounters Ido in part II in the same tenement house in which they both now reside, Ido is unemployed and unable to support his sick wife and four children. There is a corresponding alteration in his physical appearance: he is ghostly looking, his top coat hangs on his body, he has been weeping copiously, and his erect strands of hair, now red and not black, want to escape from his beaten-up hat. "The Penman" ["El pendolista"] now reveals his talent as an oral relator, updating the provincial lad on what has happened to Polo and the Sánchez Emperador girls, and sprinkling his accounts liberally with two pet words that will immediately identify him hereafter without further ado: "frankly, naturally" ["francamente, naturalmente"]. Annoyed at the injustice and contradiction of his being unemployed and without money when ten million Spaniards do not know how to write, he has the same sense of foreboding about political revolution as Morales, but welcomes the possibility of a total social change. If Morales thinks Alejandro Miquis is mad, Ido believes that he is a saint, and later, with his whole family and some neighbours, that he is also a literary genius. Both Ido and Morales agree that Miquis will suffer an early death. As Ido's financial plight worsens, much like that of Mr Micawber in *The Personal History of David Copperfield* (Ribbans, *History* 57), his physical appearance undergoes more changes: his eyes are now bulging out of their sockets, and his ghostly complexion, as he paces up and down the tenement corridor, almost carried along by the breeze, is more accentuated. When Celipín meets him begging in Madrid's main avenue, the Castellana, his head is slumped over his chest.

In the novel's last chapter (when Ido accompanies Celipín to Alejandro's burial) the unemployed calligrapher, like Cayetano Polentinos and Relimpio, undergoes a kind of cathartic ennobling of character that supercedes his function as a reflector of Don Florencio. His eloquence and articulateness are a revelation for a type whose whispery, faint voice has been stressed hitherto. From being a comic, pathetic type, he is transformed into a much more admirable and interesting character, and, as with Relimpio, this change is, to a degree, signalled by the dramatized format of the text at this point. This technique has the advantage of separating typographically the words and thoughts of the narrator from those of his character: the former's omniscience is now syphoned off into a few italicized stage directions, some of which, as well as some of Ido's sayings, were pertinently expanded at the proof-correction stage. By hilariously dismissing Ido's unusual perspicacity (Scanlon 250) as the prompting of some spirit or the miraculous reincarnation of wisdom in his body, the narrator, now as voice-off, only manages to focus more attention on these words of wisdom from the madman (Hoddie, "Reexamen" 62). Moreover, Ido's words of compassion for the distraught and unemployed Celipín are a surprise when he had previously been so given to self-pity. His philosophical advice could not be more accurate or practical: Alejandro's death will be a great learning experience for the young lad, not only about life in general but also about himself. He predicts that Celipín will soon have a better position with another master; in fact, he knows of a paraffin seller who needs a young lad to help with sales. Ido now succeeds in turning the narrator's earlier false praise of his saintliness into a moving statement on human existence: "All of us human beings, if we weren't what we are, would be saints; that is to say, if we did not have this wretched mortal flesh, which makes us men and women, we would be angels" ["Todos los humanos, si no fuéramos lo que somos, seríamos santos; es decir, que si no tuviéramos esta maldita carne mortal, por la cual somos hombres, seríamos ángeles"] (II, 4, vi). Amidst these words of Solomonic wisdom are to be found more recognizable outbursts of exaggerated sentiments, in that curious mixture of the sublime and ridiculous that was also seen in the dramatic last words of Cayetano Polentinos and Relimpio: for instance, Ido declares that, although a neighbour has removed the top coat from Alejandro's corpse, she will not be able to steal the artist's "glorious garment of immortality, nor will the sublime spirit of Miquis suffer from cold in the invisible, intangible, and immeasurable region" ["glorioso vestido de inmortalidad, ni el espíritu excelso de Miquis padecerá de frío en las regiones invisibles, intangibles e inmensurables"] (II, 4, vi). It is a measure of how much Celipín has learned about human nature during his months in Madrid that he can appreciate that Ido is showing unusual wisdom on this trip to the cemetery. He attributes the phenomenon to the calligrapher being drunk. Alcohol was certainly the catalyst that fired Relimpio's brave outburst of cautionary words to Isidora. The fact that Ido and Celipín are attending a funeral could have prompted these thoughts on life and death, but the truth is suddenly revealed, and with it the illusion of Ido's wisdom disappears to some extent. It happens that he had read these words the previous night in a book (unspecified) with the purpose (so Galdós added when correcting the proofs) of preparing for his own imminent attempt at novel-writing. Reading, especially when the words and phrases are well expressed, is a cause of spiritual regeneration and encouragement for Ido, and should be for Celipín (and the reader of the novel, Galdós implies) too. It could be argued that Ido can afford to be philosophical here, for, as he reveals in the next breath, his fortunes are beginning to change: he now has two pupils to teach. Even so, the context and the recipient of his wise words are more important: as in Cayetano's letters and Relimpio's words to Isidora, the proximity of a recent or imminent death adds a poignancy to his words, a poignancy that is accentuated by the almost complete indifference of the listener. From this point on in his fictional existence, Ido takes on another function: no longer just the voice of pedagogy or true education, he becomes a theorist and practitioner of the novelistic art.

Because Ido del Sagrario is the only secondary eccentric-mad type studied in this book who appears in more than a single novel and because this newly acquired function at the end of El doctor Centeno is treated consistently through his successive interventions (modest in scale in Torment [Tormento], That Bringas Woman [La de Bringas], and Prohibited [Lo prohibido], substantial in Fortunata and Jacinta [Fortunata y Jacinta]), Don José now deserves a chapter to himself. Montesinos (Galdós 2:90) reckons that Ido came into Galdós's imagination in a flash. What is more pertinent to note here, though, is that he fits naturally into Galdós's sequence of ongoing experiments with the eccentric-mad type.

CHAPTER SIX

Fantasy Novelist:
José Ido del Sagrario

Ido's sally into the world of novel-writing, recommended by a publisher friend – perhaps the same one who is publishing *El doctor Centeno*, in which Ido is now talking to Centeno – is obviously for financial gain, since the serialized, romantic potboilers called "novelas por entregas" he will be writing are very popular. In confessing that he had at first thought his friend's proposal absurd, but that, after reflection, he had seen that it was an easy occupation to solve his income problems, Ido reveals how much his character is developing some autonomy and complexity. He is no longer a type, even less so when he proceeds to engage in some literary theorization, discussing with Celipín the relation of the events of real life to fiction. Ido's lucid arguments are prompted by the developments in the Polo family, of which he seems to have been an immediate and accurate observer. However, for the hack writer that he wants to be and whom Galdós the theorist had attacked thirteen years previously in "Observaciones," the events of real life are just the springboard for his ever-active imagination to construct something much more sentimental and thrilling for the reader. This is why he rejects the realist aesthetic of Celipín (pertinently called Aristo/Aristóteles throughout this subsection by the narrator), who says that all Ido needs to do is recount Polo's adventures or his life as a servant to Alejandro. This is – ironically – something that has been achieved already by the same narrator who is now copying down these ideas from the young lad. More important than Ido's defence of "folletín" literature are the lucidity of his ideas and the pithiness of their expression: "Common things that happen every day do not have the nice little taste that is proper of things that are invented and taken from the imagination. The pen of the poet has to be dipped in the ambrosia of the beautiful lie, and not in the soup of the horrible truth" ["Las cosas comunes y que están pasando todos los días no tienen el gustoso saborete que es propio de las inventadas, extraídas de la imaginación. La pluma del poeta se ha de mojar en la ambrosia de la mentira hermosa, y no en el caldo de la horrible verdad"]. The irony of this sentences lies in the fact that, at a moment when Ido is showing that he is capable of progressing from a common literary type into a real individual, he is proposing to convert the real individuals of his own experience into common literary types for his novel, for, as he says, "I won't be short of types " ["tipos no han de faltarme"]. If Galdós is trying to show how types can be complex individuals, Ido as a budding novelist wants to go in the opposite direction and reduce the complex individual to a type: Nicanora will be the virtuous wife, Celipín the model loyal servant, and Polo the type of man overwhelmed by his social position. Ido's scheme of typification is not defective, for his evaluation of Polo is much more clear-sighted than the one Morales gives at the beginning of the novel, but, at the same time, it is incomplete, or partial.

Ido's last-minute promotion to the ranks of popular novelists in *El doctor Centeno* changes the dynamics of his role as a reflector of Florencio Morales: he now surpasses that conventional function in two important aspects. First, the elevation permits him to be an indirect mouthpiece of Galdós's theoretical meditations on the craft of fiction, especially about the symbiotic relation of art to real life. The basis of Ido's theory of art, as we have just seen, is that the crude reality of life can only be a starting point for a literary work: life has to be transformed. He has put theory into practice by the time he reappears in the opening chapter (dramatically formatted as a reprise to mirror the closing chapter of *El doctor Centeno*) of Galdós's next novel, *Torment* [*Tormento*] (1884). Ido has transposed the contemporary reality of the story of his neighbours, the Emperador sisters, to the Golden Age Period, using simplistic types to symbolize vices or virtues. But amidst all these distortions, he has not lost complete touch with reality, showing, in fact, that he can see it only too well and knows what to select or reject: for example, when Celipín mentions the sisters' beauty and virtue, he shows in his demurral that he can see very clearly the reality of what is happening in the building in which they all live. The same tendency to the occasional surprising insight recurs in another dramatically formatted scene between Ido and Celipín towards the end of *Tormento*: the lad accuses the hack

novelist of believing that things have to turn out the way he has imagined them. Even so, the ending Ido has imagined for his novel on
Amparo is not all that fantastic, given her previous suicide attempt
and her current nervous condition as she waits for the confrontation
with Caballero about her past. Moreover, Ido again displays his grasp
of reality when he tells Felipe not to worry about Rosalía Bringas's
pilfering of the Caballero mansion, for he knows that his master is
aware of what is happening but has good reasons for not tackling his
cousin about her actions. For Rodgers ("Appearance-Reality" 398),
Ido becomes a warning for the readers themselves: Ido correctly sees
a far more dangerous moral and ethical falsification abroad in society at large, in comparison with which his own literary lucubrations
pale in significance. The implications of this perspicacity are far-
reaching: Ido's instruction on the realities of life extend beyond the
boy: they are also directed at Galdós's readers and Spanish society in
general.

The second advantage of the change in Ido's status at the end of *El
doctor Centeno* is that it enables him, in a way not really open to the
letter-writing Cayetano Polentinos in *Doña Perfecta*, to be propelled
at whim into subsequent novels, not just one, the sequel, but several.
This explains why some critics have believed that he makes a very
fleeting appearance – again right at the end – of *La de Bringas*
(1884), when his two favourite words ("naturally, frankly") ["naturalmente, francamente"] are used by the narrator. Since the married
and moral Ido clearly cannot be the narrator, who has a sexual relation with Rosalía Bringas, Galdós must surely be teasing his regular
readers – it cannot be a minor error either (Nimetz 94n18; Ricard
59–60). As if to remind the reader of this tease and to make amends
for it, Gadós does introduce Ido – once more as a complete surprise,
and at the end of the novel, but this time unambiguously – as the narrator in *Lo prohibido* (1884–85). His appearance in this novel is the
work of God and a most unlikely ally, Pilar, aunt of the narrator-protagonist, José María Bueno de Guzmán. He is to complete, with his
perfect calligraphy, the memoirs of the now incapacitated author.[1]
Ido is, thus, performing the same service he had done an incredible
seventeen years before, in 1864, in *Tormento,* for another invalided
author. However, confusion is immediately sown in the mind of the
reader, for, on the one hand, the narrator of *Lo prohibido* indicates
that Ido only needs a couple of dozen words to faithfully re-create the
scene, as he can read José María's thoughts perfectly. On the other
hand, the narrator is quite adamant that Ido, a successful "novela por
entregas" writer, does not add any of his own material. But such
affirmations have to be treated with caution, for these words are

probably written by Ido, since he took over the redaction of the manuscript just before the passages chronicling José María's stroke. The
latter is not being completely helpful; he is even more obfuscatory,
when he reports, in a phrase that was added at the galley stage,
according to Whiston in his edition of the novel (479n481), that he
has allowed Ido to change the names of all the people he mentions.
Such a statement, however, makes no sense if interpreted literally, for
the narrator has given his name on the first page of the novel and it
is not changed in these last few pages. The other possibility is that Ido
has gone through the whole manuscript inserting fictitious names,
which would also have necessitated other re-writings and given him
the chance to add his own inventions. Uncertainty and confusion are
once more associated with Ido the writer-copyist. José María "doth
protest too much" about the accuracy of Ido's penmanship, for he
admits in the next breath that, with such an intelligent copyist as Ido,
he could so easily have dictated material for those readers looking for
excitement in the text. In the last paragraph of the novel, José María,
now feeling weaker and nearer to death, again inspects Ido's part of
the manuscript and certifies that there is no deviation from the truth.
The novel ends with a visit from the person who will publish these
memoirs and continue José María's prologue to another project. This
publisher happens to be a friend of both Ido and José María, perhaps
the same person who had advised the former to become a novelist in
El doctor Centeno. The admiration, even deference, shown Ido in
these paragraphs is very suspicious: Willem (*Galdós's 'Segunda Manera'* 174–5) is very reluctant to discount this influence of Ido on the
style of the concluding section of the novel and, therefore, on the full
sincerity of José María's final contrition. Leaving aside Galdós's obvious teasing of his regular readers, an authorial ploy that increases
even more the problematic status of the narrative and of the reliability of the autobiographical narrator, one still has to ask why Ido del
Sagrario was selected to discharge a prominent role at the end of yet
another novel. A rampant fictioner who has appeared in the creative
crucible of two novels already, Ido overshadows the last two chapters
of *Lo prohibido* in a more interventionist role, textually, than hitherto.[2] He is no longer the literary theorist who talks about his craft
with references to the plot and characterization of his own novels; we
now see what he can really produce, and it is not only facts and characters, but ideas and thoughts, all signalled to him by the voiceless
and paralyzed José María, now reduced to the status of ventriloquist
narrator.

   In part II, chapter 2 of *Lo prohibido* the narrator-protagonist
rejects for himself the label of individual or hero derived from books

of history or old-fashioned novels. He is only a type, a common man, a product of his time, race, and environment. Again, he blames traditional novels and dramas for creating the reader's expectation of heroes and heroines, a special type of men and women. Until his death, he maintains that his experiences do not differ from those of other people. But the truth of the matter is that this decadent, materialist Don Juan, labelled an ugly, eccentric monstrosity ["Feo, apunte, mamarracho"] (I, 12, iii) and a dummy and twit ["muñeco, estafermo"] (II, 8, iv), has become, unwittingly, through his autobiography, a complex, human individual rather than a stock literary type. In the last two chapters of his *Life* he becomes even more individualized and sympathetic because of his terminally debilitating illness and his change of heart and outlook – the memoirs are described in the last sentence as a book of confessions. Whether Ido del Sagrario introduced changes to the galley proofs before the text was published (the sign that José María is dead) can only be a matter of conjecture. But, if he did, the changes could well have been important additions of tone and comment – especially if Galdós's own practices when correcting proofs were followed. Consequently, Ido's role in the presentation of a more sympathetic José María in the closing stages of the novel could be as significant as the perceptive remarks he had made in the same place in previous novels. Ido, like Cayetano, *Caifás*, and Relimpio, is allowed to surprise his readers – in his own novel way.

If Ido has now outgrown his initial role in *El doctor Centeno* as a mirror figure for the eccentric Don Florencio Morales and has become the narrator's pen, or even the hidden narrator of the whole novel, both complex and perplexing, it can also be said that he is José María's alter ego, his better self, the writer pure and simple, free of the responsibility for the historical, real man's actions and feelings. To this extent, his character can stand in contrast to that of José María himself and all the other eccentrics-cum-madmen that flood *Lo prohibido* in what could be interpreted as another version, albeit greatly enlarged, of Galdós's gallery-of-mirror-characters technique, used in *El doctor Centeno* and earlier novels. At the beginning of the novel, José María Bueno de Guzmán had surrounded himself with a plethora of minor and minimal mirror characters: his own extended family of male relatives, present and past, both in Madrid and Andalusia, with their variants of the same hereditary mental disease from which he suffers. Finding the correct generic term for the disease proves difficult: it could be called "a slight nervous imperfection; eccentricity; invincible passion" ["una imperfeccioncilla nerviosa; chifladura; pasión invencible"], that derails their lives; or "a more or less strange mania" ["manía más o menos rara"], that has no effect on individual behaviour; or "a constituent peculiarity" ["singularidad constitutiva"] (I, 1, ii).[3] Heart or mind could be damaged; some relatives, male and female, have ended up in the insane asylum, whilst others have been famous for their learning. The result is that the gamut of mental disease is very wide, ranging from mild eccentricity to raging lunacy. For example, one old relative would go round Ronda dressed in a blanket as a ghost to frighten people. The narrator's own grandfather had been a most famous Don Juan who had requested that, after his death, poor children in Ronda should be buried beside him. Of those who reappear during the novel, Serafín, an uncle, is a kleptomaniac old general who likes to ogle girls on the buses and march behind the Royal Palace band at the changing of the guard. A great-uncle, Rafael, suffers periodic illusions of walking on air. A passing reference to the educational theorist of *El doctor Centeno*, Jesús Delgado – "a most simple person" ["un ser inocentísimo"] – who is another of the narrator's relatives, reminds us that the 1863 world of that novel was populated more by eccentrics than madmen, whilst the 1884–85 world of *Lo prohibido* contains a bewildering number of clinically certifiable madmen.[4]

In the novel that followed, *Fortunata y Jacinta* (1886–87) Ido's activities as a novelist take on even graver dimensions, and, at the same time, his eccentricity has evolved into a form of craziness that has well-defined symptoms equating it to that of some of the Bueno de Guzmáns. But even here Galdós multiplies the layers of irony, for the events in which Ido participates in *Fortunata y Jacinta* occur a decade before his appearance in *Lo prohibido*, whose action is rigorously contemporaneous with the novel's composition (1884–85). In other words, Ido has recuperated from the phase of mental sickness that had afflicted him a decade earlier. His entry into *Fortunata y Jacinta* (I, 8) is casual and unrelated to any of his previous fictional appearances, although the calling card as a sales agent for national and foreign publications that he has delivered to Juanito and Jacinta Santa Cruz is probably an oblique reminder for the regular reader of his manuscript writing in *Lo prohibido*. Even so, Galdós felt it desirable to re-issue a portrait: Ido has become thin again, but he still has his recognizable bumps and warts, as well as his red, scrub brush-like hair.[5] New details are added about his apparel: he has a frayed red tie, and his boots are "so creased they seemed to have been made that way" ["muertas de risa"].[6] Another distinctive item of clothing, essential for fixing a colourful "flat" character in the reader's memory, is an opera hat that must have been the first one ever made. The point of interest about this visit is not really the attempt by Ido to sell books, but rather the reaction of the couple to his strange appearance. Despite his sickness, the chair-bound Juanito, suddenly seized with a burst of energy, jumps up when Jacinta reads aloud the information on Ido's card. Juanito immediately acclaims the agent as the most entertaining madman imaginable and the most famous of types. His reason for this assessment is that, on an earlier occasion, Ido made him and his friends die of laughter – the same expression that, in Spanish, a few lines later will be used to describe Ido's creased boots. The frenetic nature of this reaction to Ido on both occasions would indicate some abnormality in Juanito's own psyche, as if he were more unbalanced than Ido, who, like a court jester (O'Byrne Curtis 138), can be turfed out of the house when they tire of him, as Juan tells his wife. Clearly, Juanito does not appreciate Ido for any words of spiritual wisdom that he might offer.[7] His greeting to the book agent is exaggerated, whereas Ido's is sincerely urbane and respectful. His appearance and new occupation are linked through art imagery: if his sample subscription-books are so grubby that the gold finish of the binding has been worn away, Ido is the "picture of poverty in decent dress" ["estampa de miseria en traje de persona decente"]. By immediately launching into the list of the books he has brought along, Ido is able to throw the dry-goods heir off balance, for he has to listen to a rather embarrassing catalogue of titles, some of which could well refer to both his wife and his former lover: *Famous Women, The Women in the Bible, Famous Courtesans* [*Mujeres célebres, Mujeres de la Biblia, Cortesanas célebres*]. Somewhat cross, Juanito cuts short Ido's demonstration by saying that he prefers to buy complete volumes. Buying works in serialized form with the attendant disruptions of service is enough to make him mad, a phrase that Galdós again substituted for an innocuous phrase when he corrected the galleys. So, a man whom Juanito had characterized as the most entertaining madman imaginable would make him mad if he sold him a subscription for serialized novels. The other irony about Juanito's rejection of the offer is that, at this moment, he is very anxious to locate Fortunata and renew his relationship with her, which already, and more so in the future, has the outline of a serialized romance (both as a relationship and as a text). Ido is, thus, a vehicle for transporting metafictional observations from Galdós to the text. Unlike those he delivers in *Tormento*, however, the examples in *Fortunata y Jacinta* are more integrated into the fabric of the plot itself, forming the casing, as it were, for major, future developments.

Don José also shows initiative, in turn, in rejecting Juanito's accusation that he was drunk at their other meeting. Whereas in previous novels physiological details had mostly been provided by the narrator, now Ido himself delivers them by way of explaining to Juanito his condition at their earlier meeting and this one: he suffers sudden attacks of a nervous shaking that affects his left eyelid and left cheek muscle.[8] He has sought medical help, but the prescribed cure – eating meat – is counterproductive, for it only makes him worse. Given this information, Jacinta's subsequent offer of a chop is surprisingly obtuse, especially when her husband had confined himself to initially suggesting a glass of water. Consequently, it could be argued that Jacinta, by causing Ido to stay in the house longer when he had wanted to withdraw, brings about the subsequent misfortunes in her life. Juanito is now able, much to his delight, to carry out his original plan of using Ido as a laughing stock. Ido does not disappoint, first when he cannot remember what a pork chop is, and next, when he attacks the meal like a ravenous tiger, laughing nervously, and with his whole body shaking, his arms waving, and the fluttering of his left eyelid and jaw muscle even more pronounced. The fact that Ido eats from the same side table from which the sick Juan had dined on earlier suggests that the latter is prone to nervous attacks too, like the duke and duchess watching Don Quixote sup at their palace in part II of Cervantes's novel (P. Smith 49). In his conversation Ido proves himself equal, if not superior, to his taunter, at least for the reader, for Juanito does not seem to be aware that some of his comments and those of Ido can describe his own character and behaviour. For example, when Ido trots out his lament, already familiar to readers of *El doctor Centeno* and *Tormento*, about the ingratitude of the nation towards its men of letters, Juanito furnishes the standard response – that there are hardly any readers in Spain, and that those that do read do not have any money – without remembering that he has just refused to subscribe to Ido's serialized novels on the spurious grounds that he, a man of money, prefers to buy complete works, something he had done only during his university days. When Ido declares that his wife, Nicanora, has the beauty of Venus, Juanito, echoing a title of one of Ido's specimen books, declares an interest in seeing this famous beauty. However, the trick, which Juanito has signalled to his wife, backfires when Ido adds that his wife's external beauty forms a contrast with her inner evil, not an inopportune observation, however erroneous in Ido's case, because, prior to his visit, the narrator had emphasized how Juan's great physical beauty is admired not only by others but also by himself. Juan now deliberately targets – again with Jacinta's unwitting connivance, through some maladroit comments that she will quickly have cause to regret – Ido's mad point ["demencia"] by declaring that Nicanora is a saint. The words elicit an immediate response

from Don José, for, after moving his chin and neck in opposite directions and indulging in heavy self-pity, the seller of novels springs up
from his chair and, with the exaggerated gestures of an opera singer,
shouts out that his wife is an adulteress. While Jacinta is aghast at
Ido's deteriorating state of mind, Juan prolongs the man's agony and
his own sadistic pleasure with the advice that these misfortunes have
to be borne with patience. The whole exchange is doubly ironic in
retrospect: first, Nicanora is not the adulteress her husband claims;
indeed, she is quite the opposite. But Juan will eventually commit
adultery with the newly returned Fortunata, and it is Jacinta who
will be forced throughout the rest of the novel to follow the advice
Juanito has just given to Ido, that is, to bear her partner's infidelity
with patience. Moreover, she will come to experience for herself the
truth of what she had just said to Ido: that nobody cares whether his
wife is a saint or otherwise.

Galdós continues to enlarge the list of physical symptoms that
chart this attack of Ido's monomania. In his electrified state, he now
tends to repeat the last words spoken by others. He rests his chin on
his chest and closes his eyes, half sunk into their sockets, just like a
bull lowering his head to attack the bullfighter. The image is most
apt, given Juan's enjoyment of visits to bullfights in his youth and the
fact that he is described on his birth by his godfather as a calf. Ido
does move towards Juan as if to attack him, and Jacinta moves closer
to protect her husband, but the charge is not that of a bull, nor even
that of a fighting turkey cock, in spite of the inflamed caruncles on
Ido's neck, which look redder than his tie. Again what appears to
Juan as an absurdly comic scene is full of more serious meaning for
his own marriage later in the novel. Ido softly sidles up to Juan to
attack him, not physically, but with a verbal crescendo, dismissing
the importance of marital honour. Ido does this rather cleverly,
for, though the luridly Romantic details of the story that he quickly
sketches clearly refer to what he imagines is his own situation, he is
able – by using the polite pronoun of address for "you" ["usted"] as
the subject of all the verbs of action – to confusingly suggest that it is
Juan who has discovered his wife in adultery. That is nonsense, of
course, so the question of adultery has to be referred back to Juan
himself – once more his flippant remarks boomerang back on his own
somewhat precarious marital situation at this moment. Ido again out-
smarts the trickster Juan, who feigns deep consternation at Ido's
predicament. Ido sarcastically rejects his suggestion of a duel with his
wife's lover; that is a game for fools, Ido retorts, again in a crescendo:
he will settle the matter once and for all, by taking the law into his
own hands and killing the adulterers in flagrante delicto. Juanito

could well have heeded these words, for the cuckolded Maxi will attempt at the end of part II – albeit unsuccessfully – to defend his sullied honour against the adulterer Juanito. Ido's maniacal attack now peaks: he gesticulates and paces up and down the room, occasionally stopping in front of the couple as if totally unaware of what he is doing or saying. The eccentric of earlier novels has now developed into a person with mental and physiological disorders. For the Santa Cruzs, for their servant, and, at times, for the narrator, Ido is an oddball who should be ushered out with a few coins; his steps then echo down the stairs.

Juanito agrees with Jacinta's diagnosis that Ido's "delusion" ["demencia"] is due to his not eating, but he also adds another cause: his writing of novels. Apart from this weakness, Ido is totally reasonable and very truthful. This is another assessment by Juanito that will soon prove inaccurate and will lead to important plot developments. Jacinta can be forgiven, then, for wanting to help the man whose nervous fits have so frightened her. But, unfortunately, her fine feelings will lead to further problems. Ido, encouraged by the help he and his family receive from her through the offices of Doña Guillermina Pacheco, returns to the couple's apartment, but this time to see only Jacinta and with a different, more complicated purpose. "The man with the stiff hair" ["el hombre aquel de los pelos tiesos"], as Ido is introduced by the servant, now behaves much more reasonably, with none of his previous extravagances, as Jacinta immediately notes. He also conducts the conversation with a certain aplomb; in fact, he controls its direction (Goldman et al 93). After first asking for some of Juanito's old clothes – for as Jacinta remarks, they are of the same height, thereby reinforcing the associations established on the previous visit – Ido steers the conversation about his own children around to Jacinta's lack of any. In a reversal of what happened at their first meeting, Ido touches on Jacinta's "demencia," or sore point, and inflames it even more by blasphemously blaming God for not making her a mother. She is immediately won over to his side, going so far as to absurdly believe that Ido is the world's greatest philosopher. She hands over more money, allowing him to again move the conversation to the point that he wishes to raise: Guillermina reserves her best hand-outs of clothes for the child *Pituso*, who lives with his friend and neighbour, José Izquierdo. Slowly and with lowered voice, in marked contrast to the crescendo of outbursts on the first visit, Ido insinuates that this three-year-old is the illegitimate child of Fortunata. With considerable astuteness and insight into Jacinta's character as a wronged and jealous wife, Ido disparages Fortunata, calling her a mad woman who wanted to abandon her child, as well as exaggerating *Pituso*'s charms. For maximum effect, Don José reserves the revelation of the father's identity – solemnly given in its full form – to the end. When Jacinta hears her husband's name, her emotional turmoil and bewilderment are complete: she instantly believes that this is another of Ido's tiresome extravagances or eccentricities, calling him to his face "a madman" who has lost his senses through writing novels. As if to prove that she, like her husband in the first scene, is crazier than he, the acknowledged madman, Ido calmly appeals to society's principal book of authority – the Bible – to support the truth of his claim, and leaves without protest but with respectful bows, when Jacinta stealthily shepherds him to the door.[9]

Almost physically, as well as morally, blind and deaf for the rest of that day, Jacinta tries to dismiss Ido's story as an oral novel, since he can no longer publish the ones he writes, or, she muses, it is an attempt to bring the products of his tubercular imagination into real life: only in bad novels are these surprise illegitimate children brought out, when it is time to complicate the plot. Thus, Jacinta is initially responsible for labelling Ido's hoax as a bad novel. This fact reveals not only her knowledge of the "folletines" and the "novelas por entregas" but also her awareness of plot directions. Ironically, of course, in retrospect, Ido's "bad novel" will emerge as the most important plot complication in part I of *Fortunata y Jacinta*, and will be re-written as a "good novel" in part II, with, in both cases, Jacinta being the destined reader, eventually disappointed with the first novel but finally delighted with the second one.[10] Ido, patently the novel's most deranged secondary character, is to be credited, then, with launching its storyline on its proper and definitive course. The plot now increases in pace: Jacinta, accompanied by Guillermina, pays visits to Ido's hovel of an apartment to see *Pituso*. Certain activities in which Ido is shown to be engaged here seem, in retrospect, to signal the possible failure of his attempts to convince Jacinta to accept his "novel." First, Ido, the erstwhile calligrapher, secretary, novelist, and soon-to-be copyist (in *Lo prohibido*), is now a stationer producing funeral paper. Such an activity suggests a not too happy outcome to the *Pituso* story, especially when Ido's task is not to put the black edging on the sheets of paper – his wife does that – but simply to arrange them in a pile ready for the edging, a process aptly called "dissembling" ["desmentir"] (I, 9, ii). This is a term whose first meaning ("to deny, refute") Ido is not able to realize either in his other confection, the *Pituso* novel.

A second task for Ido at this point in the novel is transporting bricks to the orphanage Guillermina is having built in another part of the city, and where, ironically, the principal character in Ido's novel, the three-year-old *Pituso,* will be sent at the end of part I. For the successful completion of this one-time task, Ido is given a new hat by Guillermina – the old one is bought by a carnival actor – and some money by Jacinta. Again her generosity and gratitude has some unfortunate consequences, for both Ido and herself, since the book agent, rather selfishly and unwisely, goes to spend it on a chop in a tavern, where, joined by Izquierdo, he becomes a passive listener of his neighbour's historical exploits, when not dazed, as a grammarian, by the grotesque vocabulary used.[11] Flapping eyelids and reddening caruncles signal that a nervous fit is imminent. It is now Ido's turn to monopolize the conversation, as, full of self-pity, he succumbs to his paranoia: he rates his wife's infidelities as far more serious than Izquierdo's betrayal by politicians. His movements become very jerky: labelled "the electric man," he jumps up from his seat, his hair on end.[12] The physical symptoms continue to manifest themselves as he dashes through the streets: he gesticulates, his eyes are burning, and his lower lip is thrust out. His vengeance on the adulterers is accompanied by his usual theatrical intonation, and his eyes bulge out of their sockets before he lapses into a coma, the second stage of the attack, raving but still, with eyelids closed. His wife now explains that his seizures are dengue fevers or a heating of the brain when he takes meat, and are the result of a bout of typhoid that nearly killed him.[13] His obsession with her adultery had started two years previously while he was writing his popular novels about the marital infidelities of the aristocracy, a subject that will soon be a burning concern for Jacinta, who is really not paying any attention to Nicanora here, as she is more interested in seeing *Pituso.*

For Juan there is no doubt that Ido's novel-writing and his meagre diet are the primary reasons for the hoax story about *Pituso*'s birth: Ido must have got the idea through an artistic-flatulent stroke of inspiration, Juan reckons, inventing a neat neologism, as he soft-soaps his wife about the matter. According to Juanito, the text is multi-authored by a bunch of fools and idiots: Izquierdo, Ido, Guillermina, as well as Jacinta and his mother, who went crazy with the idea (I, 10, vii). His clinching argument against the pretentious ["cursi"] *Pituso* novel is the fact that his and Fortunata's child had died. To convince his wife of this truth, he chooses to present it as the final paragraph of the story of his relationship with Fortunata that he had read to her in stages during their honeymoon (I, 10, vii). The false novel of Ido has to be trumped by the truth of the real, live novel that, as we shall see in the next chapter, Estupiñá has authored. For their part, Juanito's mother blames the contagious nature of Ido's frenzy for her falling for

the madman's trick, whereas Juanito's father attributes his acceptance
of the false story to his old age. Yet the most demented character at
the end of part I is Juanito himself, as he searches unsuccessfully for
Fortunata. The burning need to find her becomes an obsession of his
imagination that takes on a psychotic nature: the symptoms are "a
spiritual sickness mixed with nervousness aggravated by obstacles"
["mal de ánimo con mezcla de un desate nervioso acentuado por la
contrariedad"] (I, 11, iii). Increasingly, he resembles Ido, whose "novela pitusiana" he had ridiculed as a concoction of a diseased imagination. This similarity of mental sickness is underlined by a metaphorical reference to the physical sickness – typhoid – that had, according
to Nicanora, given rise to Ido's subsequent mental disorders: increasingly dominated by an investigative frenzy, Juan visits all sorts of
houses, "searching for a remedy for that typhoid – curiosity – that was
consuming him" ["buscando remedio al tifus de curiosidad que le
consumía"] (Whiston, "Language" 87). Another word that the narrator had used to describe Ido's mental condition, "desazón," is now
applied to Juanito's. His admission to his fellow playboy, Villalonga,
of a neurosis with its locus of origin inevitably recalls, with the appropriate use of Ido's tag, his earlier diagnosis of the creation of "la novela pitusiana": "Nerves, wouldn't you say, Jacintillo? It's this rascal of
an imagination that I have .... Frankly, I thought I was stronger; that
I wouldn't be so horribly neurotic about a card that won't turn up"
["Cosas de los nervios, ¿verdad, Jacintillo? Esta pícara imaginación
.... Francamente, yo me creí más fuerte contra esta horrible neurosis
de la carta que no sale"].

When in part II Juan resumes his relationship with Fortunata, he
confesses the mental derangement he suffered during this period of
delirious searching, as well as reporting that his wife lost her senses
over the *Pituso* affair. He predicts that, if Jacinta ever gave birth to a
child, she would go mad and turn everybody else mad (II, 7, vii). Juan
is prepared to categorize everything as a mania, as if, indeed, he has
caught Ido's contagious disease. Later, when he has once more broken off his affair with Fortunata, he will refer to her enduring love
for him as a mania (III, 2, iii). For her part, Fortunata is now racked
by a number of extravagant ideas going through her head: first, that
Juan should not be rich, but poor, so she could work to support him.
Then, more practically, she proposes an exchange between Juan's two
lovers that is perceptively expressed as that of a small baby (from her)
for the big one (Juanito) (from Jacinta). Fortunata calls this a great
idea. The narrator will later qualify it as her "roguish idea" ["pícara
idea"], which will become her final mania. Ido's confection of the
Pituso story, inspired by his reading and writing of popular novels,

not only launches the plot of *Fortunata y Jacinta* into full motion but also provokes a counter action that will conclude the novel: Fortunata's creation or conception of a baby son, ultimately intended for Jacinta.

So, although Ido is absent from the novel for all of part II, his role as the author of the novel's main plotline is never forgotten. It is immediately recalled with the arresting designation of "romantic feats" ["románticas hazañas"] when the narrator reintroduces him towards the end of part III (6, ii). Again, it is at an important juncture in the storyline: Mauricia la Dura is on her deathbed, and it is in her house that Jacinta and Fortunata meet at close quarters for the first time. The narrator pointedly focuses attention on the paranoiac: Ido's physical appearance is unrecognizable, at least from the rear, because he is better dressed and cleaner than when he had first visited the Santa Cruz couple in part I. But looked at from the front, his features – disjointed body, warty face, and ever-growing Adam's apple – confirm that the person is the same old Ido. The *Pituso* episode is further recalled when it is reported that Izquierdo has vacated his old room, which is now occupied by an equally strange-looking character, an Italian trombonist by the name of Mr Leopardi, whose need for warm clothes brings Fortunata and Jacinta into conversation with each other for the first time in the novel as they offer their respective husbands' old clothes. They soon turn to the topic of children, with Jacinta revealing her true mania for them, even being willing to steal them, and Fortunata saying the same, so as not to appear inferior (III, 6, v). Earlier in the visit, when sitting on the same sofa as Jacinta and looking at Mauricia's daughter, Fortunata had recalled, somewhat angrily, all the details she had been told about the *Pituso* episode. This meeting between Juan's wife and mistress, ending with Fortunata's defiant revelation of her identity, is, consequently, the important motivation first for the latter's sudden suggestion to Maxi that they adopt a child (preferably *Pituso*) and then later, more seriously, for her final decision to have another child by Juanito, so as to prove her superiority over Jacinta once and for all. Ido and his friend the trombonist preside, as it were, over this important forwarding of the main course of the plot.

Ido's presence at the novel's dénouement is, therefore, indispensable. The first step in that reappearance is taken when Maxi becomes friendly with him in the café groups. The obvious first assumption is that Ido is being used to throw into greater relief Maxi's increasingly disturbed mind. There are minor similarities of detail: in the clinical language of Ullman and Allison (15), Ido's pellagra-induced psychosis is contrasted with Maxi's schizophrenia. Like Ido, Maxi has been prescribed raw meat (by his friend and fellow-pharmacist, Ballester) as medication for his mental condition (III, 6, ix). Ido corrects the spelling of the street signs, just as Maxi corrects non-standard speech (Labanyi, *Gender* 178). At a more significant level, when Maxi first suspects Fortunata of adultery, he behaves just as Ido had done in part I, searching for her supposed lover in the apartment early in the morning and rushing home from Ballester's pharmacy in order to catch the couple by surprise. This obsession is termed an extravagance, mania, and roguish idea by the narrator (IV, 1, ii). For Ribbans (*Conflicts* 182), this is a far more dramatic situation than Ido's literature-fuelled fantasy about Nicanora's adultery. But it is in Ido's involvement in the plot's final unwinding that his relationship with Fortunata's husband assumes its greatest significance (Yáñez, "Algo más" 852). Maxi does not know who Ido is when he sees him for the first time in the café with Izquierdo, whom, of course, he does know. This allows Galdós to give yet another account, perhaps superfluous, of Ido's predominant physical features: face, neck, Adam's apple, hair. That Maxi notices these features like everybody else is less important than his interest in Ido's speech, which, because it holds the attention of his listeners, signifies for Maxi that he must be one of the café's most learned customers. At least Maxi does not make Lavaterian assumptions on the basis of physiognomic features, but rather on what he hears from Ido's lips, which is a simplistic but accurate analysis, in Maxi's opinion, of the causes of the French Revolution of 1789, the opportuneness of Napoleon's period of iron rule, and the need to find a balance between the tyranny of a despot and the anarchy of the masses. Ido has even developed a new catchphrase: "Either there's logic or there isn't" ["O hay lógica o no hay lógica"] (IV, 5, i). Maxi is full of praise for Ido's great reasoning and display of political realism, and rightly so, as the conversation is perhaps the most profound by Ido in his whole fictional existence, albeit expressed in familiar language, and certainly, as Maxi believes, beyond what would normally be expected from a primary school teacher. The praise is not out of place, coming from Maxi, who before and after this speech by Ido makes admirably sensible comments on other political and social events. Maxi shows uncommon sympathy in comforting Ido when, on his saint's day, celebrated in the Café de Gallo, he suffers another of his attacks after overeating and displays the usual symptoms: a twitching face and a deep voice. His praise for those cuckolded husbands who murder their unfaithul wives is just the sort of remark that Maxi wants to hear at this moment, as he ponders the idea of killing Fortunata. Maxi calmly and gently tells the others at the café table not to laugh at Ido, for he is unwell, and, in words of wisdom applicable to all our eccentrics and crazies, and especially to himself at the novel's close, declares: "Mental illness is the worst kind there is, and it's not Christian to laugh at these things" ["Un trastorno mental es el mayor de los males, y no es cristiano tomar estas cosas a broma"] (IV, 5, ii). He suggests, as cures for Ido's illness, diluted brandy, a lot of cold showers, and sodium bromide tablets.

Ido has a crucial role to play in those sections of the final chapter of the novel that take place in the apartment of Fortunata after she has just realized her mania or "roguish idea" of producing an heir for Juanito. The agent and author of the *Pituso* novel, Izquierdo and Ido, are once more brought together, but now as witnesses and readers of the true novel about Juan's child that has just been born. They are detailed to guard it, although they are often seen playing cards and talking in the guard room at the door to the apartment. After attending the child's christening party at a nearby café, Ido suffers his usual attack of nerves, pacing up and down the room, gesticulating and muttering to himself. It is because of this nervous fit that Maxi is able to secure entry into Fortunata's bedroom and reveal Juanito's new affair with Aurora, which will, in turn, lead to Fortunata's attack on her, and her subsequent haemorrhaging and death, after her donation of the new child to Jacinta. Again, it can be said, Ido – albeit involuntarily – unlocks the mechanism that triggers the final series of events in the novel, which he had set in motion in the first place.

Fortunata tries to enlist his help when she is startled by Maxi's entrance: she cannot recall his name at first, referring to him as that "fright" ["esperpento"], and then, eventually remembering his matronymic, calling out twice without success: "Señor Sagrario." Ironically, of course, the only time when this form is used in the novel, Ido does not live up to its meaning (IV, 6, iii). On about five occasions he comes to the door of Fortunata's bedroom, in an emblematic reversal of those two door scenes in part I when he had been bundled out of the Santa Cruz apartment. Here, with his thin, wart-marked face, he looks like a grotesque plaster or marble statue, his eyes are lifeless, and he mumbles incoherently. When chastised by Fortunata's aunt, Segunda, for letting Maxi into the apartment, Ido reacts with extreme facial grimaces, his mouth and eye arching up toward his hairline, and then defends his dignity as a professor of intellectual births (IV, 6, iv). This is an appropriate adaptation of his professional status to the reality of the new child's birth, but, at the same time, it is another reminder of his role as the author of the false natural novel that had led to this real natural novel – on his first response to Fortunata's summons, he had looked into the room at her and Maxi, as if he were inspecting a class of boys studying their books (IV, 6, iii). This role is pertinently recalled by Doña Guillermina when she advises against Jacinta and her going to see the son bequested by Fortunata, for if they did, they would deserve to be used by Ido as types for his novels. It is Guillermina who insistently recalls Ido's first novel by assuring Doña Bárbara that the new child is the authentic, real *Pituso*.

Ido does not end the novel as an inmate of Leganés, like Maxi, the self-confessed martyr and madman. Had he done so, would he have attained the sublime status that Cayetano Polentinos and Relimpio, for example, had achieved at the end of their novels, and that Ido himself did at the end of *Tormento*? Probably. Yet critics are not unanimous in their opinion. On one side, there are those who concentrate on his comic role, which is, for sure, to the fore again, and is underscored by his physical appearance and dress. Ortiz Armengol (*Apuntaciones* 34–5) believes that Ido serves as a parodic counterpoint to Maxi, even as a parodic self-portrait of Galdós himself as artist. Ribbans (*Conflicts* 43) is convinced that Ido is always "destined to be a pathetic figure of fun, never able to rise above an agonized struggle for existence." On the other hand, Shoemaker ("Galdós' Literary Creativity" 121) argues that Ido is "never a mere tipo, never an interchangeable part." The difficulty of describing Ido is summed up by Francisco Pérez (165–6), who successively labels him as abnormal, eccentric, lovable, phenomenal, and a reasonable lunatic. Montesinos (*Galdós* 2:265) admits that Ido is a commedia dell'arte mask used to turn a scene or event into a grotesque representation, but he also appreciates how moving Ido can be at times.

By deliberately choosing to develop in detail the features of mental disorder in Ido's character, Galdós signals his intention to deepen it. The result is that Ido becomes less of a comic type and more of a pathetic individual. By the same token, his moments of wise insights in the café only serve to solidify this new stature. But it is in his fabrication of the false *Pituso* novel that his true importance in *Fortunata y Jacinta* has to be recognized: he is no longer a secondary referent for principals. He now controls events in their lives through the eccentricity that had characterized him in the preceding novels: his feverish concoction of imaginary events and people fuelled by his reading of novels of romantic fantasy. He cannot foresee, of course, the eventual reception of the *Pituso* novel after it has been put into the domain of the Santa Cruz family for their reading. Once published, it achieves its own independence, and, as a literary artefact imposed on real life, it becomes subject to all sorts of different interpretations. But, above everything else, it will collide sharply with that other novel, which, unlike his, is grounded in the realities of contemporary life: the story of Juanito Santa Cruz and Fortunata and Jacinta. This true novel will have its own author, who, unlike Ido, is unaware of what he has created: Plácido Estupiñá.

CHAPTER SEVEN

Real Novelist:
Plácido Estupiñá

Comic foolishness, rather than sad mental sickness, is the main feature
of Plácido Estupiñá's character in *Fortunata y Jacinta* (1886–87), as his
name suggests; the obvious association of his patronymic with "stupid"
["estúpido"] (Yáñez, "Autores" 253–4) is not really diminished by
Galdós's insistence on the page proofs to the printers that the final vowel
of the name should carry an accent. His first name, "Plácido," which is
never given in conjunction with his surname, reinforces the connotation
of an amiable, eccentric type of person.[1] Estupiñá is slipped parentheti-
cally into the novel very early (I, 2, iv), with the promise from the narrator that he will talk more about this type later on ["(luego hablaré de
este tipo)"], just as his fellow narrator of *La desheredada* had done with
Relimpio. So, initially, Estupiñá is just a type too, for Galdós. This first
brief mention is in the context of the story of Juanito Santa Cruz's
teenage years, when Estupiñá would take him bird-hunting in the country. The second allusion occurs in association with Jacinta's family: he is
commissioned by her mother to buy potatoes for the family's meals (I, 2,
vi). So, both Ido and Estupiñá on their respective entries into the novel
are linked, albeit in different ways, with Juanito and Jacinta. But Don
Plácido's full entry into the novel cannot be delayed much longer in the
panoramic history of the Santa Cruz family that occupies the first two
chapters, and, accordingly, just like Relimpio, Estupiñá is given a full
chapter to himself. Neither the longest nor the shortest of part I, chapter
3, divided into four sections, serves as a transition between Juanito's
family history and his chance encounter with Fortunata that will start
the plot proper. Furthermore, Estupiñá's pivotal role in this meeting – all

unwitting – is pointedly underlined by the narrator when he declares that, if Juanito had not gone to see the sick Estupiñá in the Cava de San Miguel, "this story would not have been written" ["esta historia no se habría escrito"] (I, 3, iii). Estupiñá may not be responsible for writing the subsequent text, but he is the sole reason for its existence. Its direction will, first of all, be entrusted, as we have seen, to Estupiñá's counterpart and fellow novelist, Ido.

Estupiñá is a character who defines himself and his life experiences by dates: he styles himself as a calendar brother of Mesonero Romanos because he was born on the same day (19 July 1803), and his age in December 1869, when Fortunata meets Juanito for the first time, is sixty-six.[2] His eccentricity – the narrator describes it as his vanity (I, 3, i), and Estupiñá is not pleased when anyone questions it[3] – is the exorbitant claim, duly italicized in the text, to have witnessed personally all of nineteenth-century Spanish history, by which he means all of the great actors of national events – names and dates provided – and, then, only on balconies around Madrid. (By comparison, the much more sensitive observer of contemporary politics, José de Relimpio, had not seen any figure on the balconies of the Royal Palace in Madrid on the day of King Amadeo's abdication.) The absurdity of Estupiñá's claims – he would have been barely five when he saw the arrival of Joseph Bonaparte in Madrid in 1808 – is reinforced by his pet phrase, repeated after each example: "The same as I'm seeing you right now" ["como lo estoy viendo a usted"].

In this first section of the chapter, although there is only one direct reference to Mesonero Romanos – significantly, his age was the only piece of information (along with his place of birth) that Galdós confessed to know when he wrote his first pen-picture of him for *La Nación* in 1868 – there is an implicit contrast established between Estupiñá and the author's revered mentor. The former's statistical and factual grasp of Spanish history cannot match Mesonero's more spiritual sense of Madrid's history. One is the history buff or name-dropper, the other is the true historiographer (Anderson 75). The difference was deliberately accentuated by Galdós when he excised "costumbrista" examples from the list of events and scenes that Plácido had witnessed in the Alpha manuscript (Ribbans, *Conflicts* 88) and streamlined the list of political events (Ribbans, "The Making" 149–50).[4] Estupiñá is a different kind of "curious talker" ["curioso parlante"], Mesonero Romanos's pseudonym, perhaps more akin to a literary namesake whom Galdós had signalled out in his reference to Mesonero Romanos in the *episodio nacional, Los apostólicos*: Don Plácido Cascabelillo, who, as a spokesman for the aged in Mesonero Romanos's sketch "1808 y 1832" (*Escenas* 217–25), claimed that, with their physical eyes and those of their imagination, they saw distant things more clearly than objects near them. This reference to seeing is important, for it is also the key word in Estupiñá's pet phrase, repeated six times in this first chapter section. It was also the same word repeated to describe all the changes (topographical, not political) that Mesonero Romanos had witnessed in Madrid over the years (Galdós, *Los artículos* 445), but the difference is obvious: if Estupiñá's retina just registers the physical figures before him on the capital's balconies, Mesonero's eyesight is much more piercing, going to the inner core of people's characters. In other words, there is reason to interpret Estupiñá as a caricature of Mesonero Romanos, mediated through a partial likeness to one of the latter's comic creations – a caricature that is, perhaps, intended as an ironic and affectionate homage to the recently deceased mentor (Anderson 74).

Two other aspects about Estupiñá's front-line view of national history deserve mention for their relevance to the rest of this novel. The shorthand technique of listing names and events will be seen more frequently in the Santa Cruz household, and again is expressive of a lack of interest in the deeper meaning of those events. Interestingly, Estupiñá does not make any political commentary at Santa Cruz evening parties, which he regularly attends. The second feature of his catalogue of history-viewing is that a number of the events involve deaths, whether by murder, execution or assassination. When the priest Merino was garrotted in 1852, Don Plácido was on the platform in his capacity as a member of the Order of Peace and Charity, which had the duty of consoling the condemned before execution by scorning the folly of this world and extolling the glories of the next. This historical performance will have particular resonance at the end of *Fortunata y Jacinta*.

But Estupiñá has another claim on our attention: he is not only an ocular historian, he is also an essential cog in the Santa Cruz family as their business handyman. His indispensability in making the best bargains in the market each day is in marked contrast to his failure in earlier years when, as an employee of the Arnaiz firm and then later in his own dry-goods business, he preferred to talk endlessly about politics (amongst other topics) in much the same way as Morales and Relimpio do. He cannot even refrain from talking in church to Barbarita. Just as his historical name-dropping was described as a vanity, his addiction to gossiping is termed a chronic, inherited vice, almost a verbal alcoholism, somewhat akin to the liquid and carnal kind engaged in, less frequently, by *Caifás,* Relimpio, Morales, and Ido. As a type, then, Estupiñá is quickly and clearly defined in the reader's mind by these two habits-cum-vices. What is notable here, though, is the degree of detail to which Galdós resorts to establish these two basic traits, for they are not enlarged upon further in the novel. The inescapable conclusion must be that Galdós wants to convert him into more than a type. As with the principal Santa Cruz family members, details of Estupiñá's early years build up a substantial background for a figure who will now be allowed to grow in other directions.

Having been paired by virtue of his birthday with the father of the modern Spanish novel, Estupiñá is next compared to a writer of Greek antiquity, the philosopher Socrates. The comparison is very ironic, of course, for the features that prompt this comparison – an attitude of resignation and his facial appearance – are the result of his inability to run his own business, a far cry from the metaphysical problems that Socrates addressed. The narrator undercuts the comparison when he doubts whether the Greek philosopher could have sat and talked for seven hours. Furthermore, we have already seen that not long after this chapter, Jacinta will consider Ido del Sagrario the world's leading philosopher, in one of many intersections between the two eccentrics. "That great philosopher" ["Aquel gran filósofo"] is certainly a misplaced metonym for Estupiñá. His real métier in life is to serve as a travelling salesman, indulging his thirst for talk.

If the dry-goods store in which Plácido had worked was like a prison constricting his natural impulses to wander far and wide across the capital, some of his activities when he is able to enjoy this freedom (for example, when he transports goods under his cape to avoid paying city taxes) deserve the punishment of a real incarceration. But tax officials are easily bribed, and society, especially the merchant classes for whom he deals, readily condones and even encourages smuggling. One example of this illegal activity – when, with twenty-six kilos of cloth under his cape one night, he pretends to be a beggar carrying a child – will have an important echo at the end of the novel.

Further details of Estupiñá's earlier years are important for explaining his special relation with Juanito and his mother. Like all our main eccentrics-madmen, he is a simple soul ["alma sencilla"], and his blind loyalty to the Arnaiz family over the years is such that the nature of his relationship to Barbarita is confused and confusing: he is half-servant, half-friend, yet certainly to be trusted, as he is more like a father to Juanito, overseeing her son's activities outside of the house during his youth. Consequently, he must share some of the responsibility, with the parents, for the lax way in which Juanito is brought up, particularly when he encourages his ward's interest and enthusiasm for bullfighting, which leads Juanito to gain a liking for colourful lower-class types and will facilitate his association with Fortunata and her circle.[5] His relationship with Juanito is that of a male chaperon, the cervantine "ayo," which is really the archetypal relationship of all the eccentrics in this study to their respective protagonists.

Rather unusually, the full physical portrait of Estupiñá is given late in his special chapter: in section three. He is less than average in height, rather plump, and his face stands out because of its great resemblance to that of the Italian composer, Rossini, as recorded in prints and photos: the shape of "el divino Estupiñá's" head, his smile, his profile, hooked nose, sunken mouth, and mischievous eyes are an exact copy of the famous composer's rather burlesque beauty, which in old age made him look like Punch, a parrot, or a magpie.[6] Ennobled and immortalized by his likeness to Rossini, for which he is frequently called "El gran Rossini" – the epithet had also been applied in earlier novels to Relimpio and Morales – Estupiñá lacks, however, his real, live model's musical talent, unless one considers the novel as a symphony (Chamberlin Galdós) and Plácido as the composer; but even then, his work of musical composition is totally accidental. Unlike the old Rossini, he does not wear a wig, but he does protect in church what little hair he has with a cloth cap. Nevertheless, like the Italian composer, he does wear a green cloak all year, apart from summer (Chamberlin, "New Insights" 107–8). A flat, small-top hat for outdoor wear, of a style that hatmakers could not recall, also enhances this eccentric physiognomy.

For Gilman ("La palabra" 551), Estupiñá is the most Dickensian character in Fortunata y Jacinta. Certainly a number of details about his past life suggest echoes of Mr Dick, the Dickensian eccentric who seems to have influenced Galdós in the fabrication of a number of his own. In the Alpha manuscript (Alpha f. 1:144, on the back of Beta f. 1:175) a reference to his games of kite-flying with the adolescent Juan Santa Cruz on visits to the outskirts of Madrid inevitably recalls those of Mr Dick and David Copperfield on the Dover cliffs. Unfortunately, this reference was not carried into the Beta manuscript. Mr Dick and Estupiñá do have a certain resemblance of profile: if Plácido is plumpish and tends to lean forward, Mr Dick is florid and carries his head bowed (13). Estupiñá's daily task of taking young Juan to and from school (as he had taken and fetched Juan's mother in earlier years) is somewhat reminiscent of the visits of Mr Dick, co-guardian of David Copperfield, to his ward's school in Canterbury. Both are deferential to the very domineering women with whom they daily interact (Barbarita and Betsey Trotwood, respectively). Perhaps the strongest connection between the two eccentrics, albeit an ironic inversion, is their responsibility for bringing together two sets of lovers. In The Personal History of David Copperfield, Mr Dick works hard, unobtrusively and practically – as no philosopher would, Dickens states emphatically (42) – to smooth over the misunderstandings between David's headmaster at Canterbury, Dr Strong, and his young wife, Annie. That great philosopher, the Socrates-like Don Plácido, has a more pivotal role as matchmaker: if Juanito had not had his explosive first encounter with Fortunata on the staircase leading to Estupiñá's room in 11, Cava de San Miguel, then, as we already know, the novel would not have been the same. However, unlike Mr Dick, Plácido is totally unaware of the service he is providing, both before and when it happens.

This is no ordinary visit by the young master to his aged guardian. Rather it is an exceptional circumstance that sets in motion the novel's plot: a bout of rheumatism in Plácido's right leg, the effects of old age more than of anything else, for normally he is the healthiest man alive. The great man's absence is soon noted and leads to a number of visitors, of whom Juanito is the most important, but it is at the command of his mother. The subject of his exchange with Fortunata on the stairs is ostensibly Estupiñá, although the other, more important dialogue is between their eyes and minds. Even what should have been a simple, commonplace exchange at the surface level is affected by the sub-dialogue, for Juan, first of all, asks her if Estupiñá lives in the building, which is really a redundant question, for he knows that to be the case. More appropriate would have been a question about the floor on which he lived. The second cause of confusion is over the slightly pompous manner in which he refers to the old man, "el señor de Estupiñá." When Fortunata is assured that he is the same person she knows as "Don Plácido," she is able to indicate his room, but in another potentially confusing phrase: "way up, on top of the top floor" ["en lo más último de arriba"].

The figure that the sick patient cuts there is exceptional. The constant peripatetic is, for once, immobilized in a chair like a mummy, with his head covered by his black church hat, and deprived of his most essential need: conversation. Hence his great excitement at seeing his former pupil beside him. In emphasizing once more his endemic vice of conversation, Galdós now pertinently adds the obverse of the coin: Plácido detests books or anything printed. For this lookalike of a famous composer, books deserve the pejorative, second meaning of the word "música": "drivel, useless scrawl" ["música, garabatos que no sirven de nada"]. Johann Gutenberg is one of the people he least admires; instead, society is his library, life is his book, and the spoken word is his text. But there is metafictional irony in this aversion to the printed word, for, moments earlier, he has godfathered the birth of the live story of Fortunata and Juanito that is forming the text now being perused by readers. Yet, before that unwitting, authorial act, Plácido, in his enforced silence and immobility, has, surprisingly, been discovering the joys of reading a printed text, namely, an ecclesiastical bulletin for the dicoese of Lugo in Galicia, which was the only document to be found in the apartment and was left there by the previous tenant (an ex-monk). Galdós converts this reality into a lesson on the reading process: what one reads, how one reads it, and how one reacts to it can produce unexpected results in the individual reader that are not at all discernible for the outsider. The lesson is very apropos, since the reader of *Fortunata y Jacinta* is now going to start reading the story proper. Estupiñá has discovered something to his liking: that books are, after all, "mute speakers" ["habladores mudos"], so he can convert the bulletin into an interlocutor. He reads the text to himself, in a low voice, as if he were praying, sometimes repeating phrases. This reading is very clearly, for the most part, an exercise of the vocal chords, but at the same time, with his wry smiles, Plácido reveals that he is also understanding and enjoying something of what he is reading, so much so that anybody who did not know otherwise would have thought he was reading a novel by the contemporary French writer, Charles Paul de Kock. The inference is hilarious, of course, and Juanito may laugh at the bulletin, but Estupiñá thinks that it is a good read. In this scene, Plácido is the autonomous and independent reader, responsible for drawing his own meaning and pleasure from what he reads. The reader of the real live novel that he is now also responsible for launching will, it is inferred, have the same rights and privileges.

The chapter Estupiñá has been given to himself is more than a detailed presentation of a comic secondary character. More powerful and direct than Relimpio's chapter in *La desheredada*, it is a hinge, linking background or preliminary material with the action proper, and Estupiñá is the character chosen to make that join. The surprising author of a novel, albeit a live one, he continues this role in the days following the birth of the affair, reporting back to the alarmed Barbarita on the daily activities of her son. But these "stories" ["cuentos"], recounted in a low and melodramatic voice, some of which are transferred into the published text, conceal far more than they reveal, increasingly so, as the tutor, forced to avoid mention of the exact details of his pupil's amorous adventures, utters stupidities and inanities or evasive remarks in another metafictional warning to the reader on how the truth can be distorted in any novel, oral or written.

Likewise, Juanito acts as an evasive and misleading storyteller to Jacinta on their honeymoon, when his bride is anxious to read some of the recent pages of his life's story. He narrates his first encounter with Fortunata as if it were a medieval romance, and Estupiñá occupies the first line of the first page: "But let me start at the beginning. Once upon a time there was an ancient gentleman ... called Estupiñá" ["Érase una vez... un caballero anciano ... llamado Estupiñá"] (I, 5, i). The addition at the proof-correction stage of the next phrase referring to his resemblance to a parrot or magpie has the immediate effect of destroying the traditional, fairy-tale romance mode that Juanito has just initiated. But both references succeed in transforming, by comic exaggeration, the true identity of the family servant. The comparison to a parrot is fittingly recalled at the end of the honeymoon, when the newlyweds bring back as a present for Estupiñá a stick with a parrot/magpie's head on the top. None of the other presents for the rest of their family is identified, nor is any jocular comment made by the narrator or the characters about the suitability of the present. Thus, Estupiñá closes Juanito's oral account of his Fortunata story to Jacinta just as he had begun it. He was also indirectly responsible for their marriage: Bárbara had speedily arranged the match when her son's wayward behaviour with Fortunata, as reported by the old retainer, had become intolerable. Estupiñá provides the book ends to Juan's particular story recounted in part I , chapter 5, just as he does, metaphorically, for the longer and more complete stories of the two eponymous protagonists, as we shall see shortly.

If Jacinta's mania or "craze" ["chifladura"] is the desire to have children and this is momentarily satisfied by a "chiflado" called Ido del Sagrario, Doña Bárbara's mania is buying things, and that is actively encouraged and satisfied by another crackpot or "chiflado": Estupiñá, whose exceptional abilities at securing the best market bargains earn him from the narrator the epithets of "El Grande" and "that saintly man" ["aquel santo hombre"] (I, 6, v), comically appropriate in view of his habit of notifying Barbarita of the best buys during mass. Estupiñá's obsession with the produce of the marketplace is pertinently related to the memorable first meeting between Fortunata and Juanito when her sucking of a raw egg had surprised the bourgeois sophisticate: Estupiñá threatens the egg suppliers with the full force of the law if they cheat him with unfresh produce, yet he is perfectly willing to flout the same municipal business law when he deliberately smuggles the best cigars into the Santa Cruz house (I, 5, v).

An important association with his co-metaphorical-novel writer, Ido del Sagrario, is made towards the end of part I. After the book agent's second visit to the Santa Cruzs' household, Juanito's flu gets worse and he is once more confined to his bed, where the only person he wishes to see is, not the female eccentric, Doña Guillermina, but her male counterpart, Plácido (I, 8, v), because he simply wants to raise his spirits by laughing, in the same, sick way that he had earlier done with Ido, at his tutor's accounts of embarrassing episodes from his past life as a smuggler or religious penitent. But Plácido is not prepared to play court jester on this occasion.

The 23 December 1873 lottery win by the Santa Cruz family circle also forges another ironic link between Ido and Estupiñá: just as the former had rushed out of his tavern meal in order to catch his wife in the act of adultery, Estupiñá now rushes out of his master's house to take the good news to the other lottery winners. His own reluctance to buy the original ticket is conveniently covered up by Juan's parents so that he can become a beneficiary, with the connivance of Plácido himself, who reckons, in a phrase that immediately recalls Ido del Sagrario, that "well, the truth is, my head's 'pletely, you know, sort of off..." ["En fin..., la verdad, mi cabeza anda, *talmente*, así un poco ida"] (I, 10, i). Jacinta claims that it is Estupiñá himself who has brought them all the luck of the draw. For the moment, the phrase is full of pathetic irony for Jacinta, considering the old servant's involuntary part in the series of marital misfortunes that befall her. In the present context, the willingness of her in-laws to create a sham for Plácido's benefit will not extend to accepting the little deceit of *Pituso* that Ido and Izquierdo have concocted for her and her husband and which will be unveiled Christmas Day. The celebration of the lottery win brings out a similar contradiction in the attitude of the still-bedridden Juanito: his laughter on hearing about the miracle of Estupiñá's win is indescribable: he brands Estupiñá (whose suggestion of a kitchen concert on the pots and pans is vetoed by Barbarita) and the others celebrating the win as idiots.[7] Yet, all this uproar is in stark contrast with the sternness with which he dismisses the miracle of Jacinta's son. The first announcement from Jacinta – at 3 am on Christmas Eve morning – is treated as a joke by Juanito, for Estupiñá would already have been rushing to put the announcement in the newspaper. When they wake up an hour later, Estupiñá is still in their minds, as they think of him going to early mass. The unwitting author of the Fortunata-Juanito story, who had been sedentary at its beginning, now presides over an important development in the false story of Jacinta fabricated by Ido, by being his more usually peripatetic and energetic self.

The Santa Cruz household is once more the stage for festive celebration when the traditional Christmas Eve supper is described at length. What could so easily have been an easy "costumbrista" sketch of a stock scene becomes something more complex and different precisely because of Estupiñá, who really becomes the prominent character in this episode. To show the distance he has travelled since sketching the Christmas Eve supper scene in *La desheredada*, Galdós deliberately presents the other guests as "costumbrista" types; individual names represent an institution or a profession in the capital: for example, Villalonga represents Parliament, and Aparisi the Madrid City Council. At first, Estupiñá seems to be incorporated into this gallery of types, although the introductory question about his representativeness sounds an immediate note of surprise that grows with the following answer, which seems to over-identify him as a type: with his fine, black-cloth frock coat, Estupiñá represents old-fashioned practices in business, smuggling, and religious attendance (I, 10, v). This is certainly how he was first presented in his own chapter when the narrator was relating his earlier life. But this typification no longer does justice to his status as the author of the live, Juanito-Fortunata novel. That role has changed him from a type into an individual, as is confirmed by his speech now. The party guests become merry and patriotic under the influence of, first, sherry and then, more successfully, champagne, diligently plied by Juanito, whose sole purpose now, as before with Ido and Estupiñá, is to enjoy himself at the diners' expense when they start making absurd statements.

Strangely, it is not Estupiñá, but two other guests, Aparisi and Ruiz, who sing the praise of the Spanish heroes of the century's major battles (Trafalgar, El Callao, Tetuán, and Saragossa). A more important role is reserved for Estupiñá: he suddenly stands up to make a toast, glass in hand, and his listeners wait expectantly on his words, as if, proud ocular historian that he is, he is going to sing similar praises. He is emotional and weepy like the previous orators, but, pointedly, not drunk. His toast is to his hosts, to his fellow guests, but especially to Jacinta's future motherhood, expressed first as a hope, then as a suspicion, and finally as a belief, as if he had eventually – and not immediately, as originally stated in the manuscript sent to the printer – deduced the reason for Barbarita's command earlier in the day to smuggle a nativity scene into the house. Aside from equating this forthcoming family event with the nation's past glories just toasted, and from – paradoxically – rubbing in Jacinta's predicament of childlessness, Estupiñá's words have the effect of alerting Juanito and his father, as well as the rest of their social circle, to the future appearance of a child; but nobody, not even the old tutor, suspects that it will be in the form of an illegitimate *Pituso*. As author of Juanito's live novel, Estupiñá is the perfect choice to make this announcement, which Juanito had not at all foreseen when he plied Aparisi and Ruiz with drink. His attempt to use others for selfish amusement has rebounded against him, as it did in the first interview with Ido. But this announcement by his old tutor allows Juanito to later rubbish Jacinta's novel with a reference to one of Plácido's eccentricities: real children cannot be smuggled into the house by Estupiñá as if they were boxes of cigars (I, 10, vii). Juan reinforces his argument by identifying the authors of the *Pituso* novel, thereby again connecting Estupiñá and Ido.

Estupiñá returns to the text in the fourth section of part III, chapter 2, in two brief scenes in which he greets an old friend, Manuel Moreno-Isla. The landlord of 11, Cava de San Miguel, rather patronisingly thinks that the now seventy-year-old Plácido looks youthful. The latter also coincides with Ido del Sagrario and, more importantly, with Fortunata and Jacinta at Mauricia la Dura's funeral, officiously carrying out duties for Guillermina: smuggling her bronze crucifix under his cape into the tenement house, as well as arranging for the arrival of the Viaticum.

His association with Fortunata and Juanito is subtly renewed in two

more brief scenes towards the end of part III, which form a prelude to
its more climactic resumption in part IV. Fortunata, abandoned by
Juanito a second time, stands outside the Santa Cruz mansion and recognizes an old man leaving the building as Estupiñá, her neighbour in
11, Cava de San Miguel years ago. She immediately associates him with
the beginning of the continuous misfortunes in her life (III, 3, ii), an
opportune reminder too for the reader of the origins of her story, which
will soon move into its final phase. Estupiñá will now preside over the
two lovers' final reconciliation: one day Fortunata sees the old retainer
scowling at her from a carriage in a family funeral procession. She is
unable to catch sight of Juanito in one of the lead carriages, but, obviously informed by "el gran Plácido" of her sighting, her lover surprises
her the next day in the same area and hails another cab to take her for
a ride to the city outskirts (III, 7, v). Fortunata's readiness to accompany
Juanito is described as a dive into a well, a metaphor that immediately
recalls the way she had parted from him at their first meeting in part I,
when she had almost rolled headlong down the granite stairs of 11, Cava
de San Miguel and Juanito had thought that she would kill herself.

Fortunata's face-to-face re-acquaintance with Estupiñá eventually takes
place when she moves back to her original house in order to have her
second baby by Juanito (IV, 3, vii). The structural and thematic importance of this return has been noted before (e.g. Bly "Fortunata"), but
what really deserves attention in this study is the constant presence of
Estupiñá, more than that of any other character, during Fortunata's
transfer of residence. Her aunt's apartment, to which she wends her way,
is explicitly located in relation to that of Plácido: it is not enough for the
narrator to say, as Fortunata herself had said to Juanito in relation to
Estupiñá's apartment in part I, that it was "one of the highest" ["uno de
los más altos"]: more precisely, it is situated above his own apartment.
Also, he is the first person she meets when she starts climbing the stairs
on her return. In an obvious inversion of that initial encounter of the
future lovers, it is now Fortunata, not Juanito's surrogate, who wants to
make a greeting and start a conversation. He again scowls and shows no
desire to do so. Fortunata's feelings for her old neighbour are now
analysed in some detail. She clearly sees his hostility and recognizes him
as an enemy because of his closeness to the Santa Cruz family; she also
knows his weakness for constant talking. But, in spite of these defects,
she likes him, because she thinks that he is nice, inoffensive, and kind.
These positive feelings reflect, to some degree, Fortunata's own more
benevolent state of mind at this moment in her life, but they also serve
to stand as the first attempt by any of the other characters, including the
anonymous narrator, to give a more rounded and balanced picture of the
old man. He himself had started the process when he had surprised

everybody with his outburst at the Christmas Eve supper. Fortunata will now advance this conversion from "costumbrista" type to more complex individual: she coaxes out the more sympathetic and deeper side of this agent of the new owner (Doña Guillermina).[8] Plácido is the centre of her thoughts as she anticipates his likely reaction to the request for improvements in her apartment. The encounter with Estupiñá acts, then, as a catalyst for Fortunata, forcing her to re-assess her present position and her past life. The result is a picture of a more rational and reflexive Fortunata, now interested in material things like the repairs, and, most astonishingly, her chances (nil) of inheriting this building. Fortunata does broach the question of improvements when Estupiñá comes to collect the rent on 4 January 1876. Again the point of interest is not so much the improvements as Estupiñá's reaction to Fortunata, whom he obviously cannot forgive for striking Jacinta at Mauricia's apartment. "El gran Plácido" acts the despot, scowling and frowning at her as she looks through the door grille, and brandishing his parrot/magpie-head stick, an overt reminder to the reader both of the legal relationship that had supplanted Fortunata's affair with Juanito and of how she had dominated his honeymoon and, with the birth of her child, had aroused strong maternal desires in Jacinta. Overcoming Plácido's abruptness and encouraging his desire to chat, Fortunata gently elicits the news that Guillermina, as the new landlord, has mortgaged the building in order to complete the construction of her orphanage. Thus, in a very real sense, Fortunata's second child – the true *Pituso* – will be born in a satelite building of the orphanage, where the false one – Ido's invention – is now housed.

The rapprochement between Fortunata and Estupiñá continues in the final chapter of the novel, after the birth of her child. Again it is significant that in her moments of great happiness she should often think of him and want him to visit her. Segunda's reports of his surly, authoritarian reaction to the news of the birth – he looks like a judge when told the news and threatens them with eviction – seems a regression to his earlier typecasting. However, when he does come to see the newborn baby, he acts reverently by removing his hat, thereby certifying the correctness of the family likeness, as if he were the family registrar of births. Indeed, in the proofs Galdós had excised a remark by the old retainer about the likeness of the new child to the one the couple had earlier lost (g. Part IV; 2:23). Fortunata has correctly foreseen that Estupiñá, with his gossipiness and loyalty to the Santa Cruz clan, is the key to any visit from, first, Guillermina and then, perhaps, from Barbarita, who will go even crazier over the real *Pituso* than she had done over the false one ["Y si doña Bárbara se chifló por *el Pituso* falso, ¡cómo no se dislocará por el de oro de ley!"] (IV, 6, ii). After the baby's birth, Izquierdo and Ido, publisher and author, respectively, of Jacinta's novel, come to stand guard over Fortunata, heroine of the other, more authentic novel, whose author, Estupiñá, completes the ironic triptych of the Three Wise Men, as it were, around the manger of the new Messiah for the Santa Cruzs. As befits the author of the true novel, Plácido is given more important tasks to discharge at its conclusion than the other two, authors of the false novel: in contrast to his enforced sedentariness at this novel's commencement, he is constantly running up and down stairs to report on his inquiries about wetnurses, or the condition of mother and baby. Fortunata is once more remarkably affectionate in her praise of Don Plácido, who, in front of the Santa Cruzs, had not reciprocated the same generosity of feelings: "He's a good man and I like him very much" ["Es un buen hombre, y yo le quiero mucho"] (IV, 6, xii). When Fortunata realizes that she has not much longer to live, after she starts haemorrhaging, the first and only person she wants to see immediately is Don Plácido. She knows his daily routine well enough to be sure that her serving girl will find him in his room below sipping his hot chocolate after mass. Estupiñá duly comes to see her, but his officious gestures no longer have any effect, as it is now Fortunata who gives the orders, with the inveterate talker forced to listen for once, and then to fetch ink and paper after a prior, futile search for her medication. His amazement grows when the fading Fortunata tries to dictate her will-letter to Jacinta. Because she is constantly changing her mind and her wording – emphasized in the additions to the galleys – Estupiñá is given carte blanche to tidy up her words, for she is only enunciating the general outline of her idea, which is to entrust the baby to Jacinta. It is fitting that this testament of the real live novel's dénouement (the newly born baby) should be drawn up by that novel's author, whilst those of the false novel supply the desk (their checker board) as a support for the redaction of the document. The author (Estupiñá) is expressly commissioned in the will-letter, of which he is also the dutiful executor, to deliver that completed novel (the baby) to its intended dedicatee: Jacinta.

Don Plácido's next task is even more grave: he has to act as confessor to the rapidly declining Fortunata, a task that had been foreshadowed by the reference in his introductory biography in part I to his service to the condemned as a member of the Order of Peace and Charity. Despite these past experiences, he is genuinely affected by the sight of the dying Fortunata's face: he is scared and horrified, feeling pity for her in her final moments. Fortunata repeatedly calls him a friend and a good man, and he, in turn, tries to console her, affectionately addressing her as "daughter, poor woman, and good girl." His exploits as a smuggler of all sorts of merchandise for the Santa Cruzs, including the nativity scene for the false *Pituso*, are now used to effect an act of justice: in accordance with Fortunata's command, he earnestly transports the crib with the baby to his apartment before her calculating aunt and uncle return to prevent such a move. His movements are described as those of a robber or smuggler, words added at the galley stage (g. part IV; 3:2).

Estupiñá does not completely change character in this climactic scene – he is soon worrying about the legal consequences of this abduction of the baby. But he has grown to some extent in character, for, when faced by a crisis, he is transformed from a type into a person of some attraction.[9] In Fortunata's dying moments Don Plácido tries his best to help her, by searching for her medication, and to comfort her, by whispering closely into her ear words of resistance, even pretending, when those of religion have no effect, that Juanito has come to see his lady love (the word "dama" also recalls the checker board ["tabla de damas"] on which Estupiñá wrote out her will). By using this word, and by whispering the lovers' pet names for each other, he evokes the world of the sentimental romance that was Ido's forte as a hack novelist and which was also chosen by Juanito himself when describing to Jacinta his first, fateful encounter with Fortunata. Estupiñá's status as the author of the novel that the narrator has zealously penned for four long parts is enhanced, then, by this stroke of literary inventiveness.[10] The new Estupiñá takes Fortunata's hysterical aunt, Segunda, by surprise: she can only think of the old smuggler and robber type, whereas he now dismisses such crazy accusations and urges her to fetch Fortunata's final admirer and helper, Ballester. For Ribbans ("The Making" 154), Estupiñá is "a highly functional minor character" with clear, superficial characterization. If, initially, he does lack depth and seems a mere type, his display of concern, first for Jacinta's forthcoming child at the Christmas Eve supper, and then, more intensely, for Fortunata at the end of the novel, is intended to indicate the degree of feeling and common sense that he, like our other oldish eccentrics, can display, unlike some principal characters, at moments of crisis. Clearly, Estupiñá's "transformation" is not as intense and moving as Relimpio's, for example, but his efforts to minister to Fortunata's final needs are praiseworthy. He may be stupid by patronymic, but he is also placid by first name, and it is this latter side of his character that wins out in the novel's finale. Like José Mundideo, Tafetán, and Cayetano, when their respective protagonists die, Estupiñá is one of the few individuals to attend the burial of Fortunata.

JOSÉ IZQUIERDO

As the witting proposer of the false *Pituso* novel, José Izquierdo, Fortunata's uncle, is a counter-figure (visually too [Gilman, "La palabra" 551n22]) to Estupiñá. His largely fanciful accounts of participation in historical events, along with his garbled syntax and language, increase considerably this link of comic stupidity. As with Don Plácido, Juanito Santa Cruz is the cause and, moreover, the agent of his introduction into the novel, when, on their honeymoon, Jacinta prods him for more information about Fortunata's family. Juan provides a character snapshot: he calls him a "good type" ["buen tipo"], which is obviously ironic, for in the next breath he calls him the biggest libertine and animal he had ever seen. As later with Ido, he predicts that Jacinta would laugh tremendously if she saw him and heard him speak (I, 5, iii).[11] Juanito also gives a brief, but exact, summary of his chequered career. More details about "his friend," the drunkard Izquierdo, are forthcoming during the Seville stop on their honeymoon, fittingly prompted by a bout of drunkenness on the part of Juanito. His interpretation of Izquierdo's nickname ("Platón") is limited: he thinks it refers to the big plate from which Izquierdo always eats. More ironic interpretations are possible: he cannot compare, as an income earner, to his wife's first husband, a silversmith ("platero"), nor in intellectual ability to the Greek philosopher Plato, in the same way that Ido was obviously no Socrates. Izquierdo had climbed the steps to Juanito's apartment to inform him of Fortunata's first pregnancy, just as in a later chapter Ido will climb those same stairs to tell Jacinta about Juanito's illegitimate child, the false *Pituso*.

Izquierdo's grand entrance really occurs in part I during the tavern scene where he invites himself to share Ido's meal. The narrator immediately launches into a detailed physical portrait that lends some credence to the favourable introduction provided earlier by Juanito. José is in his fifties and has such a handsome figure that, shortly, with the Restoration of the Bourbons, he will become a model, much sought after by the country's leading painters. His beautiful head, arrogant stature, and manly, noble mien suggest a physiognomy that is deliberately contrasted with the more roguish appearance of the older Estupiñá, a connection that is underlined by his Italian appearance. By inserting this prolepsis about Izquierdo's future greatness as a painter's model, the narrator instantly deflates his subsequent catalogue of exaggerated political exploits and grievances, recounted to the indifferent Ido as they devour their meal, just as, by prefacing Estupiñá's catalogue of great events with the absurd claim that he had witnessed them all, the narrator had reduced its effect too. Moreover, if Estupiñá's eyes and face had been glued throughout the century to the balconies of public buildings in order to look at the country's major political figures, Izquierdo's eyes and face will soon become the focus of painters trying to recreate national, international, and biblical heroes on canvas. Izquierdo's account of events before and during the First Republic (1873–74) certainly covers a part of contemporary history from a perspective different to that of the Santa Cruz circle, including

Estupiñá (Ribbans, *Conflicts* 105).[12] Nonetheless, Izquierdo's account, as we later learn from the narrator and then from Guillermina, is largely invented and fools only a few, one of whom is Ido. Its credibility is even undermined during its narration by Izquierdo's highly individualized language, which is constructed on a whole series of pet words rather than merely one or two (Ortiz Armengol, *Apuntaciones* 259): colourful oaths, solecisms, malapropisms, metatheses, and abbreviations, many of which were often fine-tuned and standardized by Galdós on the galleys (e.g.: "endivido" for "endividu" [g. part I; 2:24]; see also Caudet ["José Izquierdo" 29n3]).[13] False and funny, Izquierdo's ramblings are characterized by a deep resentment at not receiving his just deserts, despite his attempts to curry favour with both sides in the Carlist War of 1872–76. Politics, for him and, by extension, for Estupiñá and the Santa Cruz circle too, is an excuse for personal advancement. When he includes Ido as a fellow victim of the State's ingratitude and then mentions seeing Fortunata on his wanderings in the north of the country, he is unconsciously moving towards another, equally counterfeit, source of income: the *Pituso* novel. For someone who, paradoxically, believes that writers of all kinds are the cause of the country's ruin and that his inability to write is the cause of his own lack of advancement, Izquierdo shows a surprising willingness to entrust the oral confection of the *Pituso* novel to a novelist whose teaching of calligraphy has allowed his pupils to occupy the seats of political power. But Izquierdo is a man full of contradictions: his boasting of political heroics has now crumbled into maudlin self-pity, heavily alcohol-fuelled. Why, then, at this moment of abject moaning, does the narrator indulge in a second example of prolepsis, even greater than the first in the same episode, when he informs the reader of Izquierdo's reversal of fortune a year later? This juxtaposition of contrasting pieces of information creates great comic effect, of course, and builds up suspense about the source of such a dramatic change, but, at the same time, the prolepsis exposes both Izquierdo's real material self-interest and ensures that, in the latest example of his misrepresentation of history – the *Pituso* story – he loses all room for bargaining with Guillermina. He turns into a pathetic figure – more admirable in the manuscript sent to the printer – when he acknowledges, internally, to himself, and with a look free of hatred and full of sincerity at Guillermina, that her portrait of him is absolutely correct. Izquierdo's character has taken a step forward towards a change, it appears:

the miserable man plunged into his conscience, as if it were a well, and there he saw himself as he really was, stripped of the tinseled front that his self-pride had set up. He thought what he had thought at other times: "I know I'm a real mule, a good Johnny that wouldn't hurt a fly."

[el infeliz hombre cayó en su conciencia como en un pozo, y allí se vio tal cual era realmente, despojado de los trapos de oropel en que su amor propio le envolvía; pensó lo que otras veces había pensado, y se dijo en sustancia: "Si soy un verídico mulo, un buen Juan que no sabe matar un mosquito."]

Like Estupiñá, Izquierdo is another character from Fortunata's past that she rediscovers on her return to 11, Cava de San Miguel. The re-acquaintanceship is duly highlighted by the narrator (IV, 4, ii), for he now comes to spend all his free time in her apartment and becomes a kind of servant for her, delivering messages or making purchases in the area. Consequently, there is an inverted transference of value from one job to the other: if, on the one hand, Izquierdo's crude descriptions of his work as a model for such important figures as God, Nebuchadnessar, Aeneas, Hernán Cortés, or King James of Aragón, and especially his ignorance of their importance in literature and world history, strike a hilarious note, on the other hand, with his errand-running, he contributes more substantial touches to the canvas of Fortunata that is nearing completion. Significantly, it is the transformed Fortunata who can appreciate the change that has overtaken her uncle: "[Fortunata] found her uncle morally transfigured, with a spiritual calm she'd never seen in him before, an easy talker cured of his crazy ambition and that black pessimism that had made him curse his luck constantly" ["encontró a su tío transfigurado moralmente con un reposo espiritual que nunca viera en él, suelto de palabra, curado de su loca ambición y de aquel negro pesimismo que le hacía renegar de su suerte a cada instante"] (IV, 4, ii). A big change, indeed, but one whose proportions the narrator feels compelled to reduce somewhat by immediately revealing its material cause: his prolific career as the principal male model in Madrid. The political boasting of part I is replaced by pronouncements on the historical deeds associated with the characters he models, but his ignorance is still hilarious. His change at the novel's close, then, is somewhat similar to Estupiñá's: it is not total, but it is enough to capture the reader's attention.

His activities as Fortunata's messenger will also be vital in forwarding the plot, as was his activity with the *Pituso* novel: Maxi's attention to Izquierdo's words and street movements will enable him to discover his wife's whereabouts. In the last chapter of the novel, Izquierdo's role as Fortunata's guardian becomes more pronounced, but he is as ineffectual as Ido in preventing Maxi from entering the apartment. The most famous model in Madrid cuts a far from aesthetic pose when, in his drunken stupor, he falls from sofa to floor, or quakes with fear when Guillermina appears on the scene. More effective custodial action is displayed when he escorts the excited Maxi out of the apartment on his second visit: the man of imaginary heroics in part I becomes a man of real, but limited, action in the final chapter of his niece's life, just like Estupiñá. Sure, he is no model of moral conduct, for all his success in the art world, but in the novel's last chapter he shows signs of less predictable behaviour.

MANUEL MORENO-ISLA

The other secondary eccentric or abnormal character (Walton 177) who casts some reflections on the values and roles of Estupiñá is Manuel Moreno-Isla. Within the Santa Cruz circle, he is very much a quirky exception, a loner, as indicated by his matronymic, which means "island." At forty-eight, he is slightly younger than most of our other main eccentrics, but he is tall, thin, and, with a heart condition, is of delicate health, which makes him look pale. The narrator thinks him an excellent person (I, 7, ii) but does not anticipate his later prominence in the novel as he had so clearly done with Estupiñá (Willem, "Latent Narratives" 304).

Moreno's status as a dissenter in the Santa Cruz household is always masked by his surface bonhomie, especially with his aunt, Doña Guillermina, whom he is always teasing about her obsession with the orphanage. His delight in parading his anglophilia upsets people and emphasizes his eccentricity. He even looks like a bored English peer, almost Pickwickian, with his outsized shoes and their white spats, his coachmen's gloves, dark jacket, and plaid trousers. And he speaks Spanish with a certain foreign tinge, slurring his "r"s a little, and forgetting some of the more infrequently used words. His criticisms of Spain are pertinent, but again are only laughed off by friends as the mad ideas of a funny eccentric. If his words are to be believed, he has played a more active role in contemporary history than even Don Plácido when, accompanying Alfonso XII to Dover on his return to Spain in 1875, he had presented him with a watch and encouraged him in what Manuel considers the hopeless task of ruling that country of ingratitude – shades of Izquierdo and Tomás Rufete!

He does appear, to begin with, as a caricature, a one-dimensional type (Sobejano 215). This also applies to his love life, for he has a well-earned reputation as a womaniser, like Juan Tafetán, for example, which is even more prominent in the Alpha manuscript (Ribbans, *Conflicts* 29). His aunt suggests that the purpose of his bantering proposal to become a Mormon is to spend his money on concubines. One of these ex-lovers, Aurora, ridicules his ever more obvious infatuation with the younger Jacinta as something absurd, given his age and medical condition (IV, 1, xii). By the end of part III, however, that status is totally transformed: his frustrated passion for Jacinta turns him into a complex and highly individualized character (Sobejano 217). The locale in which this process first advances is the staircase outside the Santa Cruzs' apartment: as Moreno comes panting up the stairs, Jacinta is saying goodbye to Mauricia la Dura's sister and daughter, whom she had met through Ido, who is also associated with the same staircase, as we saw earlier. The arrival of Estupiñá closely after Moreno-Isla, their friendly embrace, and conversation with Jacinta inevitably joins these staircase scenes to the momentous one which Estupiñá had involuntarily occasioned in 11, Cava de San Miguel. That Moreno could be a better Juan for Jacinta is suggested when, inside the apartment, he addresses Juan's father as his godfather, whereas, in actual fact, Baldomero's own father had been Moreno's godfather. This generational confusion enables him to be considered a valid rival for Jacinta's love, in terms of age, to the younger Juanito.

Like Estupiñá in part I, Moreno is the centre of attention for a whole chapter (2) in part IV, although his name does not entitle it. We listen to his intimate thoughts in several passages of interior monologue: when he is walking home from the Retiro park, talking to Jacinta at the evening "tertulia," or when he is lying awake in bed on two consecutive nights. The other passages in this chapter are also related from a position close to his perspective.[14] The result is that Moreno reveals directly to the reader the quickening process of his transformation from a type – he is called a number of times "the gentleman" and "the misanthrop" – into a real character with considerable inner turmoil because of his infatuation with Jacinta. In the course of this transformation, two closely allied aspects are foregrounded: sexual reproduction and infantilism. If Aurora had typecast Moreno as a faded old Don Juan, the real live consequences of that degeneration are now spelled out for the patient by his doctor: he is to give up all thoughts of love and women, but especially all sexual fantasizing, which is characterized as a mad appetite of the senses; otherwise, he will die. He is even too old for sex now. Barbarita's suggestion that he marry Jacinta's eighteen-year-old sister is totally absurd, then, in this context, not because she knows how ill Moreno is – she does not – but because of the generational difference between the two.[15] Sex, marriage, and children can only be a daydream now for Moreno. Jacinta tantalizingly paints this mental picture for Moreno when, bidding him farewell on his intended, but unrealized, return to England, she promises to be a godparent or even foster mother for any children he may have by an English bride. Returning the compliment, Don Manuel assures her that he will follow her advice and she will have her little Moreno. This innocent little make-believe receives its real counterpoint when, at the end of the novel, Jacinta fantasizes about the possibility that he could have been her husband, as she reshapes in her imagination the features of Fortunata's baby son, born in a room owned by Moreno (Caudet, ed. *Fortunata y Jacinta* 2:342n48).

Ironically, Moreno is so aroused by Jacinta at the evening gathering that, unable to envisage having a child by her, he comes to feel more and more like a child himself in the prison of her apartment: his eccentric anglophilia and hispanophobia are now replaced by a more serious form of mental derangement, clearly perceived by Jacinta, as he leaves the party: infantilism. To his credit, and in spite of his frequently maudlin self-pity, Moreno clearly sees what is happening to him, both as he steadies himself on the bannister of the staircase outside Jacinta's apartment and later that night, when lying awake: he tells himself that he wants to play the childish fool in front of her. This infantilism is underscored when he looks at the picture of St Joseph in his room, a picture he associates with childhood memories, especially with the day he had vaulted onto the unattended donkey of a water-seller and it carried him through some streets before throwing him onto the ground and leaving him with a permanent scar on his forehead. The picture is also a visual echo of his self-comparison earlier that same day to the putative father of Christ (the cuckolded spouse par excellence in popular tradition) after he had bought a lily from a street vendor (Caudet, ed. *Fortunata y Jacinta* 2:347n50). His lucidity before imminent death, similar to that of Relimpio in *La desheredada*, leads him to a deeper realization, not (understandably) shorn of self-pity, of the futility and unhappiness of his previous life: he has been stupid and those who thought him happy were equally stupid. He now has visions of the paralyzed beggar to whom he had grudgingly given a few pence earlier in the day; he is prepared to give him more if he sees him again. Moreno is a changing man, so much so that he surprises both his aunt and Estupiñá when he goes to early mass the next day. He reflects seriously on Guillermina's prediction that the crippled beggar will go straight to Heaven after death, but, once inside the church, he reverts to his more usual irreverent self. On the way back home, his banter with his aunt borders on the morbid when he agrees that he should imitate her building mania by constructing the modern insane asylum that, in her opinion, the country needs. The two of them will be its first occupants; Guillermina is aghast at the sick smile of her nephew when he says this. The distance between the caricaturesque type that Moreno initially was and the complex personality that he is becoming is neatly expressed by the collection of tourist souvenirs that his administrator, Estupiñá, is sent to buy for English friends like *miss* Newton, *mistress* Mitchell, and "amigo Davidson," names with a Dickensian ring reminiscent of those of the English eccentrics in *Rosalía*. Tambourines, a bullfighter's outfit, and a cape are regarded by the now cynical Moreno as perfect for encouraging the foreign, romanticized view of Spain and its people.

Moreno's chapter concludes with his fatal heart attack on the second night. The "agent" that triggers this final process is another staircase encounter with Jacinta, whom he had accompanied upstairs as she made her way to see Guillermina. The scene is an instant reminder of that initial doorway scene at the beginning of the chapter that had led to such an entrancing evening at Jacinta's apartment. The result of this second staircase/doorway encounter will not be so encouraging – another stair-climbing sequence by Moreno at the Santa Cruz house earlier that day was excised from the proofs (Willem, "Moreno-Isla's" 180). This final encounter also appears to be an inversion of that between Fortunata and Juanito in part I, for Estupiñá's name permeates this scene: he will bring back to the apartment some of the capes Moreno has just inspected in the Plaza Mayor and he will be the example to surpass in mass attendance, which, Moreno-Isla playfully tells Jacinta, he is going to maintain with regularity. But Moreno is mortified when, peeping out of the door as Jacinta leaves Guillermina's apartment (just as Fortunata had peeped out of her door to see who Juanito was), he notices that she does not bother to glance his way or call on him. He is even more mortified when his aunt tells him later that Jacinta had never mentioned him at all during her visit. In his despair, Moreno rounds sarcastically on his aunt, dismissing all belief in an afterlife and revealing that his attendance at mass was just an excuse to have fun with her and Estupiñá, whom he accuses of being types and eccentrics, like the tourist souvenirs he is taking back to England. This is an important statement for two reasons: "tipos" now becomes synonymous with "excentricidades," a very late addition after the galleys had been corrected. Second, for Moreno (and for the narrator), the type character is completely assimilable to an inanimate artistic object. By comparison, Galdós's own "eccentric types," like Moreno and the others in our study, are far more human and complex. Guillermina's jovial retort that her nephew is an eccentric too and should go on display in fairs receives its poignant human dimension when, before lapsing into his thoughts, he indicates that his own exhibition sign would read: "the most unfortunate man in the world" ["Se enseña aquí el hombre más desgraciado del mundo"].

As he prepares for his final night of sleep, Moreno suddenly recalls another disagreeable meeting that he had experienced in the street as he returned from viewing the capes in the Plaza Mayor, an encounter that parallels the one the day before with the crippled beggar. This time it is a horribly ugly girl, whose face is pockmarked, with her blind eyes bulging out like those of a dead fish. Her two saving graces are her beautifully white teeth and a wonderfully moving voice, to be heard when, accompanied by an old guitarist, she sings for alms. Here we have the realistic counterpoint to the beautiful image of the girl playing the guitar on the tambourine that Estupiñá has already bought for his master's package of souvenirs. More pertinently, this ugly, blind girl forms a contrast with the beautiful child Jacinta receives at the end of the novel and with the one that she and Moreno had daydreamed about in their earlier conversation, which once more in his final moments he fondly anticipates having if they ever married. More particularly, the young singer is, above all, the cause of Moreno's deepest emotional experience before he dies: as he recalls her singing even more intensely than earlier, its celestial harmony sends such waves of consoling sadness through his whole body that he is ready to burst into tears, his conscience wracked with pangs of extreme remorse for not having given her more money than he did. In a way, the ugly reality of contemporary Spain that he has derided so much in the Santa Cruz social circle surprises him with this most unexpected spiritual side. When he had first heard her singing in the street, he had been enchanted by the naturally beautiful cadences, superior to those of professional singers: "This is original" ["Esto sí que tiene carácter"], as if she were an original type. Now in his more intense reliving of that musical experience, he undergoes a spiritual experience that shakes his whole being, almost giving him a preview of the world beyond, to which he is soon to journey. Unfortunately, however, this experience makes way for one more whimsical vision of a blissful union with Jacinta when he returns to Spain the following spring. If this did take place, he would buy a silver urn for the statue of Christ to which Estupiñá is so devoted, as well as fund an asylum for the mad. For this charity, he will be called "the poor man's Providence" ["Providencia de los desgraciados"].[16] The allusions to Estupiñá, perfectly consistent with the context, remind us of the Fortunata-Juanito relationship that will ultimately produce the child Jacinta longs for, as well as the incarceration of Maxi in the lunatic asylum of Leganés, not the model institution that Moreno-Isla is willing to fund. He is closely linked to his estate agent, "the Great Rossini," in this chapter, first to cast a comic light on the latter's chauvinism, and then to anticipate his mini spiritual awakening in the final chapter. Of course, Moreno-Isla's pre-death transformation is more profound and moving, converting him into less of a type and more of an individual. His acolyte, however, will be the person charged to deliver to his beloved Jacinta the baby he had longed to give her with his own body.

CHAPTER EIGHT

Religious Acolyte:
Luis Agapito Babel

Ángel Guerra (1890–91) is typical of the novels Galdós wrote in the 1890s, with their focus on the search for new modalities with which to practice the Christian faith. Despite the riotous profusion of secondary, minor, and minimal characters, as noted by the young Ramón del Valle-Inclán (Fichter 58), our old comic eccentric is still given a prominent part to play, now adapted to the novel's religious theme. His name is Luis Agapito Babel, though he is more commonly called Pito. Following the pattern of some of our previously studied eccentrics, Pito appears early in the novel and within the context of family relations. These are considerably more complex and problematic than any seen hitherto, since the narrator immediately surrounds them with confusion: he affirms and then questions their existence: the Babel family members "[a]re totally fictitious – which in no way precludes their being quite real" ["son de todo punto inverosímiles, lo cual no quita que sean verdaderos"] (I, 1, vii). This paradox, expressed only in general terms, is passed along for the reader to accept or reject, at her/his discretion, with the narrator well aware that what follows may be labelled a fraud: "The reader is therefore free to believe or disbelieve what he is told, and although it may be criticized as a fiction or a fraud, here is the portrait, with all the falsehood of its truth, and with neither addition to nor subtraction from its incredible and incontrovertible nature" ["Queda, pues, el lector en libertad de creer o no lo que se cuenta, y aunque esto se tache de imposturas, allá va el retrato con toda la mentira de su verdad, sin quitar ni poner nada a lo increíble ni a lo inconcuso"]. The onus is upon the reader (as always in the literary equation, as Estupiñá had shown us) to decide whether to believe Pito's portrait and the others that follow, to believe, in other words, what (s)he wants to believe, but the confusion created by the narrator is sufficient for the reader to advance into the text with caution. This destabilization is increased by the non-traditional way in which the members of the family are introduced: all in a short span of text, the first three sections of part I, chapter 2, with their names capitalized and their relationships italicized, as if they were names on a list, set off with file headings. Pito and his family are first identified with reference to the House of Babel: they are the second branch. Then, Pito is presented individually and defined by his relation to his older brother, Simón, the patriarch. The impression that we are dealing with a unique, individual character is immediately qualified and restricted by the appositional phrase, which gives greater emphasis to his occupation, identifying him as a very familiar type: the mariner. The phrase "a hard-boiled man" [literally, "a man well done over by water"] ["hombre muy pasado por el agua"] adds a connotation with its humorous wording: that he is an interesting old sea dog who, we can anticipate, will have a colourful vocabulary, plenty of anecdotes to relate, and a certain liking for women and drink (although alcoholism, to a lesser degree, and womanizing are features common to a number of our other, non-maritime eccentrics), for as Nimetz certifies, "This literary type belongs to the folklore of fiction" (154). In his review article on Pereda's novels and stories two years earlier, Galdós had reckoned that the fisherman is the most universal type, in both time and place, because the element against which he strives (the sea) gives unity to the type (*Ensayos* 190–1). Pito's typecasting was hailed as perfect by a contemporary critic, Ramón D. Perés (104). Fittingly, he was born in the seaport of Cadiz and brought up by a seafaring uncle.

Pito is not a nickname, but a shortened version of his full name, Luis Agapito, which nobody ever uses. It is a most appropriate form for a mariner who would have cause to use a whistle, as well as a horn, on board his ship. Monroe Hafter ("'Bálsamo'" 48n11) believes that the shortened version implies that its bearer is also of little worth.[1] Like Estupiñá, Pito is an unabashedly hyperbolic oral autobiographer. He is also old, rheumatic, and limps on his right leg. Cursing his bad luck and always nostalgic for the sea, he now spends his time re-telling his past exploits as a slave trader plying the waters between Africa and Central America; the use of the language of intoxication also suggests that these memoirs are alcohol-fuelled. Like a good old sea dog, his weakness for drink will be a dominant characteristic throughout the novel (Fuentes Peris 9).

Pito is accorded the epithet of "grande" like Estupiñá, but it is in relation to the far-from-heroic, rather the murky, context of his marital status: it is never clarified whether his female partner was a brothel-keeper or candy-store owner, is still alive, or even was his wife. The paternity of his children is obviously in question. All of these details add proper spice to the traditional figure of an old man who has spent most of his life at sea. But they will gain extra piquancy in a novel that, in parts II and III, has a lot to do with the sexual attraction that the eponymous widowed protagonist feels for Leré, the buxom sometime tutor of his daughter. Furthermore, this typical figure of the limping old sailor full of yarns is positioned in the land-locked environment of Madrid and, later, of Toledo, for a special purpose: this transplantation to a location where his skill as a navigator and his exploits are all unknown will only encourage his morose nostalgia for his maritime past. Out of his element, he is, consequently, regarded as useless by the others.

A visit to Pito early in the novel from his niece, Dulcenombre, gives the narrator the opportunity to describe his striking physical presence: the spark in his blue eyes is like the flame of alcohol on a dry cork; his dry, withered, scarred face is like a cork tree or an old sponge; his forehead is comparable to a bunch of roots sold in a drug store; his hands are like sea rope; and his greeny white beard growing between the ruts on his face looks like the barnacle on the hull of a ship that has not docked for some time. His sea experiences have obviously contributed to this erosion of facial features, more extensive and grotesque, perhaps, than that commonly suffered by all seafarers. In fact, his face reminded Pardo Bazán (60) of a Holbein miniature, whilst twentieth-century cinema-goers might recall the cartoon character Pop-Eye. Galdós seems to have taken the familiar type of the old sea dog and exaggerated his contours. The same comment could be applied to his language: Pito is forever sprinkling his conversation with nautical terms to refer to common actions or body features.They are so common and extensive that they amount to more than the few pet phrases or tags allotted to previous eccentrics. Speaking according to type, one might say, Luis Agapito is only too ready to recommend severe punishments for landlubbers like corrupt government officials. His claim to pontificate on such matters is justified, he reckons, by his experiences of life: "I know people, I've had my share of knock-downs and dragouts with 'em, and I tell you this, they're wild animals if you don't know how to tame 'em!" ["¡Conozco la Humanidad, porque he bregado mucho con ella, y sé que es un animal feroz si no se la sabe domesticar!"] (I, 2, v).

So far, Pito seems to be no more than the old mariner type, but in his interaction with Dulcenombre after her arrival he outgrows the type mould and starts to become an individual character of some depth, being the only member of the Babel family to acknowledge her sacrifices on their behalf. He treats her with great sympathy. Limping along the corridor of the family dwelling with a stick, cursing, and belching may be colourful identifiers of "el gran Don Pito," but much more noteworthy is his feeling of excitement at seeing Dulce and inviting her into his ship cabin of a room for a drink. She is certainly in much need of this companionship in the penultimate chapter of part I. It is now that Pito begins to play a more pivotal role in the novel's plot, for he is the only member of the Babel family that Ángel Guerra can tolerate and the only relation in whom Dulce had been able to confide during her estrangement from her erstwhile lover. He will become their kind of go-between, like *Caifás* in *Gloria*. Another factor attracting Ángel to Pito is his gift for storytelling, which, at the beginning of the novel, had appeared a whim indulged by this nostalgic, ancient mariner. Guerra seems to appreciate these stories only for their entertainment value, failing to draw the obvious lesson about the savageness of human nature: "Guerra enjoyed the salty, bitter, corrupt stream of these doleful stories" ["A Guerra le agradaban el amargor salado y el vaho corrupto de estas lúgubres historias"] (I, 6, iv). In one sense, it could be claimed that Luis Agapito is only encouraging Ángel's more violent tendencies with these stories of cruelty and barbarousness. If he does, then, it could also be claimed that the widower wants to be so encouraged, for he is ready to reward Pito with supplies of his two basic needs: tobacco and alcohol.[2] This storytelling does have unfortunate consequences at times, however, for the storyteller, for when, on another occasion in the same chapter, Ángel goes to the Babel house determined to break off his relationship with Dulce, the sudden entrance of Pito provides him with the perfect excuse and opportunity. The sea captain only exacerbates Ángel's bad humour with his antics (those of a clown) and his gestures (those of a bogeyman). With his contorted face and screwed-up eyes, he appears like "a decrepit old fool who can't even walk straight" ["un carcamal incapaz de tenerse en pie"]. Pito, whose proper name was very often substituted by his naval rank in this sequence at the proof stage (e.g. g. part I; 2:97), is now given another mannerism that – besides adding to his catalogue of comic, eccentric tics – individualizes and humanizes him even more, just as with Ido's eyelid flapping, because of the circumstances that cause it: when agitated, he has the tendency to make constant movements with his stomach and right hand, as if he were trying to stop his trousers from falling down.[3] With his usual flourish of oaths ("goddammit," "dammit" ["carando" "yema" "pateta"]) and sprinkling of nautical phrases, Pito proudly stands his ground at the door, defending his dignity, calling Dulce's lover a "whippersnapper" ["párvulo"] and "my little gent" ["caballerito"]. His newly found scorn for money, while highly implausible, does serve to raise doubts in the reader's mind, if not in Guerra's, about the wisdom of dispensing food handouts and money to people like the Babels, especially when these actions are not accompanied by truly charitable feelings and are dictated by an overly literal interpretation of Christ's Sermon on the Mount.

Like Relimpio, Estupiñá, and Moreno-Isla, Pito has a complete chapter at the end of part I to himself (in the company of Dulcenombre), more obviously so in the original title ("Gin cock-tail") than in the definitive one ("Herida-bálsamo"). The chapter is deliberately designed to contrast the mariner's essentially kind and comforting advice to Dulcenombre with her ex-lover's cold ingratitude (Ribbans, "Woman" 495); the tics and mannerisms of Nimetz's cut-out type of the old alcoholic, storytelling sea captain are present, as usual, but they are subordinated to the much more important development of Pito as a person who tries to help his niece in her emotional crisis when she realizes that Ángel has abandoned her for good. Pito shows quickness of mind and agility of limb when he sees from his position in the street that Dulcenombre is prepared to commit suicide by throwing herself over the balcony: he stands prepared to catch her if she falls, but is successful in dissuading her from such madness by telling her to come to her senses and to look for another lover. Once he has rushed upstairs he does the next correct thing, which is to take the distraught Dulce in his arms and comfort her with soothing words of affection and trust, promising to protect her always. Indeed, he acts as a true and better father than his brother. Such genuine emotion and help does not prevent him from pocketing some of the coins the ex-lover had left Dulce as a parting present or from extolling the virtues of owning a little money, despite its otherwise corrupting effects (I, 7, i). Nor is he totally disinterested, of course, when he prepares a meal for the distressed woman or concocts a gin-cocktail in which she can drown her sorrows, with the resultant hang-over. But these are the usual traces of comic selfishness that puncture, without too much harm, the halo of saintliness that is beginning to form over his head. His promise of a better life free from harassment is again aimed at relieving her misery. Pito's philosophical advice about accepting the trials of life, so that any happiness is a welcome piece of luck, of course falls on deaf ears, but at least his aims and advice are admirable, however much they are made ironic by his own drinking and smoking, or by the attention of a dog. His homespun, stoic philosophy of life, derived from his experiences at sea, form a far more credible alternative to the more systematic sermon Leré had earlier directed to her infatuated pupil, Guerra. At least Pito tries sincerely to help his niece in her hour of need with practical help and advice, and at a time when, under the influence of the cocktail, he too has become depressed. For, in landlocked Madrid, his nostalgia for the ocean is relieved only by trips to the outskirts to gaze at the horizon, or by promenades along the streets ogling, or flirting with, pretty young girls, like Relimpio in *La desheredada*. At other times, he would bathe in small fountains or swing from trees, confusing places and buildings with those he had been familiar with on his sea journeys. Not unsurprisingly, he is laughed at as a madman ("el tipo aquel no tenía la cabeza buena" [I, 7, ii]) by workers repairing the street or other passers-by. When he recovers from his gin-cocktails, he again gives Dulcenombre a lesson on how to survive in life: his premise is that, as one's neighbours are poisonous animals, the best preventive self-protection is to expect the worst and, if provoked, to fight back (contrary to the passivity that Leré had earlier enjoined on Ángel).The irony of this spiel is that Pito is disproving his own theory by his current acts of kindness to his niece.

Pito's simplistic philosophizing, more extensive than that of any of our other eccentrics, including Ido del Sagrario, is to be attributed to Galdós's preoccupation in this novel with a debate between the respective merits and disadvantages of a moral-religious system that the eponymous hero, under Leré's inspiration and guidance, is trying to create for himself and her. This personal search and its origins so infuriate Dulce that Pito has to repeat his advice that she should accept the new reality of her separation and look for another lover. Luis Agapito's system of philosophy has no basis of dogma; it is just founded on the lessons of life. He encourages her to think positively: "Learn to live a little" ["Aprende a vivir"] (I, 7, iii). But such wisdom is soon drowned out by more liquor, which leads him to drag Dulcenombre on another crazy street expedition to see the boats floating in the centre of Madrid. These hallucinations are appropriately exteriorized by changes in his clothing: his hat is pulled down over his head, his jacket is closed tight, and he wears a collar made of fur.

Babel's re-entry into the novel (part II, chapter 3) occurs in the warren of streets that is Toledo. His cursing at losing his way on a cold night is the note of reality that intrudes on Guerra's enjoyment of the Romantic solitude of the surroundings. Pito is certainly not the Golden Age knight that the widower had first imagined when hearing his cries for help. However, and in spite also of their last angry encounter in Madrid, he takes the old sea dog home, where the latter gratefully accepts the offer of lodging, tobacco, and alcohol. At this juncture, Pito makes an important confession: it is not alcohol, but women that have been the cause of his downfall. The sincerity of this admission is underscored by his nervous tic of constantly hitching up his trousers; it also has pertinence for Guerra's own current infatuation with Leré. He, though, ignores the lesson by making the mariner an even more stupendous offer: to one day give him permanent lodging. Clearly, Ángel is already making plans for the establishment of a religious commune. What Pito warmly greets as an individual act of real charity (II, 3, v) may well conceal other, less altruistic motives. Luis Agapito's material need becomes, then, a test case for assaying the true value of the reborn-Christian Ángel's understanding of the virtue of charity. This is not only because Ángel's plans for a religious colony are seriously flawed but also because the perceived beneficiaries of this scheme are not free of hostile and destructive feelings towards others. At the same time as he continues to forward the plot with his constant trips from Ángel's residence to that of his relatives, Pito turns slowly into a figure of common-sense guidance for Ángel, as well as for Dulce. He succeeds in getting the ex-revolutionary to visit his former mistress: "The poor man's hints found a pious echo in Guerra's heart, for his sensibility, easily excited, responded promptly to any request made by a humble voice" ["Las insinuaciones de aquel desdichado hallaban un eco piadoso en el corazón de Guerra, cuya sensibilidad, fácilmente excitable, respondió prontamente a cualquier demanda hecha por voz humilde"]. But Pito's own susceptibility to passion and emotion, especially to hatred for the shepherd Tirso, is another warning signal to Ángel about the dangers that could face his new religious colony in its attempts to realize the utopian ideals of universal peace and love. In this respect, the sea captain's oft-repeated stories of the perils of the sea and the strange human activities he has seen in foreign lands now assume a more direct relevance for Guerra's project, but it goes unheeded by the would-be religious founder, who, sitting around the fire with other residents on his estate, has his thoughts focused on his own plans:

The lively colloquies in which the deceptions of Don Pito alternated with the rusticity of the *cigarral* folk, far from bothering him [Ángel Guerra] in his meditation on things so far removed from those they were discussing, acted as a sort of lullaby, kept time for him, if one may call it that, marking the rhythm so that his thoughts could be more easily coordinated. Thus when there was a pause in those barbarians' conversation Guerra's mind would come to a halt like a clogged machine, and as soon as their idiotic statements rang out anew his mind functioned again. What relationship could exist between the thoughts of the preoccupied master and the concepts of those poor people? None, within any usual system of logic.

[los vivos coloquios en que alternaba la marrullería de don Pito con la rusticidad de los cigarraleros, lejos de molestarle [Ángel Guerra] en su meditación sobre cosas tan distintas de lo que allí se hablaba, servíanle como de arrullo, le llevaban el compás, si puede decirse, marcándose el ritmo para que sus ideas se coordinaran más fácilmente. Así cuando había una pausa en la conversación de aquellos bárbaros, la mente de Guerra se paraba, como una máquina que se entorpece, y en cuanto volvían a sonar los disparates, la mente funcionaba de nuevo. ¿Qué relación podía existir enter el pensar del amo abstraído y los conceptos de aquella infeliz gente? Ninguna en usual lógica.] (II, 4, iv)

Hafter ("'Bálsamo'" 46) has no hesitation whatsoever in supplying the correct answer: "As Pito's stories expose the inflation of his heroism, Ángel's meditation reveals the exaggeration of his virtuousness." More seriously, though, the metaphor of the engine – an echo of Pito's previous reference to a ship's turbine – to describe the sudden interruption in Guerra's thoughts imply that the latter are too systematic, too ordered. By the same token, the mariner fails to realize that there may be dangers for him lurking in the Toledan countryside, albeit of a different kind to those he had experienced abroad. Consequently, there is some irony in Ángel's wish to become as humble as Pito. He promises the colony's first inmate that life there will be perfect, Pito will even have some of his beloved ocean – how, he does not specify – but, more practically, he is going to buy him some new boots. When Pito, in his gratitude, utters his favourite curse: "I shit on" ["me caso con"], it prompts a rebuke: "No shittings on anybody, least of all on a saint. Shittings are absolutely forbidden here" ["No se case usted con nadie, y menos con un santo. Quedan terminantemente prohibidos los casamientos"] (II, 4, iv). The irony of this admonishment lies in the literal meaning of the euphemism: "I am marrying" (Ribbans, *Conflicts* 299n41), for Guerra would dearly love to be married to St Leré. However, in his religious order, that will not be possible. The old sea captain's oath is adroitly used to mask and at the same time to reveal Ángel's real, subconscious feelings and wishes, just as slightly earlier it had underlined the falseness behind Dulce's planned marriage to her country cousin.[4] The connection, linguistic and thematic, between the two contexts advances the plot in another important direction: when Ángel again visits his former mistress, after Leré has insisted that he marry her, the drunken Dulce hurls Pito's oath at him and his newly discovered religiosity: "I shit on your mother" ["Me caso con tu madre"]. As a result of this tirade, Dulce's brother, Arístides, provokes Ángel into physically assaulting him, in a resurgence of the former's violent impulses, undoing all the good effects of Leré's Christian instruction, and with fatal long-term consequences. Likewise, Pito's simultaneous and equally predictable recourse to violence in his simmering feud with Tirso creates another parallel between master and retainer. In both men – and the language used is remarkably similar – instincts of blind anger and rage, repressed for some time, suddenly resurface with violent consequences. In Pito's case, Tirso's opinion of him is that he is "a crazy man, a lunatic who couldn't talk straight" ["un orate, un estrafalario que no decía cosa alguna al derecho"] (II, 4, vii). Guerra sympathizes with Pito in his plight, even going so far as to see a symbolism in his encounter with Tirso (the clash of civilization and wild nature with the former trying to educate the latter), but failing to see that the former slave-trader is as authoritarian and dogmatic as he is in his plans for the religious commune.

Pito's next appearance in the novel is over three chapters later, at the beginning of part III. He is glad to see his master arrive back from his five-day stay in Toledo, where his religious feelings have once more been strengthened by exposure to the artistic magnificence of the cathedral and other places of worship. Pito has missed him, partly because he has not received so much food as before, and also because he cannot get along with the others on the estate. Pito has become dependent, materially and emotionally, upon his master, as the latter has on the old sea captain for his message-running: Ángel's company can even compensate him now for his constant nostalgia for the sea. The bond has almost become akin to that between Don Quixote and Sancho Panza. The captain now assumes the role of his master's interlocutor on the cardinally important matter of his new program to establish a religious colony, details of which he has learnt on trips into Toledo to see the other Babels. Pito's exposition of the rumours not only provides a usefully brief summary of the main parts of the program, relieving Ángel or the narrator of this task, but also, through his inquisitorial formatting of the rumours, forces the colony founder onto the defensive, unable to deny the general thrust of his beneficiary's interrogation. Finally, the sea dog's repetition, in a somewhat familiar tone, of the clichés of Christian charity, along with a request to be the first inmate of the new institution, throws doubt on the proposed seriousness of the whole venture:

I know you're going to found something, a house, or a convent, or whatever the hell it was, so's you can take care of the needy, and shelter the orphans, and clothe the naked, and cure the sick, and make the lame walk straight, and everything else as goes along with a really first-class charity. It's a good idea, yessir, best trampoline you could get you for making the big old jump to Heaven, and getting yourself saved all right and tight.

[yo sé que usted va a fundar una cosa, una casa, un convento o no sé qué demonios para recoger menesterosos, amparar huérfanos, vestir desnudos, curar enfermos, enderezar tullidos y todo lo demás que es pertinente a la caridad en grande. Buena idea, buena, y el mejor trampolín para dar el gran brinco hasta el Cielo, y salvarse bien salvado.] (III, 1, i)

The confusion in Ángel's plans and thinking, perfectly illustrated in his readiness to exempt the mariner's drinking from the list of prohibitions, is even captured in the way he swings from an excessively polite address ("Don Pito," duly italicized) to the familiar second person used with close servants. Pito is really the master in this dialogue: it is he who has fleshed out the new church's gospel and got his own personal exemption written into it, so to speak, all gratefully and happily approved by the founder. It is only fitting, then, that he should now command the master to tell the servants to prepare a badly needed meal. Another unforeseen and dangerous consequence of this comfortable lifestyle is the re-arousal of Pito's sexual passion for the buxom but ugly cook Jusepa, transformed in his imagination into a goddess of beauty (Lakhdari 232), in something of a grotesque distortion of Ángel's sublimation of Leré's equally ample bosom. This infatuation of Pito's will lead directly to the novel's conclusion (Hafter, "'Bálsamo'" 45).

The scene is now set for the last (and most important) of Pito's postprandial, alcohol-fuelled speeches. This time, however, the usual account of his travels is prefaced by a short list of the main points of the brand of Christianity they should practice in the commune: the saving virtues are doing good to one's neighbours, respecting their life, honour, and property, and, paradoxically, the non-deprivation of innocent delights (by which Luis Agapito means chiefly alcohol, although he also mentions the eating of fish). However, the single matter on which he is still unclear is the matter of sex, of particular interest to him now that he is enthralled with Jusepa. It is also, of course, the major problem in Guerra's life and one that he has not been able to address in his program for the new institution: it all comes down to the question of whether women will be accepted into the order and have separate living quarters. Pito's blunt and pertinent questions – Galdós describes him here as "the inspired captain" – forces the master to reply, but he evades the issue by dismissing it as of no concern of Pito's. Unabashed, the old captain is determined to expound his theories on heterosexual love. He firmly believes that prohibiting love between the sexes, that is, enjoining celibacy on members of religious orders, is going against God's will and that loving a person of the opposite sex is not a deadly sin. If Pito's common-sense ideas may not be so remarkable, given his life's experience, his logic and articulateness in this speech are exceptional. The founder of the new order is once more forced onto the defensive, having to admit that he agrees that nobody commits a sin by loving another person. However, if he is once more prepared to make an exception by allowing Pito to go on flirting with women as he wishes, he objects that such behaviour would only cause scandal in an institution that is established for religious purposes. Pito, whom Guerra now calls his dear friend, brilliantly seizes upon the inconsistency of logic in the argument when he inquires: if the master is not going to forbid love in his new order, how is he going to incorporate it in the rules of conduct? Ángel is left appearing more like a babbling pupil than the knowledgeable master. Pito has now turned master and accurately points out the truth: that his interlocutor has not really resolved this dilemma, which goes to the core of his own existence and was the motivating force behind his desire to found a religious order in the first place. Still playing the master, the ex-slave trader dictates a lesson to pupil Ángel, citing as the textbook his life's adventures around the globe. He is deadly serious about the matter, although it is becoming apparent that Ángel, short-sightedly, is beginning not to pay him the proper attention. In this speech, Pito's role in the questioning of the cobbled-together religious doctrine is far more important than that of serving as a mirror for the landowner's growing compassion for others (Eoff 77). Rather, Pito offers constructive criticism, even providing a real model for his order to follow: the Mormon sect, which has reconciled religion and sex by encouraging its priests to marry and procreate so as to perfect the human race. His detailed recollections of a visit to Salt Lake City to see Mormonism at work and to meet with Brigham Young provoke only laughter from Ángel, when Pito's in situ examination of this valid alternative and remedy for Guerra's dilemma deserves serious consideration, as Pito remonstrates with the master. Bigamy may be widespread and encouraged in Utah, but the crime rate there is not as high as it is in Spain:

You probably think there ain't no morality over there! Hell, there's more nor what there is over here, lots more. They don't have no stealing, nor killing, nor quarrels, nor arguments. They're every whit as civilized out there as what

they are in Chicago or Boston, dammit, and the most active, hard-working
people you ever did see.
[¡Si creerás que allí no hay moralidad! Más que aquí, pero más. Allí ni robos,
allí ni asesinatos, allí ni riñas, allí ni cuestiones. Y tan civilizados como en
Chicago o en Boston, ¡carando!, y activos y trabajadores como ellos solos.]
(III, 1, ii)[5]

Pito is even prepared to compromise with the reality of Spanish society on the question of the size of the harem! Amusing details aside, the
Mormon model that Pito proposes is not totally irrelevant for the kind
of isolated, combined male and female religious order that Ángel
wants to found in the Toledan wilderness. The captain presents himself as a clear guide for his master on this matter: "you just pay attention to what I say ... Yes siree, just do it that way, and drop this other
foolishness. Love don't get in the way of religion" ["haz caso de mí ...
Sí, hombre, decídete, y déjate de simplezas. Pero si lo enamorado no
quita lo religioso"]. However, his conclusion that such a sexual
arrangement will lead to a peaceful, trouble-free society practising
Christian charity is unrealistic and absurd, the product of Pito's cere-
bral disorder, in the opinion of the narrator. As the crowning finale to
his philippic, Pito would even like to see the American city's name,
duly translated, adopted for the new colony, although a more sober
and serious name (New Zion, the City of the Elect) had originally
appeared in the manuscript, before it was changed on the galleys (g.
part III; 1:33). It is debatable whether Guerra could have retorted with
arguments against Mormonism, as he originally intended, since he
had miserably failed to rebut the old captain's previous arguments.
His weak excuse to himself is that such a sermon would not be understood by a man like Pito, whose understanding had been numbed by
senility and vice. For Ángel, unfortunately, Luis Agapito Babel is
merely a convenient object for his charity, when not making him
laugh, as if he were a court jester.

Construction work begins on the colony, and Pito's closeness to the
master becomes more emotional: he is genuinely relieved to find him
safe and sound in a cave after a storm. He was the first to locate
Guerra, and he is the one to sensibly advise him to sleep and forget
about going to church services in Toledo. Ángel, in turn, offers sound
advice to Pito, when the latter reckons that he would willingly make
a Faustian pact with the Devil to recover his youth: "the outlandish
captain" ["el estrafalario capitán"] listens to the master's exhortation
to think of death and the salvation of his soul (III, 3, vii).

Significantly, Pito opens the novel's last chapter in a perturbed state
that forebodes his master's imminent murder, for he believes that the

vision of his nephews in the kitchen the previous night is the result of a disorder of his nervous system. Refusing to believe that Ángel would have given them shelter, he resorts to further libations. But his physical and mental faculties are tested as they have never been before by the sight of his son and Jusepa appearing from behind a bush in the countryside. The comic allusions to a Faustian pact with the Devil that he had made earlier to the exhausted Ángel now take on a tragic note, forcing him to admit that Policarpo is not his own son. His self-pity turns into genuine humility when he recognizes that this concealment was due to his own weakness of character (III, 6, i). Pito is truly distraught when he sees his master dying on the bedroom floor, after being attacked by Dulce's brother, the ironically named Fausto, and Pito's newly identified stepson, Policarpo. He bursts out crying like a child, embracing his master and protector, and offering himself as a victim so that Ángel can be saved: "Kill me instead, I ain't no good for nothing" ["Mátame a mí, que no sirvo para nada"] (III, 6, iv), a phrase often found on the lips of an earlier eccentric, Relimpio, at the end of his life with Isidora. Pito's sublimity here is matched by that of his master, who, as well as forgiving his assailants, secures Pito's release from jail, by discrediting him as a reliable witness of the attack. Pito rushes back to Ángel's estate as fast as his lame leg allows him, arriving in time to see his master before he dies. Again, he cannot contain the tears that stream down his corky, wrinkled face. To hide his emotion, he deploys his full repertoire of oaths, as he kisses his master's hands, urging him not to die, much like Sancho does on Don Quixote's deathbed (III, 6, vi). His loyalty is duly acknowledged by the dying Ángel, who, in an original and affectionate adaptation of his name, calls him "Pitillo." Paradoxically, Agapito's abbreviated name, which, according to Hafter, had suggested the probable insignificance of this type, is here given a unique, diminutive suffix, or linguistic belittlement (whose other meaning of "cigarette" aptly expresses the mariner's passion for tobacco) at the moment of his greatest devotion to his master as well as of his fullest development as a more complex individual. Again, Galdós uses small details from his repertoire of type identifiers to mark the spiritual distance travelled by Pito in his transformation from type into character: he cannot now accept the bottle of rum or anis that Ángel offers him, something that the old sea dog would have jumped at before. Like his master, he overcomes pride and publicly confesses that he was no maritime hero, but a smuggler, and that Policarpo is not his son. Whether a sympathetic drunk (at least in part I [Alas, *Ensayos* 218]), or the picturesque embodiment of human nature in all its richness and contradictions (Lakhdari 26, 171), or Ángel's greatest success in human relationships

(Round 165–6), Don Pito is, above all, one of Galdós's best examples of the comic, eccentric old man who almost steals centre stage from the eponymous hero, not so much by his role in the plot, but rather through sheer force of character development. Luis Agapito Babel is the court jester who points out the serious truth of life to his landowner master: that genuine affection between human beings is more valuable than any religious do-goodism or foundation-building motivated by sublimated sexual instincts.

CHAPTER NINE

Religious Patron:
Pedro de Belmonte

In *Nazarín* (1895) it is the country squire, Pedro de Belmonte, who is characterized as a strange, strongly eccentric, rather mad, type. Though not developing any close relationship with another controlling figure as Pito did, his appearance in the novel is explained solely in terms of the need to further elucidate the religious nature of the character and actions of Nazarín.

Belmonte, unusually for our eccentrics, does not appear early in the novel, nor is his entry directly anticipated. Yet his single appearance is substantial and occurs more or less in the centre of the five-part novel: the last four chapters (6–9) of part III, or chapters 17–20 of a thirty-five-chapter novel. In effect, the Belmonte adventure is the longest and most important one that Nazarín experiences on his travels in the Castilian countryside around Madrid. Nazarín's climactic visit to this squire's mansion is prompted specifically by the confusing outline of his character that his travelling companion, Beatriz, sketches. This preview accords entirely in its ambiguity and enigmatic quality with those given hitherto in the novel, whether of character or physical appearances, especially in part I, where Nazarín and the motley collection of residents in the Madrid boarding house are presented in confusing terms. Don Pedro, the owner of a country estate, La Coreja, and with the reputation for being a good hunter and horseman, is a very rare example in our group of eccentrics-madmen of a representative of the landowning, higher middle class or aristocracy – Cayetano and Anselmo are the only other two in our group. He is rich and not very old, which probably means that he is in his fifties, just like

Moreno-Isla. But he is of quite an opposite disposition: he is the most ill-tempered man in New Castile. There is a difference of opinion about the real reasons for these temper tantrums: some think he is evil, others that he gets drunk to forget his troubles. Alcohol had, of course, been a frequent vehicle of escapism for Relimpio and Pito, but it was never accompanied by actions of physical cruelty to others, as when Belmonte had hurled a donkey and its rider down a cliff for obstructing his path. He is also supposed to have killed his wife (like Anselmo in *La sombra*). His noble relatives in Madrid no longer have contact with him, having confined him to this kind of rural prison, where he is looked after and kept under surveillance by their servants, in a way similar to that in which Jesús Delgado was confined to a boarding house by his relatives in *El doctor Centeno*. Instead of dissuading Nazarín from visiting the mansion, Beatriz's account has only whetted his appetite to confront the ogre, for he sees another opportunity to encounter the suffering for which he longs. He conveniently disguises this motivation beneath the wish to discover if there is any truth in the rumours, for, as he correctly notes, public opinion can at times make some enormous errors of judgment. The great irony of this declaration is that he himself is already the subject of similarly contradictory and controversial stories, some of which he is familiar with, but which he prefers to ignore. There will be no further excuse for ignoring or escaping these rumours after his confrontation with Belmonte.

It is also especially appropiate that Galdós should give his definitive physical portrait of Belmonte through the eyes of Nazarín, for in this way he is able to show how the wandering priest can appraise correctly and fully the external features of another person's appearance and yet, at the same time, be totally incapable of evaluating his inner character, not only through his own analytical shortcomings but also because of the inner complexity of Belmonte himself. This is precisely the challenge Nazarín presented to the reporter and the narrator of part I when they first met Nazarín in his lodging. The squire's presence is impressive: he has a most noble figure, and is very tall and handsome. His exact age is now revealed as sixty-two. The particular physiognomic features selected by the narrator – a tanned face; a slightly broad nose; lively eyes beneath thick eyebrows; a white, wavy, pointed beard; and a wide, clear forehead – all contribute to the outline of a noble type, more willing to give than to take orders. His dress befits his social station; the only slight peculiarity is a dark, light hat tilted to one side. Belmonte looks, to Nazarín, exactly the type he is: a despotic lord, as his first harsh words of greeting seem to confirm. If Belmonte soon begins to act not according to type, it is because his curiosity has been aroused, in turn, by the external appearance of Nazarín. Instead of shooting him, as Nazarín thinks he will, the squire stares at him with even greater intensity. Their continuous staring at each other is emphasized by a servant staring at both of them. Belmonte applies the same principles of Lavaterian physiognomics that Nazarín has just applied to him, again reinforced by his rather gratuitous question to the same servant: "what do you make of this fellow?" ["¿qué te parece este tipo?"][1] Belmonte's conclusion is that Nazarín is a Moor, albeit a Christian one, a conclusion to which the narrator of part I had also jumped when he first saw the priest in the Madrid tenement house. The conclusion is perfectly justifiable: Nazarín's complexion makes him look like an Arab. By the same token, his identification of Belmonte as a tyrannical lord is justifiable: Belmonte looks exactly like one. However, in both cases, the identification is made with reference back to a previous image of the type: Belmonte thinks Nazarín is an Arab because of his own experience in the Middle East whilst Nazarín's typecasting of Belmonte is made with reference to the image Beatriz had previously painted.[2] It is not that these identifications are totally incorrect. The main point that Galdós is trying to make is that determining or typecasting a person's ethnic origins or even his inner character solely from the external physiognomic evidence is a futile exercise in the long run. Already Nazarín has been perplexed by Belmonte's failure to fly into a rage, whilst the squire cannot reconcile the priest's urbane speech with his beggar's appearance. The mutual ocular scrutiny, which continues at length indoors, becomes simply comical. Belmonte's conviction, corroborated by a long perusal of documents and newspapers and announced to Nazarín at dinner, that he is an ex-Armenian bishop, Esrou-Esdras, journeying through Western Europe disguised as a pilgrim is the most hilarious of all the misidentifications of Nazarín in the novel. In his extreme frustration at not being able to disabuse Belmonte of this notion, Nazarín fails to see the importance of the lesson that is being presented to his eyes and, more particularly, to his mind. The second and most important part of this lesson in character optics is Belmonte's proud obsession with the subject of modern-day Christianity, or the future of religion in modern society, for it mirrors Nazarín's own unshakeable belief in the right of his mission to the countryside. The importance of the Belmonte episode is that, for the first and only time in the novel, Nazarín is confronted by a character with a similar religious mania and obstinacy in his eccentric ideas and beliefs. Belmonte is a mirror character in which Nazarín cannot see himself: he can only fume at the strange type the squire is:

Who'd have thought God could create such things, so many different types and species! You think you've seen it all, and you find there are still more wonders and curiosities waiting to be discovered. ... To think I came here expecting to be persecuted, humiliated, even martyred ... and what do I find but a jocular giant who seats me at his table, calls me Bishop ...! Now would you say a man like that is bad or good ... ?

[¡Y qué cosas cría el Señor, qué variedad de tipos y seres! Cuando uno cree haberlo visto todo, aún le quedan más maravillas o rarezas que ver. ... ¡Y yo que creí hallar aquí vejaciones, desprecios, el martirio quizá ... y me encuentro con un gigante socarrón que me sienta a su mesa y me llama obispo ...! Pero este hombre, ¿es malo o es bueno? ...] (III, 9)

Nazarín fails to see that this is precisely the question people are asking themselves about him as the result of his strange and unconventional priestly behaviour.

The structure of the Belmonte epsiode is also an object lesson for Nazarín and the reader on the need to constantly revise opinions in the light of experience. Beatriz's preview of the squire's irascible character had appeared at the end of part III, chapter 5, as a kind of prologue to Nazarín's visit. During the latter, Belmonte had disclosed more personal details: he now admits to have given up womanizing and resorted to the lesser vices of drink and tobacco. The information gleaned and the opinions formed by Nazarín in these two sections are resumed and expanded in a kind of third section or epilogue provided by a passing peasant woman of the area, Polonia, who, besides confirming most of this information, adds a new bit of news: Don Pedro's madness is the result of his excessive study of theology: "That handsome old dog ... is as mad as a hatter" ["Ese vejestorio grandón y bonito ... está más loco que una cabra"]. Yet Polonia's opinion of Belmonte is not totally negative: in spite of everything, Belmonte has a good heart. And Nazarín, in turn, adds a new trait, gleaned during his visit to La Coreja: Don Pedro never recognizes that he is wrong: "and a more obstinate man when it comes to admitting he's in the wrong would be hard to find" ["no hay quien le gane en terquedad para sostener sus errores"]. This is precisely the fault of which Nazarín himself is most guilty: despite his perceptive judgment of Belmonte, he fails to apply the lesson to himself. Human character is a constantly difficult enigma to decipher; even more difficult is the task of applying its meaning, if and when finally deciphered, to oneself.[3] The task is rendered even more difficult by the nature of Belmonte's enigmatic character: is he mad, or just eccentric? It is hard to determine. In Ido Galdós had explored a similar pattern of irregular behaviour, or oscillations between these two extremes, as a plot determinant. In Belmonte he succeeds in dovetailing this question of mental health with his overall pattern of indecipherable enigmas present at all levels of the narrative.

In comparing principal character, Nazarín, and secondary character, Belmonte, Galdós was, of course, only applying the well-tried formula that he had used with some other eccentrics of our group. He now adds a further permutation that incorporates a technique he had marginally employed in *La desheredada:* he adds a counterpoint figure for Belmonte, but the grotesque dwarf Ujo is given far more prominence than the minimal grotesques of Bou, Sánchez Botín, and Gaitica in the earlier novel.

UJO

Like Belmonte, Ujo only appears in one section of the novel, but that offers sufficient time and space for him to stamp himself indelibly on the reader's mind, as perhaps the novel's most impressive character, for, paradoxically – in view of the brevity of his appearance and the diminutive size of his body – he is allotted the longest physical description and the most individualized language and speech patterns of any character, principal or secondary. This is all the more surprising, given that he appears so late in the novel: part IV, chapter 6. He may be small in body and social importance, but his spiritual significance is great, which is signalled by the fact that the only scene in this very religious novel that takes place in a church is of Beatriz and Ándara meeting the dwarf for the first time in Méntrida/Aldea del Fresno. Ujo is the most grotesque and ridiculous dwarf imaginable. He is a figure of fun for all, the town's court jester, for he has access to all the houses, unlike Belmonte, who has been secreted away in his warren of a mansion. Galdós is able to subtly suggest the connection between the eccentric and the grotesque by using the popular expression "like Peter in his own [house]" ["como Pedro por la suya (casa)"] to describe Ujo's freedom to roam through any house and to provide people with an opportunity for unrestrained laughter and fun.

It is unclear whether the word "Ujo" is a first name or a patronymic, or, in fact, a combination of both. Such onomastic confusion is common in the novel; for example, the name of the eponymous protagonist was also the subject of debate in part I. Ujo's name is also ironic, if it is a distortion of the word for eyes ("ojos"), since this dwarf, who presents such a terrifying appearance to the eyes of those who see him for the first time, correctly sees the inner truth about others: he has very good spiritual eyes, although his physical ones are like those of a mouse and have a terrible squint. Alternatively, the dwarf's name could be aptly identified as the common suffix used to express a diminutive size as well as pejorative feelings. It also happens to be the name of a small Asturian village that Galdós remembered from his travels through the region with Pereda and Palacio Valdés a decade earlier (Bly, *Pérez Galdós*

71n19). The village is located very close to the Cantabrian peak of Ándara (Clarke 85), a geographical proximity that is suitably echoed by the affectionate proximity that the dwarf and the former prostitute briefly experience when Nazarín and his two companions stay in the area of Méntrida/Aldea del Fresno. The Asturian use of the same word to refer to names of caves (Clarke 87) extends the series of meanings even further, as well as establishing a physical and topographical contrast with the patronymic of Don Pedro: "Beautiful Mountain" ["Belmonte"]. The butt of the residents' sick jokes, Ujo wears the most grotesque, ragged clothes, eats awful food that he pays for in cash or kind, and has bread crusts thrown at his oversized head. For the children of the village, he is a perpetual Carnival. His body presents an optical challenge to any observer, for it looks at first as if it consists only of a big head and nose, mounted on two small feet. His other extremities are incredibly small too: they emerge slightly from the sides of his green tunic that resembles the green cloth put over the cages of male partridges. His voice may be that of a boy, but his language is quite uncouth and malicious. He is one of Nature's freaks, or, in terms of the iconography of the church where he takes refuge from the taunts of the villagers, a fearsome devil that has escaped from an altarpiece dedicated to the Blessed Souls. But Ujo totally belies this image in reality, for he is the incarnation of true Christian charity; he provides his new friends with very healthy and badly needed food (some of Nature's choice fruit, and eggs), gathered while begging from door to door, and at the cost of many a humiliation. More importantly, he also provides the party of three with encouragement, love, and advice.

In a novel that is founded on ambiguity and ambivalence, the narrator's praise of his most exceptional character is fittingly couched in humorous, contradictory terms that potentially undercut the reliability of the whole statement: "Contrary to appearances, poor Ujo was a kind man or perhaps one should say a kind dwarf or kind monster" ["Parecía que no, pero era un buen hombre, mejor dicho, un buen enano o buen monstruo, el pobre Ujo"] (IV, 4). He is such a permanent fixture in the village that he is to be included in the list of its principal landmarks: the coat of arms, the weather vane on the church tower, or the mask figure on the communal fountain tap. He is such a common type that the narrator claims that "Every carnival has its dragon, and every village has its Ujo" ["No hay función sin tarasca, ni aldea sin Ujo"].[4] However, this particular Ujo shows a surprising individuality, and, consequently, contradicts his creator: his presents of food and advice are proof of his special character, underlined by his very idiosyncratic style of speech. Apart from the significant and ubiquitous tag, "Christ Almighty" ["caraifa"], he has a special way of pronouncing certain words, all duly italicized (e.g. "dirvos," "quillotro," "vos"). As with Pito's language, Galdós integrates Ujo's into the framework of the novel and the developing plot: he is constantly saying "they says" ["diz"] not only because it is colourful and popular but also because it shows the dwarf's desire to inform Nazarín and his two followers of all the rumours going around the village and to alert them about their impending incarceration. His advice is sensible, sincere, and practical: leave the village as soon as possible, though it will be to his own dis-advantage, for he has become smitten with the ugly Ándara. He knows all about her past and can see perfectly well that she is ugly, but he still loves her, for this is the first time that he has fallen in love, although the verb used is very polite: "estimar," which originally means "to think highly": "You's ugly, you's a whore, and I fancies you ... ! I never fancied no one before" ["Tú fea, tú pública, yo te estimo ... Es la primera vez que estimo"] (IV, 5). Her failure to appreciate the depth of the dwarf's feelings leads her, like everyone else, to dehumanize him, reducing him to an insignificant animal: a tadpole or a snail. In body, he is an incomplete man; in feeling and generosity, he is a far bigger person than anybody else, far taller than the giant Belmonte. Ándara may laugh with Nazarín and Beatriz that she has found a boyfriend in the village church, yet the wording ("que le había salido un novio en la santísima iglesia") also suggests the common notion that nuns, on taking orders, become engaged to Jesus. Ujo certainly has far more Christ-like qualities than His nominal representative in this story, the priest, Nazarín. The essential irrelevance of ambiguous, external phys-iognomies like those of Nazarín and Belmonte that had fixated both in part III becomes very clear when Ujo later climbs up to the ruined cas-tle where the party are billeted to warn that the local police are com-ing to arrest them. Ujo's reappearance is in the form of a voice. The trio search in vain in the dark to see the body behind the voice. His is a happy voice and it is recognizable for the two women. Ándara acclaims him as her boyfriend, her possession, although he is "My one and only little boy" ["el chiquitín del mundo"] (IV, 5). Only then are his physi-cal features and their abnormal proportions specified once more. Respectful to Beatriz and Nazarín, Ujo lets Ándara tease him, for he is their court jester. As usual, he brings them sustenenance for their bod-ies (fresh bread), reports on recent developments (the aborted ascent of the hill by El Pinto, Beatriz's ex-lover, the previous night, and his sub-sequent departure from the village), along with sound advice about their own safety, for rumour has it that they will be arrested for rob-bery. This is a far more sensible and realistic attitude than Nazarín's eagerness to explain their innocence when the Civil Guards arrive. Shrugging aside Ándara's insults and spits, Ujo tries to console and help her when she is arrested. In the village prison, he manages to crawl through the crowd to find his beloved. Like Estupiñá and Pito, he is now called "el gran Ujo." He is Christianity in action, for he forgives Ándara for spitting on him, and he is ready to defend her against "la Verba divina," an appropriate cognate for God, given the dwarf's way of speaking. When the party of prisoners is marched off to Madrid, he accompanies "the object of his fancies" ["la estimada de su corazón"] as far as his diminutive legs will carry him, resting beside a tree and craning, with a hand over his eyes, to catch a last glimpse of her as she fades into the horizon. In a novel where visual observation is very often difficult and misleading about the true nature of the object viewed, as the Belmonte and Nazarín encounter had clearly shown, this extremely intense peering by Ujo at a disappearing point in the distance, whilst illustrating the limitations of the optical exercise, is, paradoxically, most moving, because of Ujo's great feelings for the reformed prostitute: he stares into the distance because he knows very well what Ándara is and what she means to him. There is no ocular enigma or confusion, for physical optics are no longer relevant.

The principal challenge the novel poses is not so much the representing of the unrepresentable, of which Ujo is the prime example (Labanyi, "Introduction" xviii), as one of trying to probe beyond these surface confusions and contradictions and to advance towards a deeper spiritual truth that may also be irresolubly contradictory in the final analysis. Ujo incarnates the constant theme of Carnival in the book, and as such, represents a subversive element in society in that he turns the normal world upside down (Labanyi, "Introduction" xx). This is true not only in the physical sense but in the spiritual sense. His actions and thoughts are, like those of Nazarín and Belmonte, at variance with the rest of society. But he surpasses the other two in his practice of the Christian virtues of neighbourly love and charity, about which they are more prone to talk and philosophize than to act. John Kronik (47) has expressed most succinctly the spiritual superiority that Ujo possesses: he "enters the story through a church, and he leaves with a touch of the divine." Ujo offers a model of spiritual feeling that is far superior to that of his counterpart, Belmonte, and, by extension, to that of the latter's counterpart, Nazarín. One could conclude that in *Nazarín* the valuable role of the eccentric-madman is even trumped by that of the grotesque dwarf.

CHAPTER TEN

Celestial Visionary: Frasquito Ponte Delgado

If *Compassion* [*Misericordia*] (1897) is often considered Galdós's triumphantly positive resolution of the religious problem in contemporary Spain that he had repeatedly tackled in his novels of the 1890s, then it will be argued in this final chapter of our study that Frasquito Ponte constitutes the culmination of his treatment of the old male eccentric type. In his retrospective 1913 "Prefacio del autor" to the Nelson edition of the novel, Galdós maintained that Ponte, like other characters in the novel, was a type he had met on numerous walks around the streets of Madrid when he was gathering material for *Fortunata y Jacinta*. He was the quintessentially hard-up dandy type. Yet, when *Misericordia* first appeared, Vicente Blasco Ibáñez claimed in his review of it that, whilst Ponte and the other beggar types were undoubtedly taken from contemporary reality, they had been filtered through the distorting lens of Galdós's own imagination before they appeared on the printed pages of the novel: there they had been reshaped to fit the types or "maniquis" already established in his previous novels under the guiding influence of his reading of Dickens's novels (Chamberlin, "Blasco" 214).[1] The result is, Blasco argues, that Ponte (the best type in the novel for him) is completely incredible, with the stupid things he says and does. Eccentricity was appropriate in the novels of Dickens because eccentricity is a feature of the national character of the English. Ponte and the other Madrid types were simply not as eccentric in real life as Galdós painted them, Blasco firmly believed. The very important implications of his criticisms will be examined more fully in the conclusion, but for the moment sufficeth it to say that he could see that in Ponte Galdós had wanted to create his version of the eccentric type and that he was the best of this and all other types in the novel.

Ponte's names are symbolically appropriate: "Frasquito" suggests the small containers of substances he needs for his toilette, especially the dye to put on his hair, as well as his basically nice, inoffensive character. "Ponte" may express his role as a bridging character between Paca and Benina, but it may also suggest his constant efforts to bridge or cover the gap between his social standing as a member of the bourgeoisie and his current impoverished status, which is reflected in his frail physique and echoed by his matronymic "Thin" ["Delgado": the patronymic of the paranoiac educational reformer in *El doctor Centeno*] (Barr 98). This fundamental contrast between his present and past social positions is stressed in the early conversations of Benina and Paca, and when the former meets "gentleman Ponte" ["caballero Ponte"] (as he was known in his youth in Andalusia) for the first time at Obdulia's apartment, it is his colourfully nostalgic storytelling of past social glories that stands out, along with a flowery style of speaking, full of stock-in-trade clichés that he punctuates with perceptible pauses. Benina pricks this bubble of words by laughing and mimicking the style. In retrospect, though, some of Ponte's fancy compliments for Benina here, like "you shine by your absence" ["brilla usted por su ausencia"], will assume a very real and poignant meaning.

In the narrator's introductory portrait, Don Francisco is presented as a simple soul ["era lo que vulgarmente se llama *un alma de Dios*"], a designation commonly applied by Galdós to many of our crackpots. He is so old and senile that church records in Algeciras no longer exist to verify his age, a fact that makes him the oldest of our group, appropriately so, perhaps, as he is the last to be used in Galdós's social novels of this period. In physical appearance, Don Frasquito seems to be a mummy: his shiny, black hair, with its side parting and locks that he is constantly puffing out over his ears as a personal mannerism, is the same as it looked in his heyday of the 1850s. But he has to dye his beard black to cover up the effects of time, which are also very evident in the upper part of his face: his formerly lively eyes are now dim, the corners bleary, the eyelashes thin, the eyelids wrinkled, and the crow's feet extensive. But his looks, affectionate and melancholic, innocent and trustworthy, are those of a child's face. Ponte is both senile and childlike, a mixture of opposites that permeates this novel and was prefigured in the opening description of the façades of the Madrid church of San Sebastián.

His dress presents a similarly ambiguous picture: the faded dandy makes every effort to maintain the good appearance of his clothing: he removes dirt with benzine, smoothes down ruffles or mends knee holes, and manages to find a cheap tailor to make changes or repairs to his clothes. The style of his hat is so ancient that nobody would be able to name it, and yet it looks so modern because Ponte has kept the felt shiny. His second, great anatomical pride – his pretty, small feet – must never be shod with old shoes that could spoil their wonderful shape. His outer clothes may pass inspection, but what he uses underneath is another (unknown) question. His long morning toilette also succeeds in transforming his corpse-like appearance when first waking: after the hour-long operation, he emerges completely unrecognizable, all clean and shiny. In character, a more inoffensive or useless person had never existed, in the narrator's opinion: "Ponte no había servido nunca para nada." The same had been said of Relimpio.

Ponte's function in life had been that of the social partygoer: a regular attendee at bourgeois soirées, he had devoted all his attention and financial resources to cutting an acceptable figure in these circles. In fact, he was a well-mannered nobody, tolerated by the men and considered pleasant by the women. This world of external show crumbles and is lost when his money runs out and he is no longer able or willing to support his lifestyle by doing menial jobs. Not permitted by his innate sense of dignity to beg on the streets, he does eventually find help at Obdulia's, where, on a full stomach, thanks to Benina's efforts, he can again delight in recalling the past. Like his body, his mind has fossilized: he really does not know what has happened in the world since 1868, which only reinforces the impression of naïveté and innocence that he gives: he seems to have fallen out of a nest or from the clouds. His judgment of people and events is totally innocent. He is mentally retarded, with hardly any ideas. His constant desire to avoid the centre of Madrid, where his former acquaintances reside, is labelled a pathological monomania. Ponte's comic eccentricities, then, have a medical basis: the obsession with social appearances and position affects the stability of his mind when he can no longer satisfy it. The result is that he retreats within his imagination, where he can recreate the past with all sorts of poetic distortions and changes. These accounts are all the more comical, for they "contained every variety of ingenuous libertinism, impoverished elegance and honorable foolishness" ["contenía[n] todas las variedades del libertinaje candoroso, de la elegancia pobre y de la tontería honrada"] (17). His storytelling is such that he is accorded the designation of narrator. His tales of yore certainly occupy a sizeable proportion of these chapters (15–19) and interrupt the narartor's central thread (O'Byrne Curtis 93). But the question remains: why does Galdós give so much space to the old dandy's ramblings as well as to the narrator's own background information about him? The whole sequence is probably the longest given to any in our group of eccentrics. The answer is to be found in the new role that Ponte will shortly discharge in the present of the textual action.

Always the model of social correctness, Ponte's gratitude is such that he calls Benina an angel. That Ponte should be the first to acclaim her in this way is very significant. It says as much about him as it does Benina: he can appreciate her efforts for what they are. The narrator may call him a "proto-snob" ["*proto-cursi*"] (17) (for Obdulia he is the prototype of elegance [18]), and Ponte may employ a number of his flowery clichés, all highlighted in italics by the narrator, but there can be no doubt that, postprandial satisfaction aside, he has perceived something special in Benina:

I assure you on my word of honor, that you are an angel. I am inclined to believe that some beneficent and mysterious being has been incarnated in your body, a being who is a pure personification of Providence such as is revered in ancient and modern belief.

[yo aseguro, bajo mi palabra de honor, que es usted un ángel; yo *me inclino a creer* que en el cuerpo de usted se ha encarnado un ser benéfico y misterioso, un ser que es *mera* personificación de la Providencia, según la entendían y entienden los pueblos antiguos y modernos.] (17)[2]

Benina gently laughs off this and more examples of hyperbole from Don Frasco by distorting it; "yes, the kind [of angel] carved on buildings ... angel stuff" ["sí [ángel] ...de cornisa ... *angelorios*"]. But Ponte is genuinely overcome with gratitude, when, having confronted him about his complete lack of funds, she presses a coin into his hand. Once she has disappeared down the street and he is alone, he bursts into tears, partly because of an eye irritation common in old men, but also out of happiness, admiration, and gratitude to her. With no audience to play to, Ponte cuts a moving figure, the sincerity of his feelings, despite his dire plight, very much in evidence. So, from his first appearance in the novel he is presented as a possible spokesman for Galdós about the divine character of Benina: less egotistical and sex-driven than Almudena, who comes to mistakenly see him as a rival for Benina's affection (24), he represents an unbiased appreciation of her virtues that will grow during the remainder of the novel. He seems to have continued where the senile and intoxicated Relimpio had stopped in his adoration of Isidora in *La desheredada*. For this reason, Paca's malicious and jealous characterization of her distant relation as a dirty old man, or faded Don Juan, who will spend Benina's alms on toiletries, is only half true.

It is Benina who next searches out Ponte, alarmed that he has not been able to pay the bed fee at his lodging house. She discovers him stretched out in a kitchen attended by the two prostitutes who had been the cause of his injuries. Benina defends his respectability to the others, calling him a very important person, a big shot. When he does recover his senses, Ponte is delighted to see his benefactress beside his bed and kisses her hand, continuously calling her a saint. She believes that he has gone really mad when he reports that he has spent her coin, not on some dye for his beard, but on a postcard of the Empress Eugénie for Obdulia. The phrase she uses ("está ido") immediately suggests a link with José Ido del Sagrario.

With typically practical kindness, Benina lodges the injured Ponte in the kitchen of Doña Paca. There is perhaps some kind of echo here of Miss Betsey Trotwood's lodging of her distant relation, Mr Dick, in *The Personal History of David Copperfield*, after his brother had sent him to a private asylum because he thought he was a little eccentric and he did not want him about the house (14). But Paca is not so warm or appreciative of her eccentric relation as Betsey, for, after the initial enjoyment of childhood reminiscences, she soon becomes jealous when he shows more affection to Benina, for whom he reserves his gratitude, his smiles, his languid looks (like those of a half-dead sheep), and his most refined phrases. It is the constant use of his favourite word for her ("angel") – repeated almost two hundred times during one meal (25) – that arouses Paca to launch what will be the fundamental argument of the novel, as it is of the conclusion to *Fortunata y Jacinta*: is Benina (like Fortunata) really an angel? Whilst acknowledging her virtues, Paca believes that Benina's past sexual life would disbar her from full rights to this overemployed epithet. Recovered from his injuries, although still with a limp in his right leg, Ponte is now prepared to follow Benina's advice and resume a minor job, but her arrest with Almudena for vagrancy forces him to stay in the house; Ponte is now accorded by the narrator such epithets as "Kind Frasquito, the faded old man" ["el bueno de Frasquito, el desteñido viejo"] (32).

Ponte's inspired idea to send for Benina's invented priest, Don Romualdo, to help them locate her after her arrest leads nowhere initially, but when a real priest of the same name informs him and Paca of a true inheritance bequest, Ponte is overcome with excitement, constantly smoothing down the famous puffed-out locks of hair over his ears and hanging on to his chair as if he were going to fly into the air in a hot-air balloon, perhaps another subtle allusion to Mr Dick's liberating experience of flying his kites on the cliffs at Dover. Again, Ponte's appreciation of the reality of their current financial situation and Benina's role in alleviating it through begging is far more accurate than Paca's. He suddenly demonstrates a more robust attitude: when Paca refuses to believe that Benina could be a beggar, he repeats, timidly at first, then emphatically, that, regardless of whether she begs or not, she is an angel. He does not know for sure whether she herself begs, but he feels honour-bound to tell Paca and the priest that he had seen Benina in a square with Almudena. When Romualdo returns next morning with the first pension payment, Ponte's initial doubts about his sudden good luck evaporate and he now feels an overwhelming urge to go outside to run and fly, for he feels he now has wings, much like Mr Dick's mind seems, to David Copperfield, to fly, free of his obsession about the *Memorial*, in the Dover sky with his kite. Ponte's words are almost a cry of desperation: "It is imperative that I leave ... Besides, I must get a bit of air ... I feel a little dizzy. The exercise will do me good, believe me, it really will" ["Me es imprescindible salir ... Además, necesito que me dé un poco el aire ... Siento así como un poco de mareo. Me conviene el ejercicio, crea usted que me conviene"] (34). He will also need to see his tailor at once, it is true, but he is honest to admit that clothes are his weakness ["Soy muy dificultoso"], because he takes his time picking the cloth. In another surprising display of candour, more than Relimpio ever admitted to himself in this matter, he confesses that, after futile previous attempts, it would be pointless for him to keep an account book of his expenditures. He luxuriates in the wonderful feeling of renewed vitality as he ambles through the streets, ogling female pedestrians, just as Relimpio and Pito had done in the same urban setting.

Ponte now has the means to change his lifestyle: better accommodation and a good meal are his first priorities, and they awaken a new conscience of his own independence, in which he rejects his previous identification as a type. First, he is reluctant to go to his usual cheap tavern because he has not dyed his beard, but such scruples about keeping up his type are soon overcome by a more important consideration: he now wants to repay the landlord the debts he has incurred. Second, during his meal, he is incensed by the way a person, whom he calls a type, looks at him, which he attributes to the same cause: his lack of make-up. Instead of being cowed by such thoughts, he now asserts (to himself) his freedom to do what he likes with his face:

But whose business is it if I fix myself up or if I don't? I can do whatever I feel like with my face. I don't have to satisfy men by always presenting them with the same façade. I know how to win the respect of old women as well as young.
[Pero ¿qué le importa a nadie que yo me *arregle* o deje de *arreglarme?* Yo hago de mi fisonomía lo que me da la gana, y no estoy obligado a dar gusto a los señores, presentándoles siempre la misma cara. Con la vieja, lo mismo que con la joven, sé yo hacerme respetar y dejar bien puesto mi decoro.] (35)

Ponte could not have chosen a more significant way to demonstrate his new personality: he has moved from type to character. Paca's son, the undertaker Antonio, who joins him at the table in the tavern, may rile him when commenting on the comic effects of his antiquated fashions, but the old man controls his anger and forgives the impertinent jokes because of Antonio's youth. He is even more impressive when he declares, without hesitation, that the first purchase he will make with his windfall will be some new boots and an outfit for Benina. This, he proclaims, is only just and charitable, presumably for all she has done for him and for Paca, although Ponte does not elaborate (35). And it is he who, when informed by Antonio of Benina's imprisonment for unlicensed begging, takes the initiative in proposing that they secure her release from the civil governor. Here again, there is a new direction in Ponte's thinking: typically, he has no idea who is the current occupant of that position of authority, and, as in his previous conversations with Paca or Obdulia, he cites a name from his heyday of the late 1850s. But this does not matter any more. Ponte is a new man, and that fact is illustrated succinctly and emphatically by this tic taken from his past type character. It is Antonio and the initially hostile, staring type who now waste time in history talk, whereas Ponte is the one who wants to solve the crisis in hand: "'Be that as it may, gentlemen,' Frasquito added returning to reality, 'Nina must be gotten'" [" – Sea lo que quiera, señores – añadió Frasquito, poniéndose en la realidad – hay que sacar a Nina"]. If they are successful next day, he will treat everybody in the tavern.

Ponte's generosity had, moments before, also extended to accepting a bizarre and ominous wager proposed by Antonio: the rental of the vehicle chosen for the trip to the El Pardo jail (horse by Ponte, bike by Antonio) will be paid by the other, if the rider does not break his neck when they go to free Benina. Juliana, Paca's imperious daughter-in-law, who now runs the house, ejects Don Frasquito, calling him a painted orangutan (36). In his new riding gear, though, he cuts a fine figure as he displays his skills on a big horse in front of Paca's balcony. It seems that Ponte the old dandy has resurfaced, a figure that Benina later recognizes as foolhardy: "Frasquito was not up to such tomfoolery and his age did not permit such ridiculous flaunts of vanity" ["no estaba Frasquito para tales bromas, ni su edad le consentía tan ridículos alardes de presunción"] (37). Yet even Benina cannot foresee the extent of the spiritual transformation Ponte is now undergoing.

A reappearing limp in one leg is minor compared with the mental confusion he now suffers: his speech becomes incoherent and rushed, his face as red as beetroot. He later gets out of bed and goes to his favourite drinking hole, where he upbraids the owners in a display of emotion that is totally out of character. The following morning Paca is able to witness the same behaviour for herself when Ponte comes back to her house, spouting terrible nonsense (39). Ponte is now possessed by a monomania: he is determined to search out Almudena and demand an apology for the insult to his honour when the beggar publicly accused him of courting Benina. Almudena's reaction is to laugh off the threat from the "fancy gent" ["mi galán *bunito*"]. Benina, who has tried to show Christian love and care equally to both of her admirers, now feels great sympathy for the plight of Ponte, who, for her, is "Poor Don Frasquito ... , the miserable man, such a kind-hearted person" ["¡Pobre D. Frasquito ... , cuitado, alma de Dios!"], whereas the heartless Juliana calls him "What a fright!" ["¡Valiente estantigua!"]. Her subsequent rhetorical question could really resume the general attitude of the "normal" characters in this and the other novels to Ponte and all our crackpots: "What do we care though if that painted-up old fool goes off his nut or not?" ["¿Y a nosostros qué nos importa que ese viejo pintado se chifle o no se chifle?"] (39). Juliana's own reply is interesting, if only for its absurd, but novel, attempt to discover the cause of his mental disturbance in trivial, external physical details: "You know what I say? This comes from the drugs he puts on his face – they're poisonous and they've attacked his senses" ["¿Sabéis lo que os digo? Pues que todo eso proviene de las drogas que se pone en la cara, lo cual que son venenosas y atacan al sentido"]. Frasquito cuts an even more deranged figure when he furiously rings the doorbell of Paca's apartment another morning: his hat is pulled down over his ears, he is waving his stick, and there is dirt all over his clothes; the limp in his right leg has become more pronounced. The women of the house are scared by his appearance. Obdulia is shocked that a man of such refinement should be so noisy. Since he believes that the false rumour about his courting Benina has originated in Paca's house, he has come for some explanation from her and the other women. He feels insulted because he venerates Benina as an angel who has "heavenly white wings and immaculate purity" ["de blancas alas célicas, de pureza inmaculada"] (40), and he respects angels, whereas, if she were an ordinary woman, he would have added her to his long list of conquests. This comic resurgence of a Don Juan's pride is only temporary and soon vanishes before his sublime declaration to the three women that the Benina they have shut out of their house and their lives is divine: "Nina is not of this world ... Nina belongs to heaven" ["la Nina no es de este mundo ... la Nina pertenece al cielo"]. With great determination and energy, he confronts them and himself for the first time with the bitter truth: "Dressed as a beggar, she went begging for alms to support you and me" ["Vestida de pobre ha pedido limosna para mantenerlas a ustedes y a mí"]. In an expression of comic, yet also curiously sublime humility, he contrasts himself with Benina: "My beauty is human, and hers is divine; my splendid face is of mortal flesh, and hers of celestial light ... she belongs to God" ["Mi hermosura es humana, y la de ella divina; mi rostro espléndido es de carne mortal, y el de ella de celeste luz ... es de Dios"]. He then contrasts himself with Paca; she cannot move because she is filled with ingratitude towards Benina, whilst he is like a feather flying through the air because he is filled with gratitude for her former servant. Again the simile of an airborne object inevitably recalls the figure of Mr Dick and his kite. That eccentric's most sublime moment, comparable to that of Ponte here in *Misericordia*'s penultimate chapter, and also ending with a remarkably similar reference to the levity of air, occurs when he informs the admiring David in chapter 45 that he will reconcile Dr Strong and his wife:

"A poor fellow with a craze, sir," said Mr Dick, "a simpleton, a weak-minded person -present company, you know!" striking himself again, "may do what wonderful people may not do. I'll bring them together, boy. I'll try. They'll not blame *me*. They'll not object to *me*. They'll not mind what *I* do, if it's wrong. I'm only Mr Dick. And who minds Dick? Dick's nobody! Whoo!" He blew a slight, contemptuous breath, as if he blew himself away.

In both instances, the simpleton/crackpot breaks out of his previous inhibitions through sheer force of inner convictions and determination to declare aloud the truth of what he feels or wants to do, mindless of what others think of him.[3] This is the moment of truth for Paca, one of the principal figures in the novel, and madcap secondary character Ponte is charged with telling it, just as simpleton Relimpio had confronted the hapless Isidora with the truth of her situation as her novel closed. Ponte's tirade does not seem to have any immediately visible effect on his listeners: Juliana, unable to stand his impertinent ravings, threatens to throw him over the balcony with her usual epithet: "you monstrosity" ["so mamarracho"].

Since there is no substantial dramatic action in the novel's final chapter, entitled "Final," Don Frasquito's death at the end of chapter 40 constitutes a significant climax to the novel. It occurs as he goes downstairs for the last time, after his harangue to Paca and the others. The former shouts to the doorman from the landing that Ponte, once the model gentleman, has now gone completely mad. At this juncture, Ponte looks back, and, as he angrily begins to shout the word "ungrateful" to Paca, he suffers what appears to be a heart attack or stroke, since his facial features become distorted, his eyes bulge, and his mouth moves close to his ear, in a fashion similar to one of Ido's fits. He only has time to raise his hands and groan an "ay!" before falling dead to the ground, just as Relimpio had fallen onto the sofa before eventually dying at the end of *La desheredada*. Unlike Relimpio, Ponte is not drunk. His end is spiritually moving because of his noble declaration of the truth about Benina's character and actions. Ponte is the voice of reason that has to shout out the truth against the materialism and egotism of useless bourgeois characters like Paca and Obdulia. His appearance and actions paint the figure of an eccentric old man, but his words reveal him to be a new kind of person: the prophet of heavenly truth. That they are not without some effect, especially on the person who has most insulted him (Juliana), is conveyed in the "Final" when the names of both are pertinently juxtaposed: "But since no happiness is complete in this rascally world, about a month after the change of residence, a date which would be marked in the Zapata annals by Frasquito Ponte Delgado's disastrous death, Juliana began suffering strange transformations in her health" ["Pero como no hay felicidad completa en este pícaro mundo, al mes, poco más o menos, de la mudanza, señalada en las efemérides zapatescas por la desastrosa muerte de Frasquito Ponte Delgado, empezó a resentirse Juliana de alteraciones muy extrañas en su salud"]. If, as Russell (127) comments, Juliana is the only person to be affected by Ponte's final ravings, his role assumes even greater significance in that he prepares the way for her to approach Benina with a desperate appeal for advice and spiritual help in her domestic crisis. Ponte is not a guide figure for the protagonist, as many of his fellow eccentrics are. On the contrary, saintly, divine Benina is the role model for the crackpot Don Frasquito, who, in turn, when reborn after his fall from the horse, becomes a lesson to be pondered by the remaining women in Paca's household.

X Ido the informant

Conclusion

Galdós's claim in the "Prefacio" to the 1913 edition of *Misericordia* is representative of others he made during the last years of his life. His revelation that Almudena and Benina, for example, are faithful copies of characters he knew in real life in Madrid was repeated when talking about two of our eccentric characters in *Fortunata y Jacinta* in his fictionally framed autobiography of 1916, *Memoirs of an Absent-Minded Man* [*Memorias de un desmemoriado*]: Galdós recalls that when he returned from his trip to Germany in the summer of 1886 he received a visit from his great friend Ido del Sagrario, who gave him news about the other characters in the novel. Later he talked with Estupiñá. Galdós is not confusing fiction with reality, but rather merging them, just as he had stressed in his 1870 manifesto before he started publishing social novels: the best characters in novels should strike the reader as reproductions of acquaintances in real life, just as a character seen in the street could look like a character that the reader had come to know when reading a novel. Consequently, a stall holder in the Plaza Mayor called José Luengo was the model for Estupiñá, and, as his readers knew this character very well, he did not need to describe him (6:1679).[1] Such pronouncements would seem to justify the assertion, made by José Rodríguez Mourelo in a 1929 interview with Enrique Ruiz de la Serna, that all of Galdós's characters were based on real live models, as if this fact also certified the novel's realism. Such an extravagant view of Galdós's characterization was, fortunately, qualified by Rodríguez Mourelo: his characters were really composites, constructed with traits taken from one or another real person. The result is that they become universal types that are too real to be found in life, if not in literature. Indeed, the existence of literary precedents did weigh heavily in Galdós's conception of the kind of character that is the subject of this book and which I have generically called the "eccentric old man." Given his familiarity with and enthusiasm for Dickens's work from his earliest days as a journalist, culminating in his translation of *The Pickwick Papers,* it is not unreasonable to believe that examples of this type in that novel, but particularly in *The Personal History of David Copperfield* in the figure of Mr Dick, were the inspiration for the creation of his series of old eccentrics.[2] In a number of short stories and journalistic sketches of this period ("La novela en el tranvía," *La sombra,* and the unpublished *Rosalía*) Galdós experimented with various prototypes of this figure. By the time the outline of this type is definitively drawn in *Doña Perfecta,* he is no longer a principal character like Anselmo in *La sombra.* Neither is he just a minor or minimal character flitting through the text with the occasional comic eccentricity, whether of speech, dress, or habit.[3] Nor is he merely a secondary or "ficelle" character linked through interaction with the principals, acting as a plot facilitator. Rather, he is entrusted by the narrator with a special mission that enhances his status within the fiction very considerably. In this higher role he ceases to be a variant of the stereotypic wise fool or village idiot and assumes a certain individuality. He reappears in Galdós's contemporary social novels between 1870 and 1897 with a far greater frequency than previous critics have noted, even those who, like Benítez, Montesinos, O'Byrne Curtis, and Rodríguez, have studied them in some detail. He does not appear in every novel written in those twenty-seven years, in part, no doubt, because Galdós did not want to be overrepetitive. But the important fact to note is that in thirteen of the twenty-five contemporary social novels written in this twenty-seven-year period, Galdós felt the need to give this type a prominent function in the narrative. This can not be haphazard, a mere coincidence, especially when in one or two of the novels he adds even more figures of the same kind or of a grotesque nature for a compound, contrastive effect.

The nine "major" eccentrics of our study (Cayetano Polentinos, *Caifás,* Relimpio, Morales, Ido del Sagrario, Estupiñá, Pito, Belmonte, and Ponte) exhibit certain homogeneous features: they are old or look old (that is, between forty and seventy years or so), even the exceptional Ido, despite the age fluctuations demanded by the time periods of the various narratives in which he appears. Some have symbolic names. They have a distinguishing corporal (especially facial) appearance, mode of dress (specifically, the hats they wear), speech tag, or behavioural tic. Above all, they appear to the narrator and other characters in the novel as odd, strange, eccentric, or even mad types that make other people smile or laugh in some manner. Because these characteristics are repeated to varying degrees in the presentation of the nine characters, it is very reasonable to conclude that, at least at the initial level of artistic conception, this figure was meant to be, in Forster's terms, a "flat" character, who could be quickly sketched and therefore instantly memorized, and subsequently recognized, by the reader (Muir). Galdós's regular readers may not have been able to remember all these characters in the series, but their common typeness, recognizable as traditional, was probably sufficient to trigger some associations, as Alas showed very clearly in his 1883 statement with which this study began. The appendix that follows this conclusion summarizes in full these characterological devices, so they will not be discussed here, except to indicate that Galdós is able very often to go beyond the mere background notes of comedy they certainly provide: for example, Pito hitches up his trousers at moments of great emotional tension; Ido's tag "frankly, naturally" is used to perplex the reader about the authorship of *La de Bringas*; Ponte's refusal to dye his beard after receiving the first portion of his inheritance marks the declaration of his newly found independence of mind after coming under the spell of Benina's charity. Galdós's extensive elaboration of some of his eccentrics' favourite words and phrases into veritable idiolects (for example, that of Pito) attests to his desire and ability to go beyond mere automatic snatches of colourful speech and to blow up these types into secondary characters with some degree of personal identity, such as that evinced by Sam Weller in *The Pickwick Papers*. In many ways, the eccentrics who are so individualized linguistically dominate the text more than the nominal principals in the way Dickens's types did (Harvey). Kay Engler (134) has remarked that secondary characters in Galdós's novels are only separated by breadth from the major figures. Our eccentrics certainly fit into this pattern.

The question of what I have frequently called the eccentricity of these characters is perhaps the most difficult to address, for definitions of terms are important, both in English and Spanish. "Eccentric" seemed, following Maudsley, a good, intermediary, generic term with which to categorize the group as a whole. For example, Morales's eccentricity is quite mild (the odd posturing and declamation) compared to that of Relimpio, with his use of cosmetics and leering at pretty girls. The range of eccentric behaviour, speech, or dress is extensive, naturally so, for the sake of variety from one novel to another. More importantly, by being different from the rest of so-called normal society, they inevitably invite from the reader some questioning of the values and attitudes of that society. This reaction increases when the eccentric also displays symptoms of madness or mental sickness. All of our group are eccentric, but some have also crossed the borderland into true madness for a while before returning back to eccentricity (e.g. Cayetano Polentinos, Ido del Sagrario, and Belmonte).[4] Some, like Relimpio and Ponte, are considered by the other characters as mad, but, in reality, their worsened mental state, if it can be so called, is due to physical pressures and accidents and has more to do with the visionary mission with which Galdós then wishes to entrust to them. It seems that after Anselmo, Galdós scaled down the mad side of these old male types, for, if they were too mad, they would tend to lose some of their comic appeal and become more worthy of pity and compassion. The component of madness is downloaded, as it were, to more minimal characters (Tomás Rufete, Canencia, Delgado, and the Bueno de Guzmán extended family) who are included to form a counterpoint to our group of eccentrics. Sometimes the use of psychiatric descriptors creates a comic effect (*Lo prohibido*). In *La desheredada* the frightening reality of the insane asylum at Leganés produces a far more chilling effect on the reader, acting as a reference point for the questioning of so-called "normal" obsessions, like social ostentation.

By nature and by habit, the eccentric should be a loner, set apart from the rest of society even when living within a family unit. But with the exception of Belmonte, none of the nine eccentrics are recluses. On the contrary, they show an exceptional willingness to interact socially. This is particularly noticeable in their relationships with the principals, which, in the case of *Caifás*, Relimpio, and Ponte, are often of a very close nature. Some are responsible for launching the action of the novel (Ido and Estupiñá). Cayetano and Pito contribute to important plot developments by actions of their own initiative. Because of this role, they are very often introduced early into their respective narratives. But more than plot facilitators, these characters are also reflectors of, and, at the same time, guide characters for, their protagonists, whether they are close to them, like Ponte and Relimpio, or distant and casual, like Belmonte. That is to say, they do more than move the plot along; they also reflect the values and attitudes of the principal characters to varying degrees and, in so doing, become potential counsel figures for the latter: they are living lessons from whom the principals can learn some wisdom. This is best illustrated in the relationships of Relimpio and Isidora Rufete, and of Pito and Ángel Guerra. This is not to say that the eccentrics are the protagonists' only interlocutors or guide figures; far from it. But because their peculiar and often comic features instantly capture the reader's attention, they are perfect vehicles for telegraphing an instant message, whether understood or not, both to the protagonist and the reader.

In these close relationships, a number of our eccentrics (Cayetano, *Caifás*, Relimpio, Estupiñá, Ido [in *El doctor Centeno*], Pito, and Ponte) rise to an almost sublime level of behaviour and speech at the novel's close. This metamorphosis, again of varying kinds, is the result of a sudden confrontation with the death or loss of their master or mistress. This cathartic development, sometimes aided by the liberating effects of alcohol (e.g. in the cases of Relimpio and Pito) elevates them to a category of quasi-principal character. Their sudden illumination or vision of what is afoot is somehow intense and moving. If previously they were common, recognizable types and figures of fun, in this final moment they are very wise men of the spirit, telling the truth about themselves and others: they are the wise fools or court jesters of literary tradition. Betsey Trotwood expresses very well this aspect of the eccentric's character when informing David Copperfield, soon after he has arrived at her Dover home, about the character of Mr Dick: "he is not half so eccentric as a good many people .... He is the most friendly and amenable creature in existence, and as for advice! – But nobody knows what that man's mind is, except myself" (13). Later, she proudly tells Mr Micawber that Mr Dick is "not a common man" (49). David himself sums up this quality when later he is able to appreciate Mr Dick's great service to Dr Strong and his young wife: "there is a subtlety of perception in real attachment, even when it is borne towards man by one of the lower animals, which leaves the highest intellect behind. To this mind of the heart, if I may call it so, in Mr Dick, some bright ray of the truth shot straight" (42). Galdós's eccentrics resemble Mr Dick by and large (apart from Belmonte) in their sympathetic, amiable character towards all, and their friendliness and devotion to the masters they serve and help. Laughed at and dismissed as useless for any conventional, productive activity, they are worth more than conventional, normal people because of this warmth of human feeling. They have Mr Dick's "mind of the heart." If they are mad, eccentric, or crackpot, then the rest of the world must be equally mad or more so (O'Byrne Curtis 49), as Galdós had declared in the narrator's famous aside when describing Leganés's inmates in *La desheredada*. A madman or eccentric is able to point out the basic madness of the world, as Mr Dick does to David: "'I'll tell you what,' he added, in a lower tone, 'I shouldn't wish it to be mentioned, but it's a' – here he beckoned to me, and put his lips close to my ear – 'it's a mad world. Mad as Bedlam boy!' said Mr Dick, taking snuff from a round box on the table and laughing heartily" (14).

As obviously older men, the eccentrics are given to nostalgically reminiscing about their exploits or those of others in the past (e.g. Cayetano, Estupiñá, Pito, and Ponte). Very often, this tripping down memory lane leads to a comic distortion of such matters as contemporary Spanish politics, which "normal" people in their circles (e.g. in *La desheredada, El doctor Centeno, Fortunata y Jacinta,* and *Ángel Guerra*) treat much more seriously, for reasons of self-interest.

Some of our group are also described as old roués, dirty old men, faded dandies, or Don Juans. However, this strongly sexual dimension to their existences is always presented as a comic feature that is outweighed by a greater warmth of human kindness shown to the woman in question (e.g. Relimpio to Isidora, Pito to Dulcenombre, Ponte to Benina). These eccentrics present a more comforting, less threatening, maleness for the females that is not patriarchal or domineering. In other eccentrics, there is a certain indifference to sex and romantic love (e.g. Cayetano) that is replaced by an interest in different matters. The status of respect and admiration that Galdós feels for his eccentrics is often conveyed by the use of "Don" and their first name or by the fleetingly ironic accolade "Great" preceding some surnames. This practice conforms too with Dickens's way of addressing his eccentric: Mr Dick is obviously the familiar form of his first name, "Richard," used with the nomenclature of politeness as a sign of affectionate respect by Dickens and Betsey Trotwood. In fact, Mr Dick cannot bear to be called by his proper names: Richard Babley.

One last important role that a great number of our eccentrics play is that of being storytellers or writers, as if they were an ironic device Galdós inserted into his text to remind his readers of the basic truth that novels are the written products of a single author, who uses the people, events, and ideas of real life to create a text of fiction that gives the illusion of a mimetic reproduction in words of the real world. In *Fortunata y Jacinta,* Estupiñá and Ido are the unwitting and witting authors, respectively, of the real live novels that form the text of Galdós's novel about two married women. Ido is also the supreme example of the eccentric type who creates novels from his life experiences, albeit with disturbing distortions at times, and yet, at others, with accurate aperçus on the contemporary reality around him. In many respects, he is a mole in the novels in which he appears, for he points to the twin dangers for the reader of relying completely upon the narrator's written word or, alternatively, of completely rejecting it. The reader is challenged to sift the verbal evidence and make her/his own conclusions, which, because of the nature of fiction, will always be partial and tentative. Other eccentrics in our study are readers or writers of other sorts of compositions. Again, this activity is given particular resonance in the respective works: Belmonte pronounces what he believes is the true identity of Nazarín on the basis of what he reads in newspapers; Cayetano's personal letters to his anonymous friend in

Madrid convert the dénouement of *Doña Perfecta* and the writer himself into the most baffling of mysteries. Our eccentric types, like other minor types and the principal characters themselves in the respective novels, emphasize, through their varying relationships to literature and the written word, the gap that must separate fiction and the real world and, yet at the same time, the interpenetration that must obtain between both.

It is abundantly clear that, even at their most sublime moments, our eccentrics conform to a recognizable, but never monotonously identical, pattern of creation that has as its basic structure the same formulae of dress, physical appearance, speech, and tics. Galdós employs most of these eccentrics for the same purpose and often in similar situations, as he did with other characters, whether major or minor. Yet they are all unique and different, one from the other, for they are both type and individual at the same time, like all human beings. And like all human beings, in moments of great stress and emotional challenge, they can become surprising individuals and oracles of wisdom – figures of fun no more. In Balzac's terminolgy, they becomes "types individualisés." If Galdós qua ventriloquist author could have mimed this conclusion to one of his eccentric characters, let us say, to one of his earliest and minor ones (and not an old male one), the irascible English matron of "La novela en el tranvía," she would have perhaps expressed this view of the performances of our nine eccentrics and their supporting cast of confrères with these words in Dickensian English: "Tush! 'Twas not all Tosh!"

Checklist of Features
of Galdosian Male Eccentrics
(in alphabetical order)

LEGEND

1 Age
2 Name
3 Family
4 Relationship to women
5 Head and face
6 Other body features
7 Dress
8 Speech
9 Occupation
10 Mental illness
11 Eccentricities and tics
12 Connections to literature and the arts

I ANSELMO

1 Old, not well preserved
2 Anselmo means "protected by God"
3 Wealthy, aristocratic father with manic hatred of lawsuits
4 Jealousy of wife leads to mental breakdown
5 Small, sunken eyes, which only become significant when he talks. Very expressive mouth movements
6 Smallish in stature and sickly looking; limps for some unknown reason and has difficulties moving his left hand

7 His dress coat has an exceptionally high lapel and a sheen of fifteen years' dirty use; wears an oversize waistcoat; his strange-shaped tie is positioned at the back of his neck

8 Consummate storyteller; narration personified; speaks in a very hoarse and cracked voice

9 No useful occupation in society, except when telling stories

10 Complete mental breakdown after wife's death

11 Constantly talking to himself; walks forward in a straight line

12 After breakdown, he reads a lot of books through the night

2 BELMONTE

1 Sixty-two years old

2 His patronymic suggests his handsome appearance

3 He is supposed to have killed his wife; his aristocratic, rich family have confined him to the country estate of La Coreja under the surveillance of his servants

4 Very much a Don Juan earlier in his life; he has given up this vice for those of drink and tobacco

5 Has a tanned face, slightly broad nose, lively eyes beneath thick eyebrows; white, wavy, pointed beard; wide, clear forehead; he is very tall and handsome

7 Dark, light hat tilted to one side; wears hunting boots and carries a shooting gun over his shoulder

9 Idle, rich landlord; formerly in diplomatic service in the Middle East

10 He goes mad whenever the subject of religion is broached

11 Stares intensely at Nazarín

12 Studies theology in great detail; reads foreign and national publications

3 CAIFÁS

2 Both patronymic (Mundideo) and nickname (*Caifás*) have symbolic meanings

3 Abused by wife, who steals money from him to drink with her fellow miners; he is a single parent who has to look after three youngish children

4 Adores Gloria as the Virgin Mary; is dominated by his wife

5 Has the eyes of a mole and an angular face

6 He is bow-legged

8 Tends to construct phrases in groupings of three

9 First he is the sexton of Ficóbriga's abbey church, then he becomes the gravedigger for the town's cemetery

10 Prone to extremes of depression and exultation

11 Adores Gloria, as if she were the Virgin Mary
12 Repairs ecclesiastical art objects; sings in abbey choir; recites psalms

4 CANENCIA

1 Elderly
2 His patronymic suggests his age as well as his need to gasp for air at times
3 Has spent thirty-two years in Leganés mental asylum because of a lawsuit brought against him by his children
5 Face is totally shaven, like that of a priest; fairly dark-skinned
6 He is small and has a wrinkled body
7 Wears a small, circular beret and green elbow pads
8 Has a sweet, melodious voice; his verbal tic is the phrase "complying with the sovereign will"
9 Bookkeeper for the mental asylum
10 He is attacked every two to three years by the belief that he has an electric machine on his head and that people are insulting him; his lips tremble, his hands shake, and his speech becomes slurred; then he runs around until he quietens down
11 Twirls pen; rolls cigarettes; opens mouth wide to take big gasps of air at times
12 He is a distinguished calligrapher

5 CANÓNIGO

1 Old
2 His surnames (Quijano-Quijada) are strongly reminiscent of the real name of Don Quixote. His nickname, the Canon, is also a reference to a character from Cervantes's novel
3 Has lived with female cousins and nephews in La Mancha for over thirty years; first cousin to Tomás Rufete
8 Speaks and writes in a refined and discreet way, more appropriate to Madrid than to the country
9 Had been steward and then administrator in Madrid mansions before retiring to the countryside, where he now eats, hunts, and reads
11 Preoccupied with Spain's past greatness; knows history of the country's aristocratic families
12 He writes letters; reads novels

6 DELGADO

1 Close to fifty years old

2 His first name (Jesús) suggests his status as a victim of abuse by the student lodgers; the patronymic indicates his sensitive nature; his Greek nickname expresses his habit of writing letters to himself

3 His family pays for his lodging monthly but have no direct contact with him

8 His tags are short exclamations, both written and oral: "oh! ah!"

9 He was dismissed from his Ministry of Education position after twenty years of service

10 Constant facial grimaces, which intensify when he is feeling pressure; then he suffers an attack of St Vitus's dance; otherwise, a shy, modest, sensitive man

11 Writes and send letters to himself about educational reforms

12 Writes letters; always consulting the books on the theories of education by Froebel and Pestalozzi

7 ESTUPIÑÁ

1 Sixty-six–years old in 1869

2 Both the first name and the patronymic sum up his character. He is not given a nickname, but he is compared to Mesonero Romanos, Rossini, and Socrates

4 Very subservient and deferential to Barbarita

5 His face is instantly recognizable for its similarity to that of Punch, a magpie/pigeon, and Rossini: mocking smile, hooked nose, sunken mouth, and mischievous eyes

6 He is of less-than-average height, rather plumpish

7 Wears green cape all year, except in summer; flat, small-topped hat with flat rims

8. When defending his political reminiscences, he uses the phrase "just as I am looking at you"

9 Originally a sales clerk in the Arnaiz dry-goods store, he was a failure when he set up his own business; then employed as an agent by many former customers for purchases of all kinds in the city; finally, personal servant to Barbarita and her family; rent collector for the owners of 11, Cava de San Miguel (Moreno-Isla, then Guillermina)

11 Great talkativeness; claims that he has seen all of nineteenth-century Spanish history

12 Hates the printed word, preferring the oral literature of human contact and communication. On 23 December 1873, he leads the kitchen celebration of the Santa Cruz lottery win with pots and pans. In the Alpha manuscript, he had composed verse on the occasion of Barbarita's wedding

8 IDO DEL SAGRARIO
[EL DOCTOR CENTENO, TORMENTO, LO PROHIBIDO]

2 His surnames refer respectively to his mental condition and the ecclesiastical connotations of his figure; nicknames by schoolchildren and Polo underline his stupidity, as well as referring to his candle-like figure

3 Four sickly children

4 Has fits of suspicion about his wife's fidelity

5 His face is as pale as a church candle; warts are spread over his face; a lock of spooky, black hair falls over his forehead; moist eyes with flickering eyelashes; huge Adam's apple

6 Thin, bloodless figure, like that of a ghost

7 Clothes are worn low

8 A pair of tags: "frankly, naturally"

9 School assistant for handwriting; collaborative author of popular sentimental novels

11 Takes breaths in order to articulate syllables; very emotional, starts crying when under stress; as sensitive as the plant mimosa

12 Penman of great skill, writes novels; his figure is painted on street walls in cartoons

[ADDITIONS IN FORTUNATA Y JACINTA]

4 and 11. Now suspects wife of infidelity

7 Wears a very antique opera hat, which, when he is given a better one by Guillermina, he sells to a carnival actor; very threadbare and frayed, red tie

8 In his electrified state, he tends to repeat the last word spoken to him by another speaker

9 and 12. Door-to-door agent for subscriptions to serialized novels

10 In his electrified state, the nervous shaking of his left eyelid and cheek muscle increases; he rests his chin on his chest or stretches his neck; he moves arms around a lot; he begins to shout or raise his voice in a crescendo; his whole body shakes and he gives a nervous laugh; the caruncles on his neck become redder; he finally loses sense of where he is. The suggested cure for these attacks – eating meat – only increases them. Maxi suggests to Ido these remedies: diluted brandy, cold showers, and sodium bromide tablets

9 IZQUIERDO

1 He is in his fifties

2 His first name links him with Ido; his matronymic suggests his political leanings, as well as his devious character in the matter of hoaxes

5 Has a beautiful head, an arrogant stature, and a noble mien

8 His speech is full of all sorts of uneducated, linguistic distortions that become his trademark tags because they are repeated so often, as interjections and oaths. In effect, a sizeable proportion of his conversation is constructed on these lingusitic peculiarities

11 His boasting of imagined participation in recent political events in Spain

10 MORALES

1 Respectable age

2 His first name suggests his rather artistic appearance, appropriate enough, given the neo-classical architecture of the Observatory. His surnames sum up his old-fashioned, middle-of-the road moral and political values

3 Has pleasant and domesticated wife

5 Dark, bushy eyebrows like two strips of tapestry; black and white moustache is short and bristly like a scrub brush

6 Tall, solemn, polite figure

7 Two kinds of clothes that sum up his character: well-kept overcoat, black silk tie and gold-capped tie-pin express his affluence, whereas his cloth cap suggests its lack; wears boots in the house

8 Has a sublime voice; often gets lost in his own convoluted syntax; ideas are expressed in triplicate form. Has a number of verbal tags: "by the way," "I am old," "I have the satisfaction," "stop, stop," "order, order," "if I weren't convinced"

9 Caretaker of the Madrid Observatory

11 He refuses to drink wine, except Valdepeñas; has a passion for the pure waters of Madrid; in politics, he believes that personal freedom is compatible with a régime of extreme law and order; has fossilized ideas about the Progresista Party; boasts of knowing important political figures

12 Reads newspapers in bed at night. The only book he believes in is the book of life

11 MORENO-ISLA

1 Forty-eight years old

2 His matronymic suggests his outsider status within Spanish society

3 Bachelor; nephew of the social do-gooder, Guillermina

4 A famous womaniser, whose victims include Aurora, Juanito's later mistress

5 Has a scar on the forehead after falling from a donkey as a child

6 He is tall and thin, and in poor health – he has a heart condition

7 He wears outsized shoes, with soles an inch thick, coachman's gloves, a dark jacket, and plaid trousers that make him look like an English lord

8 Because of his residence in England, he has lost some of his Spanish fluency: he slurs his "r"s and forgets some of the less common words

9 Rich capitalist; owner of 11, Cava de San Miguel

10 Under the spell of Jacinta, he becomes gaga and childish

11 Anglophilia and hispanophobia; teases his aunt about her charity campaigns

12 PITO

2 One of his abbreviated first names has an appropriate nautical connotation

3 Two sons, one of whom is not his own; an unfaithful wife

4 His attraction to women is one of his two great weaknesses

5 Withered, scarred face; wrinkly forehead; sparkling blue eyes; greeny white beard

6 Knotted hands

7 Sometimes he has his hat pulled down over his head; wears a furry collar

8 His ordinary speech is full of nautical terms; uses a wide repertoire of oaths; his most memorable one, especially in parts II and III, is the euphemistic "I am getting knotted with"

9 Retired sea captain; former slave-trader and smuggler

11 Nostalgic for the sea; often gets drunk; hitches up his trousers when agitated

12 A great raconteur of his past adventures

13 POLENTINOS

1 Middle-aged

2 First name could refer to local Santander paper of the 1870s; the patronymic, with a letter change, could refer to inhabitants of the old historical Castilian city of Palencia

3 Sister-in-law is Doña Perfecta, with whom he has a very harmonious domestic relationship

6 He is tall and thin, and shows the ill effects of constant studying; does not eat or drink much; takes the odd picnic in the countryside

8 Has a tendency to repeat phrases; very correct, refined speech

9 Amateur local historian and archaeologist

10 He reckons himself to be cured of his youthful tendency to suffer manias

11 Passion for old history books and archaeological digs; always note-taking in his library, even late into the night

12 Great reader of history books; letter-writer and substitute narrator of the penultimate chapter of *Doña Perfecta*

14 PONTE

1 He is older than a palm tree, according to Paca; it is impossible to say what age he is; very senile, regressing to childhood

2 His first name suggests his toiletries; his patronymic indicates his role as a bridge character between Paca and Benina, or Obdulia and Paca, and his matronymic is a verbal reflector of his thin body

3 Distant relation of Paca, with whom he reminisces, when he stays with her, of their childhood experiences in Andalusia. Had finally decided against marriage; bachelorhood was the ideal state for him

4 Boasts of many conquests in his past as a dandy and partygoer in the houses of the rich bourgeois

5 Dyes his beard; very proud of his black locks of hair, which he smooths over his ears; has hair style of the 1850s; small nose; deathly looking eyes, childish face; bleary corners of eyes; thin eyelashes; wrinkled eyelids; extensive crow feet

6 His other source of body pride is his small, pretty feet

7 Mends and repairs his clothes so that they keep their original appearance

8 Very polite speech, with a number of refined, social, clichéd phrases; great conversationalist

9 Had a few minor office jobs, but he was, essentially, a social fixture at house parties

10 Innately innocent, a simple soul with a fossilized mind, he is somewhat mentally retarded; but after his fall from a horse, he pronounces the truth about Benina's charity, which leads his relations to think that he has gone completely mad

11 Devotes great attention to the appearance of his body and clothes. Has the tic of constantly smoothing down his locks of hair over his ears

12 In the past, he took part in amateur dramatic productions; he recites poetry or opera pieces for Obdulia in their escapist conversations

15 RELIMPIO

1 Sixty years old

2 Both surnames are ironic: his patronymic refers to his constant shortage of funds, his matronymic to his intermittent sewing work with his daughters

3 Two daughters and a son

4 Has a domineering wife who ridicules his attempts to keep young. Inveterate Don Juan

5 Uses rouge on cheeks; has a little blond moustache; purses lips; has syrupy, overripe-grape eyes; he is the incarnation of sweetness

7 Wears a cap with a gold tassle

8 He is affectedly polite; has verbal habit of repeating three pet political peeves

9 Failed Militia volunteer, government bookkeeper and tailor; he is the incarnation of uselessnesss

11 Obsession with pretty young girls and bookkeeping; gets drunk at Christmas Eve party

12 Bangs children's drum in tenement house procession on Christams Eve. In an earlier draft of a section, he played the bandurria and composed popular poems. He reads newspapers at night; keeps diary of events; writes treatises on bookkeeping

16 RUFETE

1 Has lost all sign of age; he is either middle aged or old

3 Wife predeceased him; two delusionist and psychotic children; deranged father

5 Has a confusing face: sparkling eyes, mobile features; he is almost bald; has a thin, half-grey beard, half-shaven like a half-cut meadow; drooping upper lip constantly shaking like a rabbit gnawing at cabbage; pallid face; papyrus-like skin

6 Thin legs; has short build and a slightly bent back

9 Formerly secretary to three provincial governors; his last job was working in a printing press

10 Delusions of grandeur; when unemployed, goes to Congress debates and makes a commotion; rambles to himself about figures, which he sees as mercury rushing around inside his head; he is a paranoid schizophrenic

11 Preoccupation with what country owes him; anger at ill-treatment by the State

12 Writes up private reports on public finances and corrupt practices

17 TAFETÁN

1 Oldish, but age is not specified

2 Patronymic denotes a fabric used for women's dresses

4 An original Don Juan in his youth, now a dirty old man

5 Puts rouge on his cheeks, dyes his moustache black, and combs his hair to hide up his bald spot; he has very lively little eyes; he laughs a lot, and when he does, his whole face is covered with grotesque wrinkles

6 A poorish build

9 Formerly an employee of the civil service in the provincial capital, he now works in the welfare office in Orbajosa

11 Ogling pretty young girls

12 He has a great talent for telling funny stories; he supplements his regular income by playing the clarinet in processions, at ceremonies at the cathedral, and at the theatre whenever a touring troup gives a performance

Notes

INTRODUCTION

1 In the opinion of Scholes (*Elements* 17), however, to laud the reality of characters is the greatest mistake to be made in interpreting fiction, for, if they can be like real people, they can also be unlike them.

2 The Greek source word, "kharattein," originally meant a drawn or written sign, and then a title that confers a rank or right (Cixous 383).

3 For Communist literary theorists and critics of the early and mid-twentieth century, like George Lukacs, the type was the perfect instrument to represent the totality of the contemporary human and social experience. The type captured the organic and indestructible connection between the private man and the social individual as participant in public life (*Ensayos* 16).

4 E. Dale A. Randolph (51) pertinently reminds us that, for the description of characters with relatively minor neuroses, Galdós could have had access to the English editions of Maudsley's *The Physiology and Pathology of the Mind* from 1867 to 1873, and then, from 1879 to 1886, to both the French and Spanish translations.

5 The serialization of the chapters continued until 8 July 1868. Leonardo Romero Tobar (*La novela* 174) gives different dates: 9 May to 9 July 1868. Pedro Ortiz Armengol (*Vida* 210–11) believes that Galdós could have possessed the French translation of *The Pickwick Papers* by the beginning of 1868 or even by the autumn of 1867. He had in his library an English edition published in Philadelphia in 1847. Walter T. Pattison ("How Well" 149) believes that this edition belonged to his distant

Cuban relations, the Tates, who returned to live in Las Palmas in the mid-1860s. He used the 1865 French translation for his own translation, although only the first volume is to be found in his library (Wright 264, 269). Galdós's limited knowledge of English was probably the reason, along with the serialization schedule, for the translation failing to capture the linguistic flavour of Dickens's original text, as well as for simplifying and shortening it.

The Pickwick Papers was not the only translation of Dickens's work that Galdós made. The short story "The Battle of Life," whose 1865 French translation he had partly annotated (Wright 264n9), was also translated, although never published; some of the folios of the manuscript (132–4; 136–9) are found on the reverse sides of folios 162–8 of the manuscript of Doña Perfecta.

Galdós's interest in Dickens was not unique in Spain; it was widely shared by his compatriots, much to the surprise of a modern critic (José Prades 515). Rodolfo Cardona (Galdós 67), noting that the Pickwick Papers translation appeared as Galdós was composing his first published novel, La Fontana de Oro, claims that the similarities between both authors encompass descriptive technique as well as an interest in the unusual and the grotesque. For Timothy McGovern (3), the surprising fact that Galdós never mentioned the name of Dickens or of any of Dickens's characters in any of his novels is compensated by his incorporation of such Dickensian techniques as the use of type characters as symbols.

6 The last phrase seems to echo a passage in chapter 10 of his translation: "Mr Pickwick era un filósofo. Pero después de todo, los filósofos no son otra cosa que hombres revestidos de una armadura de sabiduría" (Aventuras 1:145).

7 Philip Rogers (23) also notes this change in the direction of the novel: what starts as a satire of Pickwick's bumbling naïveté becomes a celebration of his innocence.

8 This is not to say that Galdós completely understood the cockney English of Sam Weller. Isabel García Martínez (224), disagreeing with Arturo Ramoneda (20), maintains that Galdós failed to convey the full comic flavour of that character's original speech.

9 In the 1864 "Prólogo" to the first volume of the Proverbios ejemplares, Ruiz Aguilera had cited this same reaction from his readers as the criteron by which he would judge the success of his stories, that is, if they said to themselves, when reading them, that they knew these types of individuals or had seen them in the streets of the capital (1:xi). Galdós's interest in Ruiz Aguilera's work preceded his 1870 review article. Just before his study on Dickens and his translation of The Pickwick Papers, he had reviewed for La Nación (on 9 January and 2 February 1868) Ruiz Aguilera's collection of poetry, La Arcadia moderna, and then included

him as the fifth subject in his "Gallery of Wax Figures" in the same journal. He praises Ruiz Aguilera's shepherds for their life-like quality: they are types and individuals at the same time, as memorable as the figures painted by Velázquez (*Los artículos* 374).

10 In using the exclamation, "Ooooh!," as a kind of verbal tag with which to identify this indignant Englishwoman, Galdós shows that he had learnt a Dickensian technique that he will later employ to even greater effect in the creation of his eccentric old men (Erickson 429).

11 Walter Oliver (258) assumes from this allusion that the narrator is dedicating the entire story to the English matron.

CHAPTER ONE

1 We are later told (1, ii) that Anselmo has no medical degree and that the word "doctor" is really a nickname coined by friends to poke fun at his scholarly ways.

2 In Galdós's library there is an 1836 number of the *Semanario Pintoresco Español* (the "costumbrista" magazine founded and edited by Mesonero Romanos), in which the anonymous author of an asterisked, unsigned article on the various faces of Napoleon claims that life experiences and other factors change people's faces almost completely, impressing on them a new type ["concluyendo por imprimir en ella un nuevo tipo"] (Anonymous 78).

3 Anselmo's marriage is reminiscent in some respects of that of the mad nobleman in Dickens's "A Madman's Manuscript," a short story intercalated in *The Pickwick Papers* (11) with which Galdós would have been very familiar after completing his translation of the novel. The unnamed writer, who suffers from a hereditary mental disease, gives an account of his attempts to kill his wife in bed, believing that she loved another man and that she had been forced by her family to marry him instead for his money. The wife dies of shock some time later. A note at the end of the manuscript, written in another hand, casts doubt over the more exaggerated parts of the account whilst maintaining that the general outline is true, in much the same way as the narrator comments on the veracity of Anselmo's story.

4 Rafael Bosch (30) thinks that Galdós could have listened to the lectures of Pedro Mata Fontanet at the Madrid Ateneo in the late 1860s. He is far more categorical when affirming (37n16) that Galdós had read Ambroise-Auguste Liébault's study on sleep, *Du sommeil*, because, when Galdós uses in *La sombra* the term "idée fixe" and its synonyms, "tenaz idea, monomanía, una tema," he is fully aware of their meaning.

5 The narrator's full text is much more complex than O'Byrne Curtis (42–4) grants, when she calls it merely an echo of Anselmo's lies and stupidities.

6 Don Cayetano Guayaquil, a returned, native son of Juan Crisóstomo's
  village or "indiano," who moves to Madrid to press his suit of Rosalía, is
  an example of a type of character that Galdós will introduce alongside
  some of his later eccentrics. He is a rather grotesque person – Rosalía's
  brother describes him as a "frightful sight" ["un esperpento"] (5, ii) –
  with his oiled moustache, waved hair covering his premature baldness,
  outsized abdomen, and short legs; he commits all sorts of stupidities, as
  well as saying every kind of foolishness (6, i). His clothes, including the
  abundance of gold chains and trinkets, are the usual garish sort worn by
  these returning nouveaux riches, like Pereda's Don Apolinar de la Rega-
  tera, who appears in "Two Systems" ["Dos sistemas"], a story included
  in *Types and Landscapes* [*Tipos y paisajes*] (1871). Apolinar also has a
  sallow complexion and a short body, although the hair on his head is
  more abundant than Guayaquil's. As it happened, Galdós had penned an
  unsigned review of this collection of sketches by his friend for *El Debate*
  of 26 January 1872. Galdós praises Pereda's gift for vivid characters; significantly, some of those he cites are comic, eccentric types, like the bourgeois Don Anacleto Remanso in "The Carmen Pilgrimage" ["La romería
  del Carmen"]: it is his funny actions and words ("sus graciosas simplezas") and his old-fashioned attitudes ("sus absurdas manías") that are
  so laughable (Barbieri 110).

7 Pattison (*Benito Pérez Galdós* 53) believes that, at this point in his career,
  Galdós could only present English people as eccentric or Romantic,
  according to what he had read in Dickens. Even the more "normal" Englishman among the shipwrecked guests in Gibralfaro's house, Horacio
  Reynolds (the Anglican priest whose ultimately frustrated love for Rosalía will form the novel's main storyline), is given to behaviour that,
  according to the narrator, earns him "fame as an eccentric amongst the
  eccentrics of his country" ["fama de excéntrico entre los excéntricos de
  su país"] (12, ii). Later in Madrid, Reynolds himself describes his
  redemption of Gibralfaro's debt as an act of eccentricity for which the
  English are famous: "Los ingleses tenemos fama de extravagantes ...: no
  será ésta la primera excentricidad" (47). His love for Rosalía, he claims
  in a letter to his sister (whose husband's name, Sam, is perhaps an echo
  of Sam Weller of *The Pickwick Papers*), has transformed him into a madman, an eccentric ("un loco ... un extravagante" [50]), the juxtaposition
  of the two words signifying the proximity of the two mental states for
  Galdós.

CHAPTER TWO

1 Enrique Rubio Cremades ("Galdós" 252) also relates Cayetano Polentinos to another type from Galdós's previous short fiction: the philosopher

husband of Doña Cruz in "La mujer del filósofo": both are learned bib-
liophiles and have moderate food intake. But for the significant presence
of the youthful Rosario, Doña Perfecta's mansion would resemble the
decayed household of Cantabrian aristocrats like Don Robustiano and
Don Ramiro in the story "Coats of Arms and Bags" ["Blasones y tale-
gas"], in Pereda's *Tipos y paisajes*.

2 Seventeen years later, in one of his "costumbrista" sketches on contemporary types for *La Prensa* of Buenos Aires, "The Collector" ["El colec-
cionista"], Galdós was to remark that collectors of archaeological items
were the collectors most liable to suffer mental disorders as a result of
this passion, as well as driving those around them mad: "Say what they
like, in this business of archaeology, there is plenty of insanity" ["Digan
lo que quieran, en esto de la arqueología hay mucho de demencia"]
(*Fisonomías* 203).

3 Miss Betsey Trotwood's idyllic Dover cottage and surroundings also
proved to be a welcome refuge for Mr Dick after his brother had con-
signed him earlier to a private insane asylum. David Copperfield's great-
aunt thinks that Mr Dick's father was mad too. Mr Dick's obsession with
the date of King Charles I's execution is the outward manifestation of the
trauma his mind suffers when remembering the fear he felt of his brother
and his sympathy for an unhappily married sister (14).

4 Geoffrey Ribbans ("*Doña Perfecta*") claims that a seven-page, undated
document entitled "Conclusión" and recently discovered in the Casa-
Museo Pérez Galdós in Las Palmas de Gran Canaria may be a first draft
of the ending to *Doña Perfecta*, dictated by Galdós, for it is not in his
handwriting. However, it is not given in epistolary form but rather continues the style of the omniscient narrator predominant in the rest of the
novel. The subsequent adoption of the epistolary form, then, changes
fundamentally the presentation of the dénouement.

5 In a macabre sort of way, it is fitting that the disclosure of the circumstances surrounding Pepe's death should be made in the form of letters,
for an exchange of letters (between Perfecta and her brother) about the
possible marriage of Pepe and Rosario had led to the engineer's visit to
Orbajosa in the first place (Turner, "The Shape" 129).

6 In fact, he had read his most recent section of the study to Pepe Rey after
the latter's return from the casino and the house of Las Troyas in chapter
13.

7 Ribbans ("*Doña Perfecta*" 213n12) remarks that in the manuscript this
reference to the Las Troyas's visit to the grave was squeezed in as an
afterthought. The sentence that follows, conveying Cayetano's reaction to
their praying, it should also be noted, was only added at the galley stage,
for it does not appear on f. 483 of the original manuscript.

8 Galdós strengthened this deft show of polite sarcasm from the greatly

underestimated Cayetano by adding the adjective "prudent" at the galley correction stage, for it is not to be found in f. 486 of the original manuscript.

9 Letters four and five were the only ones changed in some detail in a second edition of *Doña Perfecta,* published by Guirnalda in December 1876 (Jones). The first edition, published by Noguera in June 1876, contained a rumour in the first paragraph of letter four (dated 12 December) that Perfecta was going to marry Jacinto, although Perfecta is reported to be laughing at the rumour. This paragraph is excised from the second, definitive edition of the novel. The last letter, written eleven days later, underwent a far more extensive revision in this second edition. The first two paragraphs that had related how Jacinto was accidentally killed by the knife in his mother's hand as she and her staff were preparing the food for Christmas celebrations were removed. These changes may well have been prompted by the reaction of colleagues and admirers like the young novelist Armando Palacio Valdés who believed that Cayetano's letters should never have been written, since they greatly reduced the merit of the novel and Galdós's reputation (Valis 708). What is of interest for our study is that Cayetano shows in the excised passages the same sudden moments of insight that surfaced in his first three letters: he relays a rumour (without attribution of sources, of course), and he quotes Perfecta's reactions to that rumour. Then, he advances his own very sensible objections to such a marriage, if the rumour were indeed true: age difference and incompatibility. In another display of surprising perceptiveness, he records how Jacinto is not too keen on the plan himself, and it seems that his mother, María Remedios, is the main instigator of the rumour. Jacinto's death in the fifth letter is reported almost as soon as it happens, the details supplied soon after Cayetano's exclamations of disbelief and horror.

10 The reference to proof-correction is, of course, pertinent to *Doña Perfecta*'s and any book's manufacture. Cayetano's addition of new material reflects what Galdós had done, was continuing to do, and would still have to do with the text of this novel, even after it had been published.

11 The picture of the old rake at the beginning of the nineteenth century, as sketched in an article by a certain "Diógenes," "Letter Sent to Us by the Dirty Old Man" ["Carta que nos ha remitido el viejo verde"], in the Madrid journal *El Regañón General* of 1803, had focused on the daily toilette and dress operations that he needed to complete in order to appear young and attractive to the ladies on the dance floor: he had to shave and put a wig over his bald head, as well as wear a frock coat, waistcoat, and thin trousers. The wide shoes he had to wear for his gout were, however, the clue to his real age. Tafetán, with his recourse to cosmetics, resembles the picture of "El viejo verde" by Francisco de la Corti-

na in *Los españoles de ogaño,* the collection to which Galdós had contributed the sketch "Aquél." This type, described as a bit of a buffoon,
and quite a funny clown or eccentric ["algo de bufo, mucho de cómico, y
no poco de extravagante con ribetes de divertido"] (371), never owns up
to being older than fifty, and has a dressing table full of cosmetics with
which to dye hair, beard, and eyebrows, as well as to paint nails and lips.
A well-conserved wreck ["una ruina bien conservada"], he appears more
effeminate than other men. As a bachelor or a widower, he generally has
no profession and lives off his own income or, more cleverly, off that of
others. His life is somewhat monotonous, for he is always to be found in
the same places, in the same company, and cultivating the same habits,
like attending theatre rehearsals, where he leers from all angles at the
movements of the ballet dancers – his favourites – or the actresses. He is
the spoilt child of the girls at the gambling tables. The saddest aspect of
this behaviour, de la Cortina concludes, is that he does not realize that he
is cutting a ridiculous figure; he is horrified at the idea of death, for he
would like to be immortal, playing the fool forever ["para no dejar nunca
de hacer el *oso*"] (376).

12 Another old roué compelled to use facial cosmetics in order to attract
young women is the impecunious Marqués de Tellería in Galdós's *The
Family of León Roch* [*La familia de León Roch*] (1878). But he lacks
Tafetán's warmth of heart and humour, and is a mere type who incarnates the obsession with outward appearances.

CHAPTER THREE

1 Benítez (*La literatura* 56) sees in this scene an echo of some involving
Quasimodo in Victor Hugo's *Notre-Dame de Paris.*

2 In an earlier version of this section, the narrator concentrated on the
events that had caused *Caifás* to lose his faith in Morton (Pattison, *Benito Pérez Galdós* 303–4), something that had already been treated in their
preceding conversation. The substitution in the final manuscript version
of more abstract considerations that emphasize bewilderment rather than
certainty about Morton adds a deeper dimension to *Caifás*'s character.

3 The sentence is one of those spine-chilling phrases on death that surface
from time to time in Galdós's writing; in fact, one had appeared in
"Forty Leagues through Cantabria" ["Cuarenta leguas por Cantabria"],
a report that Galdós wrote of a trip he made around the region of
Cantabria from his summer residence in Santander (Bly, *Vision* 33–4).
The travelogue appeared in December 1876 in the *Revista de España.* It
is quite possible that these impressions were still in his mind when he
wrote part II of *Gloria* in the spring of 1877.

4 Not surprisingly, a gallery of eccentrics and mad, oldish men appear in

the two series of *Episodios nacionales* that Galdós also worked on during
this period (1873–79): Don Pedro del Cangosto (*Cádiz*) (1874) is clearly
patterned on Don Quixote. Perhaps Patricio Sarmiento (*El terror de
1824*) (1876) is the most interesting example for our study, for, in an
important anticipation of the culminating development of the eccentric
figure in the social novels, this oldish schoolmaster develops from a
comic minor type into a tragic protagonist of sublime proportions, ready
to die a martyr's death for the cause of liberty. The crux of the narrator's
argument summarizing the sacrifice of his schoolmaster (again in a final
chapterette) is that it is virtually impossible to separate madness, eccentricity, and sublimity, and, more arrestingly, that this fictional character is
far worthier of occupying a place in the history of Spain than those historical figures who, as mad as Sarmiento, but far less sublime, achieve
posthumous fame as heroes:

> ¿Habrá quien marque de un modo preciso la esfera donde el humano
> sentido, merecedor de asombro y respeto, se trueca en la enajenación
> digna de lástima? Siendo evidente que en aquella alma [Sarmiento] se
> juntaban con aleación extraña la excelsitud y la trivialidad, ¿quién
> podrá decir cuál de estas cualidades a la otra vencía? ... ¡Cuántos
> tienen ésta [posthumous fame] con menos motivo, y cuántos ocupan
> aquélla [the pages of history] habiendo sido tan locos como él
> [Sarmiento] y menos, mucho menos sublimes! (1:1818)

CHAPTER FOUR

1 Ignacio-Javier López (*Galdós* 33) claims, without providing any evidence
or reason, as far as I can see, that Don Juan Crisóstomo de Gibralfaro of
Rosalía is, undoubtedly, the prototype of Relimpio.
2 In Galdós's first wording of Chapter 2 in the manuscript of *La desheredada*, Relimpio was not named when he was introduced, merely
being described as "a type who is not from this place" ["un tipo que no
es de este lugar"; f. 1:67, on the back of f. 1:70] (Entenza de Solare 153).
3 James H. Hoddie ("The Genesis" 32–3) claims that certain details of
José's physical appearance make him a parodic figure of the god Apollo.
4 Jesús Páez Martín (442) interprets Relimpio's patronymic as an allusion
to a double cleanness (spiritual as well as material), which would be a
secret sign of approval from the narrator.
5 A greater affinity with Don Juan Tafetán is discernible in some rejected
sentences at this point in the manuscript. Just as the civil servant in *Doña
Perfecta* had played the clarinet at public events and in the local theatre,
Relimpio could play the bandurria with moderate passion (f. 1:273). If
Tafetán had been an original Don Juan in his youth who later bragged of
his conquests, Relimpio had played such roles in plays when young, and

now in old age wrote popular verse for distribution ("coplas" and "aleluyas") (Entenza de Solare 153).

6 For López ("Génesis" 119n19), Relimpio dates this historical sequence, but it is the narrator who arranges it in the text. Romero Tobar ("*La desheredada*" 199) maintains that the information supplied to the narrator by José was written. Antonio Ruiz Salvador (54) also believes that Relimpio had been keeping a diary of the events.

7 That Galdós intended to make some kind of change in the character of Don José is conveyed by the different wording appended after his name in the lists of dramatis personae inserted in the first edition of *La desheredada*: in the list for part II, he is now referred to as a bookkeeper, whereas in the corresponding one for part I, he had been described as a model for the lazy (Krow-Lucal 151).

8 C.P. Snow (233) calls the Relimpios "toned-down and semirealistic Micawbers."

9 There is a corresponding division of opinion amongst critics over Relimpio's character in these closing scenes. On the one hand, López (*Caballero* 59) believes that Relimpio has become grotesque. Enrique Miralles (xxxv) declares that Relimpio's alcoholic end was a necessary punishment by Galdós for his decadent, romantic dreaming, although his friendliness saved him from a truly hellish, Naturalist fate. On the other hand, Montesinos (*Galdós* 2:15) believes that Galdós does not overplay the grotesque: grotesque tragedies can still be very tragic. For M. Gordon ("'Lo que le falta'" 35), Galdós strikes a fine balance: we are made to feel sympathy for the dying Relimpio, yet without falling into excessive sentimentality, because of the use of irony. Joaquín Santaló (101) also considers Relimpio a character who embodies both tragic and comic traits.

10 "I never heerd, mind you, nor read of in story-books, nor see in picters, any angel in tights and gaiters ..., but mark my vords ... he's reg'lar thoroughbred angel for all that" (45). Galdós's own translation is reasonably faithful to the sense, if not to the form, of the original wording: "No he oído jamás decir, ni leído en ningún libro de historia, ni visto en ningún cuadro, un ángel con pantalones y chaleco ... os digo ... que es un verdadero ángel, un ángel de pura sangre" (*Aventuras* 2:173).

11 Hafter ("Galdós' Presentation" 28) contends that this repetition of terminology is designed merely to emphasize the unsentimental nature of the final moral by the narrator. Ribbans ("*La desheredada*" 73) recalls that the same image of wings and soaring flights was used to describe Isidora's delirious ravings in jail about her failed lawsuit at the end of part II, chapter 15, just before what Galdós had orginally planned as the main event of the novel's last chapter: her brother's attempt to assassinate King Alfonso XII.

12 Julio Santiago Obeso diagnoses Tomás's madness, according to modern
    psychiatric categories, as paranoid schizophrenia (residual type).

13 The possibility that Galdós's thoughts were turning to a story about mad-
    men is raised by a brief allusion to Leganés in his previous novel, *La
    familia de León Roch,* the only one of the "Primera Epoca" to be set
    largely in Madrid, when Leopoldo Tellería had suggested that he and his
    companions should take a horse ride to the village in the suburbs to see
    the mental asylum (III, 9). This passing allusion comes a year before the
    account of a visit to the same institution by a journalist, M. Alhama
    Montes, published in late August 1879 in *Los Lunes del Imparcial.* The
    remarkably strong similarities (both in content and tone) between his
    description of the facilities and the inmates and that of Galdós's narrator
    in *La desheredada* lead one to conclude, with some reason, that Galdós
    probably had this article in front of him as he wrote chapter I of *La
    desheredada* (Robin 28–9). Galdós had also visited the institution with
    his friend, the writer and journalist José Ortega Munilla (Schmidt, "José
    Ortega" 108).

14 In his *Responsibility in Mental Disease,* published in 1874 – a Spanish
    translation appeared in the same year as *La desheredada* – Maudsley
    also presents a variety of types of inmates in a mental asylum: those
    who were hyperactive or hypervocal, those who were listless and silent,
    and those who looked like normal people. This would be what an
    untrained eye would see. But the skilled observer (the psychiatrist),
    Maudsley says, would recognize all the traits of human character from
    the real world, now seen in its true, stark bareness, and he cites in sup-
    port words by the doyen of nineteenth-century psychiatrists, the
    Frenchman Jean Étienne Dominique Esquirol: "man is then seen in all
    his nakedness, because he does not dissimulate his thoughts, because he
    does not conceal his defects, because he lends not to his passions the
    charm which seduces, not to his vices the appearances which deceive"
    (2–3). A more novelistic description – again surprisingly free of profes-
    sional jargon – of the actions and features of the inmates of a Valencian
    insane asylum was penned fourteen years after the publication of *La
    desheredada* by José María Escuder, who criticized the institution for
    imposing on the inmates a harsh penitentiary or military régime that
    stressed uniformity at the expense of individual attention and treatment
    for mental disorders, which, by definition, are multiple and diverse.
    Interestingly, these kinds of reforms, long advocated by Esquirol and his
    followers, had been foreseen as established procedures in the mental
    asylum of the turn of the century by Antonio Flores in his witty "cos-
    tumbrista" sketch "The Prison Madhouse, and the Voluntary Mad-
    house" ["El Manicomio penitenciario, y el Manicomio voluntario"],

published in his 1864 collection "Tomorrow, or the Electric Spark in
1899" ["Mañana, o la chispa eléctrica en 1899"], part III of the volume
Yesterday, Today and Tomorrow [*Ayer, hoy y mañana*]. Private compa-
nies hired to run the asylums ensure that the criminally insane are separated from those sent there by their fee-paying relatives. Inmates are
separated according to the nature of their illness, are well fed, and all
physically violent treatment is forbidden. Visits to the asylum cost
money but are valuable, as the character Venancio tells his mother, for
the sane can learn truths from the insane (233). The recipe for a cure is
to treat the patient's mania by feeding it to saturation point: the political maniacs, for example, are given musical instruments, like a drum
and bells, that, reminding them of the sounds in Parliament, cause them
to constantly shout out their respective ideological clichés, just as
Rufete does in Leganés.

In the fee-paying section of Leganés where Tomás is first lodged, modern psychiatric therapies are mentioned: for example, a doctor examines
Rufete and prescribes a drug (potassium bromide) as treatment. He is
courteous and solicitous in conversation with Rufete and the others, listening to their manic talk, just as the real doctors at Leganés were accustomed to do (Robin 93). Rufete is also subjected to another therapy: the
Scottish shower treatment, when jets of water are blasted at him. But it is
true to say that Galdós prefers to exploit the symbolic value of the insane
asylum rather than probe into the scientific aspects of mental diseases
(Gordon, "Medical" 75).

15 Alhama Montes (Robin 94) was equally upset by what he saw at
Leganés, but perhaps expressed himself more explicitly than Galdós when
he bitterly criticized the failure of the government to set up proper facili-
ties for the treatment of madness. The scenes are truly Dickensian, reminiscent of those of the debtors' prisons in *The Pickwick Papers* and *Little
Dorrit* (Erickson 427).

16 Despite repeated attempts by various committees, including one in 1874,
Leganés never became the model psychiatric centre it was intended to be:
"scientific and beneficial; curative for the curable madmen, and a refuge
for the uncurables" ["científico y benéfico; curativo, para locos curables,
y de refugio para los no curables"] (Espinosa Iborra 102; see also Villasante). But in reality, the asylum, like others in Spain in the last quarter
of the nineteenth century, was just an inhuman isolation area for all
kinds of mentally sick people. No medical doctor was appointed as its
director, and the admission of patients was not the task of the medical
staff. In 1895 Escuder (307) was more outright and scathing in his
denunciation of the poor management of Leganés – the only state asylum
in the country – by the governing board of women and by the nuns who

operated it. No report, study, or discovery of any psychiatric kind or value was ever issued from this institution.

17 Alhama Montes (Robin 91) also avoided physiological detail: for example, he regarded dementia as a catalepsy of the soul. It is generally assumed that Galdós's ideas on psychiatry mainly derived from his friend Manuel Tolosa Latour, a paediatrician who was close to Spain's most prominent psychiatrist, José María Esquerdo (Gordon "Medical"), as well as being a collaborator of younger psychiatrists like Ángel Pulido, Escuder, and Antonio Ramón y Vega. If Tolosa Latour did keep Galdós informed of advances at home and abroad in psychiatry as they appeared in publications, it is somewhat surprising that none of the Spanish translations of the four books by Maudsley, which appeared between 1880 and 1881, is to be found in Galdós's library, and that the founder of modern psychiatric studies in Britain is not quoted by Galdós in *La desheredada* (Ullman and Allison 23).

18 The emotional intensity and the central idea of this passage are very similar to those expressed by Alhama Montes, who confessed to being troubled for many months after his visit by recurring, nightmarish visions of the inmates and by strange doubts about his own sanity: "I am still overwhelmed by strange ideas about whether they are the sane ones and we are the mad ones, they the rule and we the exception" ["todavía se apoderan de mí extrañas ideas sobre si son ellos los cuerdos y nosotros los locos, ellos la regla y nosotros la excepción"] (Robin 95).

19 Alhama Montes described a very similar character in the director's office when he visited Leganés: a gentle, weak-faced man, he, too, is seen writing at a desk, and he carefully cleans his pen. He talks with great philosophical sense about the vanity of the world, and shows compassion for human weakness. It is only when the conversation turns to modern inventions that he starts uttering nonsense, claiming that the coming of the train engine has changed the number of seasons in the year into one for every village because he confuses the two meanings of "station" in Spanish ["estación"] (Robin 92).

20 Canencia's patronymic is also appropriate, given his habit of gasping for air, since it is also the name of a mountain pass close to Madrid (G. Gullón, "Originalidad" 44).

21 In part II, the series of eccentric old men that had formed a point of reference for Relimpio's guidance of Isidora in part I is now substituted by another set of contrastive figures: her succession of lovers, whose grotesque physical features, exaggerated reflections of some of Relimpio's, are indicative of their corresponding lack of noble feelings for his goddaughter. Bou is the closest to Don José in his slavish affection for her, but he is an animal of a man, successively described as a bull, donkey, ox, and bear. His cyclopic pair of eyes are far more off-putting than

Relimpio's, which are sweet- and syrupy-looking. As a printer of all sorts of minor industrial objects, he is far more successful than the unpublished Relimpio, and in politics, he is far more revolutionary and anarchistic than the Progresista godfather. He wins the lottery, Don José does not. Sánchez Botín's sexual appreciation of Isidora is far more intense and perverted than José's: he becomes very excited watching her remove her boots. He may have pretty hands and feet, but his eyes look like two hard-boiled eggs with red veins. He too uses cosmetics, but on his piliary outcrops, which, when the colour or cream wears off, are far from flattering. The epitome of the ambitious career politician, he has been more successful at milking the government than Tomás Rufete. *Gaitica*, Isidora's last identified lover, is effeminate-looking like José, with a smiling face, red lips, a shaven face, and dyed sideburns. Compared to a dummy by Isidora, just as Relimpio had been by his wife and the narrator, he is Don José's opposite in his treatment of Isidora.

CHAPTER FIVE

1 In a first draft (on the back of f. 1:42), Don Florencio was given the name of "Cándido Lucas," a more immediately obvious indicator of his simple character.

2 A number of critics have taken a negative view of these political idiosyncrasies. Ribbans (*History* 116) remarks that Don Florencio "voices an astonishingly incoherent mixture of patriotism, liberalism and religion." Geraldine M. Scanlon (246) considers Florencio's repertoire an imperfect assimilation of the ideals of liberal democracy that is comparable to his unawareness of Polo's shortcomings as a priest. Gloria Moreno Castillo (387) argues that his opinions are derivative and that his conversation is full of commonplaces.

3 Slightly more pompous and officious than Morales, he fulfills the same purpose of furnishing background information about political developments. However, his delight in being the first to break the news, along with his rhetorical way of speaking (including verbal tags) and his constant report-writing about the national financial crisis only manage to deflate the worth of this preoccupation.

4 Galdós had juggled with other names for Don Jesús, like Eladio Fernández de la Valleina and Juan Estanisalo de Kosca de la Concha (Schnepf, "Galdós's *El doctor Centeno* Manuscript" 37–8).

5 It appears that Galdós never recorded the age or birthdate of Ido (Shoemaker, "Galdós's Literary Creativity" 93), but judging by the reference in *Tormento*, set in 1867, to his eldest son as a compositor earning a living in a printing house, it would not be out of place to guess that he had married some time around 1850, having been born circa 1830.

6 María-Paz Yáñez ("Algo más" 862) notes another meaning: the Latin root word for "Sagrario": "sacrarium" meant a secret place, which could refer to the mind.

CHAPTER SIX

1 In the first draft of the novel, the possibility of José María withdrawing to Leganés and writing his memoirs there was expressed (Whiston, "Change" 39).

2 Romero Tobar (*La novela* 171) argues that, if Galdós's warmth to Ido, the "novela por entregas" writer, contrasts with his opposition to the genre in his 1870 manifesto, it is because he now feels that the new Spanish social novel he had called for is no longer threatened by this popular type of novel.

3 Galdós had tried quite a number of variants of these terms in earlier drafts in the manuscript: "A chronic ill, a neuropathic disorder, a constituent neurosis, a constituent eccentricity" ["un mal crónico, un desorden neuropático, una neurosis constitutiva, chifladura constitutiva"] (*Lo prohibido* 117n13).

4 This extensive cataloguing of the family pathology is too much of an overkill to be taken seriously – López-Baralt (27) calls it ridiculous, Alfred Rodríguez and Luz María Rodríguez (53) a parody of Naturalism. However, when it is discovered that real people did exhibit such strange symptoms, the effect is less comical; in fact, it becomes more pathetic. As James Whiston has pointed out in his edition of the novel (120n21), one sample bears a striking resemblance to a case reported by Henri Huchard and repeated by José Armangué y Tuset in his *Clinical Studies* [*Estudios clínicos*] (211). Undoubtedly, part of this superabundance of clinical detail in *Lo prohibido* about the host of eccentrics and crackpots can be attributed to Galdós's continuing close contacts with members of the medical profession. But the matter goes deeper than mere recycling of medical data. Both Galdós and his doctor friends emphasized a connection between the novel and medicine. Tolosa Latour, under the pseudonym of "El Doctor Fausto," wrote in an article on Galdós in 1883 that medical students had been among the most avid and knowledgeable readers of the *Episodios nacionales* and the contemporary social novels of the "Primera Época." In a speech at the Madrid Ateneo in 1884, the year in which *Lo prohibido* appeared, he emphasized the value of contemporary character novels for psychologists, because of their quick assessment of people (quoted in Lakhdari 81). As a return compliment, Galdós was to voice similar affinities five years later in the prologue he wrote for the 1889 edition of Tolosa Latour's book, *Niñerías*, where he recognizes the need felt by some doctors and psychiatrists to express in artistic form

Bky comforts the purely satirical assertion of the Rodriguez

their daily experience with patients (*Obras completas* 6:1493). He welcomes this sort of literary science-reporting because it allows him and other novelists, whose job is to paint life and its pain, to understand more easily the workings of the mind and body. Tolosa Latour's pleasing literary style makes, paradoxically, the reality of the therapeutic or neuropathic details all that much easier and more attractive to read. Novelists like himself, Galdós continues, are necessarily removed from the reality of hospitals and infirmaries, and their focus is different: it is moral rather than psychotherapeutic. If psychiatrists were to discover the truth about functional disorders, they would make the diagnosis of passions less mysterious and complicated for the novelist. Galdós envies doctors and has a kind of constant flirtation with medicine, which he is not able to turn into a truly serious relationship.

Armangué y Tuset also cultivated an artistic style in the two clinical studies he published in the same year in which *Lo prohibido* came out, copies of which he sent, with a personal dedication, to Galdós. In *Mimicismo o neurosis imitante,* his observations (marginally annotated by the dedicatee) on the force of habit in human actions, especially those shared by husband and wife – as Galdós's 1871 sketch, "La mujer del filósofo," had already illustrated – is more a description of physical examples (verbal tags, idioms, tone of voice, dress, even ideas) than a scientific disquisition. Armangué pointedly refers to *La familia de León Roch* and *Doña Perfecta* as examples of the contribution that literature, with its classification of types, has made over the centuries to the understanding of human psychology. Given Galdós's admiration for the clinical studies of his doctor friends, it is rather unlikely that he is poking fun at them in his own extraordinary sample-catalogue of cases that launches *Lo prohibido*. It is likely that the comic appeal of its first chapter has more to do with the characters of the fictional narrator and his great-uncle, Rafael, who acts as the family's oral medical archivist, so to speak. The laugh is really on them, not as carriers of the family mental disease, but as actors in the fiction. When Rafael comes to the end of his account, José María does not know whether to call it a "prolix short story, a history or chap book" ["prolijo cuento, historia o pliego de aleluyas"] (I, 1, iii). At the beginning of his uncle's account, he had been nearer the mark when he commented that Rafael would have made a good novelist. This is precisely what he himself will become by narrating the insanities of his own family.

5 Galdós himself forgot to include in the manuscript Ido's famous tags, for they are inserted at least five times in heavy black ink on the margins of the galleys in this episode (as well as in later ones).

6 In the galleys, Galdós toned down the colours of Ido's clothing by excising references to his green coat and brownish trousers.

7 Alas, in his review of the novel on 22/23 September 1887 in *El Globo* (*Galdós* 163) did not see any wisdom either: in praising everything about Ido in the novel as "unsurpassable" ["inviolable]," he considered this episode one of the funniest Galdós had ever written.

8 In the short story "Un tribunal literario," which Galdós published in 1872, the aristocrat on the panel of literary judges, an idealistic writer, has a nervous tic: he pulls violent faces every two minutes, which make those looking at him die of silent laughter (*Ensayos* 135). Armangué y Tuset had reported in one of his 1884 studies somewhat similar symptoms experienced by a patient who suffered from migraine: his attack would begin after drinking milk and also produced blurred vision in one eye (*Estudios* 121). The absence of marginal annotations, both in Armangué y Tuset's book and in the 1885 Spanish translation of Sigismond Jaccoud's 1869 *Tratado de patología interna* (sent to Galdós by Tolosa Latour) – even though there is a pertinent section in volume 2 on the infirmities of the nervous system – as well as in Antonio Ramón y Vega's 1888 work, *Compendio de práctica médico-forense* (with its generous acknowledgment of Galdós's clinical observations and his literary talent), does not necessarily invalidate the idea that Galdós might have consulted these studies.

9 Ido is not as "totally inoffensive" or "pitifully eccentric" as Willem (*Galdós's 'Segunda Manera'* 72) believes him to be on this second visit.

10 López ("El poder" 10) calls this dual process one of poetic creation (poiesis) followed by its mimetic assimilation (mimesis). Ángel Tarrío (154–5) fails to see that, as well as ridiculing the popular "folletín" literature on which it is modelled, the false *Pituso* story does, inevitably, transfer some of that genre's melodrama to the subsequent text of *Fortunata y Jacinta* itself (see also Yáñez, "Algo más" 857).

11 Fourteen months after completing this scene (which takes place on 21 December 1873) and shortly before another café scene (on 19 March 1875) between the two Pepes in part IV (Ribbans, *Conflicts* 309n30), Galdós wrote an article for *La Prensa* of Buenos Aires (19 March 1887, but only published 4 May 1887) on that day's patron saint: St Joseph. This article is, in fact, a recycling (pace Shoemaker "'Los Pepes'"), with minor changes, of a text that Galdós had published almost twenty years before in *La Nación,* in 1868. The day's festivities centre on various sorts of meals according to social rank. The namesake that Ido most resembles is the pauper in ragged clothes who only eats scraps and is sombre and quiet: he is no tramp, beggar, pickpocket, or criminal, but simply a sad, old Joe (*Las cartas* 233).

12 This bristling of the hair is, according to Charles Darwin (294), following a Dr Browne, most apparent during the paroxysms of chronic maniacs.

13 Some of these symptoms are listed by J.E.D. Esquirol in his diagnosis of
monomaniacs (*Mental Maladies* 378): heat within the cranium, voracious
appetite, and insomnia. In his psychiatric study of Ido, Ildefonso Gómez-
Feria Prieto (196–7) comes to the conclusion that he suffers from the
paranoia of jealousy, but that this does not develop into madness; nor
does he suffer visual or auditory hallucinations.

CHAPTER SEVEN

1 His patronymic seems to be Catalan in origin; there is, in fact, a small
town in the province of Huesca called Estopiñán (Ribbans, "The Making"
155n6), a strange onomastic origin for a type who is insistently described
as a "hipermadrileño" (Ortiz Armengol, *Apuntaciones* 161). Galdós also
toyed with a number of first names (Serafín, Zacarías, Isidoro, and José
Quintín) before selecting "Plácido" (Ribbans, *Conflicts* 19, 289).
2 In the Alpha manuscript of the novel, Estupiñá himself (and not the narrator) takes great delight in comparing his age to those of three other
famous writers, one French and two Spanish: Victor Hugo, Manuel
Bretón de los Herreros, and Juan Eugenio Hartzenbusch (Ribbans, "The
Making" 148). If the irony of the Mesonero Romanos comparison
emerges more clearly by excluding the other writers, their status as writers of Romantic drama would have contributed, on the other hand, to
the Romantic overtones of Juanito and Fortunata's first meeting in the
Cava and their subsequent relationship. Rubio Cremades ("El costumbrismo" 106) reminds us opportunely of the fact that, even though
Estupiñá is associated with Mesonero, he is not given the latter's famous
bluish glasses or a family of wife and four children to support.
3 For María del Pilar Palomo Vázquez (228), Mesonero Romanos was
guilty of the same vanity in his *Memorias de un setentón* (1877).
4 Ribbans perceptively notes that the "costumbrista" dimension to
Estupiñá's life history in the original Alpha manuscript is "subsumed into
his role as consultant on the commercial history of Madrid" ("The Making" 150).
5 Ribbans (*Conflicts* 40–1) points out that in the earlier manuscript versions of the novel, Estupiñá's role as tutor ["ayo"] to Juanito in this for-
mative period was much more extensive and obtrusive.
6 Perhaps this comparison to the magpie is a subtle allusion to Rossini's
opera, *The Thieving Magpie*, all the more appropriate, of course, in view
of Plácido's smuggling activities (Chamberlin, "New Insights" 107–8),
although it is wise to bear in mind Julio Caro Baroja's observation that
many of Rossini's compatriots would display the same smile, and that
just as many Italian men could be physically compared to Verdi (272).

Galdós had been attracted nineteen years earlier by the same physiognomic features of the sixty–year-old Rossini in an article he wrote on 13 November 1867 for the *Revista del Movimiento Intelectual de Europa*. For Galdós the journalist, Rossini has an expressive, kind appearance, although he can be grumpy. He also indicates other characteristics (a moderate liking for drinking port, smoking, eating well, and gossiping), some of which can be perceived in Estupiñá. A more significant resemblance is the composer's loquaciousness and eccentricity (Hoar 242). Galdós's purpose in that journalistic bio-pic had been to emphasize how ordinary Rossini looked in his old age. In *Fortunata y Jacinta* the process is reversed. It is interesting to note that in his 7 January 1866 *La Nación* article on Mesonero Romanos, Galdós had noted something of Rossini's kind, mocking smile in the Spaniard's face (*Los artículos* 259). Mesonero Romanos had praised the composer's sublime genius in one of his articles, "La Filarmonía" (*Escenas* 388–94). In his second bio-pic of Mesonero two years later, Galdós repeats the similarity, but in greater physiognomic detail (*Los artículos* 444). So, one could say that Estupiñá, Rossini, and Mesonero Romanos formed a physiognomic trio in Galdós's mind.

In the Alpha version of the novel, Estupiñá's physical appearance had been likened to that of a person at prayer in the religious paintings so favoured by Spanish artists (Ribbans, "The Making" 148–9). This is not, ironically, an inappropriate iconical referent, for Estupiñá is a great mass-attender, with or without Doña Bárbara, but he is never seen praying devoutly.

7 The type of musical serenade proposed by Don Plácido hardly seems suitable for a Rossini-lookalike. Relimpio had conducted a slightly more harmonious concert when banging drums with younger musicians on the following evening – Christmas Eve – one year earlier (1872), in *La desheredada*. In effect, Galdós originally had Estupiñá suggesting the use of drums, but this detail was changed at the galley correction stage (g. part I; 2:89). Another member of the Santa Cruz circle, Samaniego, had first suggested that they celebrate the win with tambourines and Christmas carols. In the Alpha manuscript, Plácido had also composed some very funny verses at Barbarita's wedding (Ribbans, "The Making" 151). In an article he wrote for *La Prensa* on 28 December 1886, that is, almost a year after he had painted this scene in part I (*Las cartas* 217–18), Galdós admits, rather disingenuously, to his Argentinian readers that he has never won a lottery share or even knows anyone who has, so he could not describe for them the emotional experience of the winners.

8 Fortunata remembers during this encounter that Estupiñá had been made administrator of the building a year earlier, in 1875, by the then landlord, Moreno-Isla, which was later than the old factotum had hoped when Juanito had visited him in his apartment in 1869 (I, 3, iv).

9　Ortiz Armengol (*Apuntaciones* 529) talks of Plácido's sublime status here. Ribbans (*Conflicts* 41–2), on the other hand, is much more critical, calling his attitude "appallingly narrow-minded." In actual fact, in the very schematic version of the last chapter in the Alpha manuscript, his kinder side was more to the fore: Fortunata even goes to his apartment, and not her aunt's, to have her baby. It is worthy of note that when Galdós corrected the proofs, he wisely deleted a conversation between Estupiñá and Ballester in which there was a repeat description of the recent scene with Fortunata (g. part IV; 3:13). The other unfortunate impression conveyed in this excised passage was that Estupiñá's usual penchant for talking, as well as his moral comments on Fortunata's life, eclipsed the new, more admirable side of his character.

10　In fact, María de los Ángeles Ayala (126) compares the importance of Estupiñá in *Fortunata y Jacinta* to that of Mesonero Romanos in the development of the Spanish novel in the nineteenth century.

11　Montesinos (*Galdós* 2:246) calls Izquierdo an odd, eccentric character, whilst Tarrío (137) claims that, because of his language, he is a Spanish – not a universal – type.

12　Izquierdo's escapades may be largely invented, but his tavern ramblings can be considered an example of an emergent, working-class political consciousness (Caudet, "José Izquierdo" 26). His matronymic might also suggest his deviousness in the *Pituso* affair much more aptly than his original Alpha manuscript name of "Mayor" ["Alcalde"] with the nickname of "Pilate" ["Pilatos"] (Ribbans, *Conflicts* 104).

13　In a section that was unfortunately erased on the galleys, Galdós summarized the salient features of the peculiar language of Izquierdo: "Izquierdo spoke worse than he thought, mixing with his disjointed syntax underworld slang and vulgar words. Popular philology had no secrets for him, and he brayed in all the dialects of the ignorant rabble" ["Hablaba Izquierdo peor aún que pensaba, mezclando con su descoyunturada sintaxis términos de germanía y vocablos soeces. La filología popular baja no tenía secretos para él, y rebuznaba en todos los dialectos de la plebe ignorante"] (g. part I; 2:28). One of Izquierdo's pet phrases that was removed during the correction of the proofs, undoubtedly for being too direct an allusion to the *Pituso* business, was "I do not sell kids" ["yo no vendo criaturas"] (Ribbans, *Conflicts* 104).

14　Ribbans (*Conflicts* 219–20) believes that this chapter was intended to balance Fortunata's story, which was threatening to take over the whole narrative as the novel came to its close. Sobejano (222) is more inclined to see it as an expression of Galdós's growing interest in the unsuccessful lovers of his two heroines.

15　The sister's name is Barbarita, and in order to avoid confusion with Juanito's mother, Galdós calls the latter in this scene Barbarita I – on the

galleys (g. part IV; 1:85) Galdós added the Latin numeral in heavy ink –
and the former Barbarita II in the same way that he had distinguished at
the beginning of the novel the two generations of Santa Cruz patriarchs,
by calling them Baldomero I and Baldomero II. Of course, this generational numbering is asymmetrical and made even more so by Moreno's
erroneous custom of calling Baldomero II his godfather. The inference is
only too obvious: Moreno-Isla would have made a better son for the
Santa Cruzs and a better husband for Jacinta than Juanito.

16 Francisco Caudet (ed. *Fortunata y Jacinta* 2:363n53) believes that, in
these final words of Moreno, Galdós is being sarcastic, that he is attack-
ing the old Don Juan with pitiless scorn. This interpretation is difficult to
accept.

CHAPTER EIGHT

1 In one of the *Proverbios ejemplares* (1864) by Ventura Ruiz Aguilera that
Galdós reviewed in his "Observaciones" of 1870 – "Hasta los gatos
quieren zapatos" – the pretentious, ridiculous admirer of a married
woman is called Agapito, and when he slips on an apple in the street, the
merchants in the adjoining buildings make fun of his name " Señor D.
Agapito! ... pito! ... pito!... pitirrrriiiiito!" (159).

2 Mariano Baquero Goyanes (159–60) believes that Pito's picturesque language increases the ironic perspective of the account of his slave-trading
days; rather than a cruel slave-trader, Pito is an unconscious fool.

3 Evidence from the galleys suggest that, as in other novels, Galdós at times
either forgot to include this tic in the original manuscript or felt that its
inclusion for greater impact and immediate recognition by the reader was
easy enough to effect at this late stage of composition; for example: g.
part I; 2:95.

4 The bridegroom is the appropriately named Casiano. The idea of the
marriage had come from an area priest, called, again with appropriate
alliteration, Casado, a relative of this cousin.

5 Leonard J. Arrington and Davis Bitton (199) claim that between 1850
and 1890 – the period during which, at some time, Pito must have travelled through Utah on his way from New York to San Francisco – only
about five to twelve per cent of the state's population was involved in
polygamous marriages. This percentage is confirmed by another historian (O'Dea 246). It is ironic that, in the same year (1890) in which the
first two parts of *Ángel Guerra* appeared, the Mormon president, Wil-
frid Woodruff, presented a manifesto indicating a willingness to obey
the laws of the United States on this issue and that the vote in Utah in
support of the manifesto was practically unanimous (Arrington and
Bitton 203).

CHAPTER NINE

1 Galdós substituted the word "tipo"when correcting the galleys (*Nazarín,* ed. Arencibia, 150n725), as if to make it conform with Nazarín's application of the same word to himself when examining the appearance of Belmonte (III, 6).

2 Belmonte's international experience and interest in the foreign press links him to some extent to a sub-type Galdós had described for his Argentinian readers in a *La Prensa* series of type sketches he had penned two years earlier, between May and August 1893: the out-of-work diplomat, who is constantly updating himself on current political developments and taking notes from all he reads, including not only the foreign newspapers that Belmonte will read but all the official documents published by foreign diplomatic circles. He seems to possess the same urbane, modest character that, in his saner moments, Belmonte displays: "A person of simple customs, of irreproachable integrity, and exquisite urbanity, the unemployed diplomat lives off a modest leave salary" ["Persona de costumbres sencillas, de honradez intachable y de exquisita urbanidad, el cesante diplomático vive de un modesto sueldo de excedencia"] (*Obras inéditas* 1:266–7). But he exhibits all the registers of his insanity when he is teased and plagued with questions on international politics by fellow diners in restaurants, in much the same way that Belmonte will appear at his craziest during the dinner he puts on for Nazarín.

In *Torquemada in Purgatory* [*Torquemada en el purgatorio*] (1894), written the year before the publication of *Nazarín,* the narrator had expounded in a lengthy aside on the impossibility in contemporary Spain of deducing the professional identity of people just from their external, physical appearance and dress, as had been the norm in previous decades: arrogant-looking, bewhiskered men who strike one as the perfect military types turn out to be examining magistrates, piano teachers, or officials in the Ministry of Finance. Other types who appear elegant and have exquisite manners are, in fact, extortive moneylenders. A brawny young man who looks like a horsebreaker is, in reality, a pharmacist or a University law professor. Another type who looks like a regular member of a religious procession turns out to be a marinescape painter or a town councillor (I, 11). This is precisely the same conclusions that Galdós had expressed in *La desheredada* thirteen years previously, when discussing the lawyer type Muñoz y Nones (see pp. 80–1). And, as on that occasion, the tone of extreme exasperation in the voice of the narrator of the penultimate number in the Torquemada tetralogy sounds suspect. The very length of the list, as well as the wide disparity between the appearance (primarily physiognomic features rather than dress) and the reality of the profession, strike a comic

note that deflates the seriousness of the narrator's purpose, just as much
as the first reason he had given for this great social levelling of generic
types – people had become cleverer ["se va despabilando"] – took away
from his other, far more credible reasons: industrial progress and tariff
reductions. In fact, the sardonic, overfamiliar tone that pervades the
narrator's digression (which reaches its peak when considering the disappearance of the old pedant type established by the literature and arts
of the past), far from making his lament at the disappearance of these
traditional types sound convincing, succeeds, paradoxically, in justifying
what he says is the only solution to this modern problem: if you want
to know what people really are in life, as well as in literature, you have
to study them one by one, family by family. The mystifying external
appearance has to be the starting point for a much deeper penetration
of the type's character. The danger of relying exclusively on external
appearances in modern society is fully illustrated here in *Nazarín* in the
person and actions of Don Pedro de Belmonte.

Two years after the publication of *Nazarín* and three after the narrator's digression on types in *Torquemada en el purgatorio*, Galdós again
had reason to expatiate on the same topic in his 1897 acceptance address
to the Real Academia Española, "Present Society as Material for the
Novel" ["La sociedad presente como materia novelable"]. Generic types,
representing large blocks of humanity in contemporary society, were disappearing, a fact that was also reflected in art. The human face is at the
root of this change: faces are just not what they used to be; faces no
longer express, in an explicit Lavaterian correspondence, the character or
the profession of the person. The faces of types were usually masks
moulded by the conventionalism of repeated customs. Society is still the
first and last source of all literary work, but it no longer delivers this
material to the novelist in an already-made format: the generic type
(*Ensayos* 224). But this is all to the good of the novel – and this is where
Galdós the author differs from his somewhat depressed narrator of three
years previous – for, now stripped of the mask of typical appurtenances,
the human character reveals itself in its stark nakedness: this is the new
area for art to explore. In a memorable phrase, Galdós concludes: "We
have lost the types, but we can see the man more clearly" ["Perdemos los
tipos, pero el hombre se nos revela mejor"] (*Ensayos* 225).

3 In arguing that in this central episode Nazarín partially resembles Jean
   Jacques Rousseau and Belmonte Count Alexey Tolstoy, Franz (*Remaking
   Reality* 49–50) claims that both "men represent 'types' existing in all
   ages, and each type is capable of assuming greater (Rousseau and
   Tolstoy) or lesser (Nazarín and Belmonte) stature."

4 In his contemporary review of the novel, Hilarión Frías y Soto is quite
   sure that Ujo is no Romantic Caliban or Quasimodo; he is a type: "*Ujo*

es un ser vulgar, como hay algunos entre el pueblo, un tipo natural digno de ser retratado en una novela realista" (reprinted in Sinnigen and Vieyra Sánchez 160).

CHAPTER TEN

1. For Nimetz (42), Ponte's literary pedigree goes back almost four hundred years to the proud, impoverished, but stoical, squire in *La vida de Lazarillo de Tormes*. María del Mar Mañas Martínez (141–2) reckons that Ponte, like Paca and Obdulia, is too individualized to be a mere type, although she agrees with Nimetz that Ponte is, in outline, a reproduction of the eighteenth- and nineteenth-century "costumbrista" types, the fop and the dandy ["el petimetre," "el elegante"].

2 Both Varey ("Charity" 185) and Robert H. Russell (127) tend to dismiss the sincerity of this praise for Benina because it is couched in Don Frasquito's usual, mannered speech.

3 Theodore S. Beardsley (43) suggests that, in his relationship with Benina, Ponte, the faded roué, is pencilled in as a male equivalent of Mary Magdalene. In his review of the novel, Uruguayan writer José Enrique Rodó refers to Ponte as a most curious example of a tragicomic, exhausted old "lion" (877).

CONCLUSION

1 It is pertinent to note that in the same passage of his autobiography, Galdós did not claim historical truth for some of the events in *Fortunata y Jacinta* with the same eagerness. Indeed, he preferred to emphasize their fictional nature: the honeymoon of Juanito and Jacinta Santa Cruz and the "*Pituso* novel" are imaginary, though they seem real (6:1679).

2 In a 1910 interview with the journalist El Bachiller Corchuelo [Enrique González-Fiol], Galdós claimed that with his translation of *The Pickwick Papers*, he was the first person to introduce Dickens to the Spanish (47). Some years before (25 March 1894), he had revealed to the Argentinian readers of his *La Prensa* articles the identity of the mentor in Madrid who had steered him towards reading Dickens in the 1860s: it was the critic and poet Federico Balart, whose contagious enthusiasm for the English novelist had encouraged Galdós to translate *The Pickwick Papers*. For Galdós almost thirty years later, Dickens is still primarily a creator of comic characters (*Las cartas* 521). His debt to Dickens was emphasized by Menéndez y Pelayo (67) in his official reply to Galdós's acceptance speech to the Spanish Royal Academy in 1897; he also drew attention to the common interest of both novelists in the creation of mad characters, but without referring to the allied category of eccentrics.

3 This is not to say that Galdós limits eccentricity or madness to these secondary old males. Quite the contrary: characters of both sexes, of all
   ages, and with different functions, share these mental weaknesses.

4 For Leota W. Elliott and F.M. Kercheville (27), Galdós's eccentric characters, whom they call mildly peculiar or borderline cases, are distinguish-
   able from the psychotic or psycho-neurotic because, unlike the latter, they
   exhibit no breakdown of personality nor definite disease symptoms, even
   though there is a lack of mental balance. On the other hand, Benítez
   (*Cervantes* 119–20) positions the extreme eccentrics like Ido in an intermediate group between the polar extremes of normal people with an
   occasionally dangerous imagination and the true madmen, who are readily identified as such by their physical characteristics, dress, and behaviour. These intermediate characters are the most memorable, because
   their presentation combines sympathy with humour. Elliott and
   Kercheville's classification has more affinity with mine than Benítez's
   does.

Works Cited

Alas, Leopoldo "Clarín." "Crónica literaria." *Artes y Letras* (1 April 1883): 59.

- *Ensayos y revistas*. Madrid: Fernández y Lasanta, 1892.
- *Galdós, novelista*. Ed. Adolfo Sotelo Vázquez. Barcelona: PPU, 1991.
- *Solos de Clarín*. 4th ed. Madrid: Librería de Fernando Fe, 1891.

Albaigés Olivart, José M. *Diccionario de nombres de personas*. Barcelona: Edicions Universitat de Barcelona, 1984.

Alcalá Galiano, José. *Estereoscopio social*. Madrid: Imprenta de José Noguera, 1872.

Alhama Montes, M. "Una casa de locos." *Los Lunes del Imparcial* (29 August 1879). Reprinted in Robin, 91–6.

Anderson, Farris. "Madrid, los balcones y la historia: Mesonero Romanos y Pérez Galdós." *Cuadernos Hispanoamericanos* 464 (1989): 63–75.

Anonymous. "El semblante de Napoleón." *Semanario Pintoresco Español* 9 (19 May 1836): 78–80.

- *La vida de Lazarillo de Tormes*. Ed. R.O. Jones. Manchester: Manchester University Press, 1963.

Armangué y Tuset, José. *Estudios clínicos de neuropatología*. Barcelona: Ramírez, 1884.

- *Mimicismo o neurosis imitante*. Barcelona: Sucesores de Ramírez y Cía, 1884.

Arrington, Leonard J. and Davis Bitton. *The Mormon Experience. A History of the Latter-Day Saints*. 2nd ed. Urbana: University of Illinois Press, 1992.

Austin, Karen. "Don Anselmo and the Author's Role." *Anales Galdosianos* 18 (1983): 39–47.
– "Madness and Madmen in Galdós' Early Fiction and in *La desheredada*." *Galdós' House of Fiction*. Eds. A.H. Clarke and E.J. Rodgers. Llangrannog: Dolphin, 1991. 29–40.
Ayala, María de los Ángeles. "Galdós y Mesonero Romanos." *Galdós. Centenario de 'Fortunata y Jacinta' (1887–1987). Actas (Congreso Internacional, 23–28 de noviembre)*. Ed. Julián Ávila Arellano. Madrid: Universidad Complutense de Madrid, 1989. 121–7.
Bachiller Corchuelo, El. [González-Fiol, Enrique]. "Nuestros grandes prestigios. Benito Pérez Galdós (Confesiones de su vida y de su obra)." *Por Esos Mundos* 11.185 (June 1910): 790–807; 11.186 (July 1910): 26–56.
Balzac, Honoré de. "Avant-propos." *La Comédie humaine*. 19 vols. Paris: Furne, Durochet, Hetzel and Paulin, 1842. 1:7–32.
– *Lettres à Madame Hanska. 1832–1844*. Ed. Roger Pierrot. 2 vols. Paris: Robert Laffont, 1990. Vol. 1.
Baquero Goyanes, Mariano. "Perspectivismo irónico en Galdós." *Cuadernos Hispanoamericanos* 250–2 (1970–71): 143–60.
Barbieri, Marie E. "Más 'Observaciones sobre la novela': tres reseñas de Galdós dedicadas a obras de Pereda." *Anales Galdosianos* 31–2 (1996–97): 105–16.
Barr, Lois Baer. "Social Decay and Disintegration in *Misericordia*." *Anales Galdosianos* 17 (1982): 97–104.
Barthes, Roland. "Introduction to the Structural Analysis of Narratives." *Image-Music-Text*. Tr. Stephen Heath. London: Flamingo, 1984. 79–124.
Beardsley, Theodore S. Jr. "The Life and Passion of Christ in Galdós' *Misericordia*." *Homenaje a Sherman H. Eoff*. Madrid: Castalia, 1970. 39–58.
Benítez, Rubén. *Cervantes en Galdós*. Murcia: Universidad de Murcia, 1990.
– "Génesis del cervantismo de Galdós (1865–1876)." *A Sesquicentennial Tribute to Galdós 1843–1993*. Ed. Linda M. Willem. Newark, Delaware: Juan de la Cuesta, 1993. 344–60.
– *La literatura española en las obras de Galdós (función y sentido de la intertextualidad)*. Murcia: Universidad de Murcia, 1992.
Bergson, Henri. "Laughter." *Comedy*. Intr. Wylie Sypher. Baltimore: Johns Hopkins University, 1956. 61–190.
Bly, Peter A. "Fortunata and No. 11, Cava de San Miguel." *Hispanófila* 59 (1976–77): 31–48.
– *Galdós's Novel of the Historical Imagination*. Liverpool: Francis Cairns, 1983.
–*Pérez Galdós: Nazarín*. London: Grant and Cutler, 1991.
–*Vision and the Visual Arts in Galdós. A Study of the Novels and Newspaper Articles*. Liverpool: Francis Cairns, 1986.

Bonet, Laureano. "Introducción: Galdós, crítico literario." In Pérez Galdós, *Ensayos*, 7–101.

Bosch, Rafael. "*La sombra* y la psicopatología de Galdós." *Anales Galdosianos* 6 (1971): 21–42.

Brooke-Rose, Christine. "Dissolution of Character in the Novel." *Reconstructing Individualism. Autonomy, Individuality, and the Self in Western Thought.* Eds Thomas C. Heller, Morton Sosna, and David E. Wellbery. Stanford: Stanford University Press, 1986. 184–96.

Buard, Marie-France. "Les rapports ville-campagne dans *Doña Perfecta* de Pérez Galdós." *Hommage à Louise Bertrand (1921–79). Études ibériques et latino-américaines.* Paris: Les Belles Lettres, 1983. 65–85.

Cardona, Rodolfo. *Galdós ante la literatura y la historia.* Las Palmas: Ediciones del Cabildo Insular de Gran Canaria, 1998.

– "Introducción." In Pérez Galdós, *Doña Perfecta*, 11–55.

– "Introduction." In Pérez Galdós, *La sombra,* ix–xxiv.

Cardwell, Richard A. "Galdós' *Doña Perfecta*: Art or Argument?" *Anales Galdosianos* 7 (1972): 29–47.

Caro Baroja, Julio. *Historia de la Fisiognómica. El rostro y el carácter.* Madrid: Istmo, 1988.

Casalduero, Joaquín. "*La sombra.*" *Anales Galdosianos* 1 (1966): 33–8.

Caudet, Francisco. "*El doctor Centeno*: La 'educación sentimental' de Galdós." *Studies in Honor of Bruce W. Wardropper.* Eds Dian Fox et al. Newark, Delaware: Juan de la Cuesta, 1989. 41–66.

– "José Izquierdo y el 'cuarto estado.'" *Actas del tercer congreso internacional de estudios galdosianos.* 2 vols. Las Palmas: Ediciones del Excmo Cabildo Insular de Gran Canaria, 1990. 2:25–9.

Cervantes Saavedra, Miguel de. *El coloquio de los perros.* In *Obras completas.* 997–1026.

– *Don Quijote de la Mancha.* In *Obras completas.* 1027–524.

– *Obras completas.* Ed. Ángel Valbuena Prat. 15th ed. Madrid: Aguilar, 1967.

Chamberlin, Vernon A. "Blasco Ibáñez's Mistaken Evaluation of *Misericordia.*" *Romance Quarterly* 37 (1990): 209–15.

– *Galdós and Beethoven. 'Fortunata y Jacinta': A Symphonic Novel.* London: Tamesis, 1977.

– "New Insights Regarding the Creation and Character Delineation of Maxi Rubín and Plácido Estupiñá in *Fortunata y Jacinta.*" *Anales Galdosianos* 36 (2001): 99–110.

Charnon-Deutsch, Lou. "The Pygmalion Effect in the Fiction of Pérez Galdós." *A Sesquicentennial Tribute to Galdós 1843–1993.* Ed. Linda M. Willem. Newark, Delaware: Juan de la Cuesta, 1993. 173–89.

Chatman, Seymour. *Story and Discourse. Narrative Structure in Fiction and Film.* Ithaca: Cornell University Press, 1978.

Chesterton, G.K. *Charles Dickens. A Critical Study*. New York: Dodd, Mead and Co., 1911.

Cixous, Hélène. "The Character of 'Character.'" *New Literary History* 5 (1974): 383–402.

Clarke, Anthony H. "*Ándara*, Ujo and a Handful of 'amazonas,' 'peludos' and Outcasts: A Footnote to *Nazarín*." *Anales Galdosianos* 26 (1991): 83–8.

Correa Calderón, E., ed. *Costumbristas españoles*. 2 vols. Madrid: Aguilar, 1951.

Cossío, Manuel B. "Galdós y Giner: una carta de Galdós." *La Lectura* 20 (1920): 254–8.

Culler, Jonathan. *Structuralist Poetics. Structuralism, Linguistics and the Study of Literature*. London: Routledge and Kegan Paul, 1975.

da Cal, Margarita Ucelay. *Los españoles pintados por sí mismos (1843–1844). Estudio de un género costumbrista*. Mexico, D.F.: El Colegio de México, 1951.

Darwin, Charles. *The Expression of the Emotions in Man and Animals*. Chicago: University of Chicago Press, 1965.

Davis, Earle R. "Dickens and the Evolution of Caricature." *Publications of the Modern Language Association of America* 55 (1940): 231–40.

de la Cortina, Francisco. "El viejo verde." In *Los españoles de ogaño*, 2:371–6.

de la Nuez, Sebastián. *Biblioteca y archivo de la Casa Museo Pérez Galdós*. Las Palmas: Ediciones del Cabildo Insular de Gran Canaria, 1990.

Demetz, Peter. "Balzac and the Zoologists: A Concept of the Type." *The Disciplines of Criticism: Essays in Literary Theory, Interpretation, and History*. Eds Peter Demetz, Thomas Greene, and Lowry Nelson, Jr. New Haven: Yale University Press, 1968. 397–418.

Dickens, Charles. *Little Dorrit*. Eds Stephen Wall and Helen Small. New York: Penguin, 1998.

– *The Personal History of David Copperfield*. Ed. Trevor Blount. Harmondsworth: Penguin, 1966.

– *The Pickwick Papers*. New York: Bantam Classics, 1983.

"Diógenes." "Carta que nos ha remitido el viejo verde." In Correa Calderón. 1:632–3.

Docherty, Thomas. *Reading (Absent) Character*. Oxford: Clarendon Press, 1983.

Doctor Fausto, El. See Tolosa Latour, Manuel.

Dutch, Robert A., ed. *Roget's Thesaurus of English Words and Phrases*. Harmondsworth: Penguin, 1966.

Elliott, Leota W. and F.M. Kercheville. "Galdós and Abnormal Psychology." *Hispania* 23 (1940): 27–36.

Engler, Kay. *The Structure of Realism: The 'Novelas Contemporáneas' of Benito Pérez Galdós*. Chapel Hill: University of North Carolina, Department of Romance Languages, 1977.

Entenza de Solare, Beatriz. "Manuscritos galdosianos." *Actas del tercer congreso internacional de estudios galdosianos.* 2 vols. Las Palmas: Ediciones del Excmo Cabildo Insular de Gran Canaria, 1990. 1:149–61.

Eoff, Sherman H. *The Novels of Pérez Galdós. The Concept of Life as Dynamic Process.* Saint Louis: Washington University, 1954.

Erickson, Effie L. "The Influence of Charles Dickens on the Novels of Benito Pérez Galdós." *Hispania* 19 (1936): 421–30.

Escuder, José María. *Locos y anómalos.* Madrid: Sucesores de Rivadeneyra, 1895.

Las españolas pintadas por los españoles. Ed Roberto Robert. Madrid: Imprenta de J.M. Morete, 1871–72.

Los españoles de ogaño. 2 vols. Madrid: Victoriano Suárez, 1872.

Los españoles pintados por sí mismos. 2 vols. 1843. Madrid: Dossat, 1992.

Espinosa Iborra, Julián. *La asistencia psiquiátrica en la España del siglo XIX.* Valencia: 1966.

Esquirol, J.E.D. *Mental Maladies. A Treatise on Insanity.* New York: Hafner, 1965.

Fichter, William L., ed. *Publicaciones periodísticas de don Ramón del Valle-Inclán anteriores a 1895.* Mexico: El Colegio de Mexico, 1952.

Flores, Antonio. *Ayer, hoy y mañana, o la fe, el vapor y la electricidad. Cuadros sociales de 1800, 1850 y 1899.* Part III: *Mañana, o la chispa eléctrica en 1899.* Madrid: Imprenta del Establecimiento de Mellado, 1864.

Fokkema, Aleid. *Postmodern Characters. A Study of Characterization in British and American Postmodern Fiction.* Amsterdam: Rodopi, 1991.

Fontanella, Lee. "*Doña Perfecta* as Historiographic Lesson." *Anales Galdosianos* 11 (1976): 59–69.

Forster, E.M. *Aspects of the Novel.* Ed. Oliver Stallybrass. Harmondsworth: Penguin, 1963.

Fowler, Roger, ed. *A Dictionary of Modern Critical Terms.* London: Routledge and Kegan Paul, 1973.

Franz, Thomas R. "*Doña Perfecta* and *Il Barbiere di Siviglia.*" *Anales Galdosianos* 21 (1986): 127–33.

– *Remaking Reality in Galdós. A Writer's Interactions with His Context.* Athens, Ohio: Strathmore Press, 1982.

Fuentes Peris, Teresa. "Drink and Degeneration: The 'Deserving' and the 'Undeserving' Poor in Galdós's *Ángel Guerra.*" *Romance Studies* 29 (1997): 7–20.

Galef, David. *The Supporting Cast. A Study of Flat and Minor Characters.* University Park: Pennsylvania State University Press, 1993.

García Martínez, Isabel. "Galdós y M. Ortega y Gasset: traductores y resucitadores de *The Posthumous Papers of the Pickwick Club.*" *Livius* 2 (1992): 221–31.

Gilman, Stephen. *Galdós and the Art of the European Novel: 1867–1887*. Princeton: Princeton University Press, 1981.
- "La palabra hablada y *Fortunata y Jacinta*." *Nueva Revista de Filología Hispánica* 15 (1961): 542–60.
Giner de los Ríos, Francisco. "Sobre *La familia de León Roch*." *Ensayos*. Ed. Juan López-Morillas. Madrid: Alianza, 1969. 64–77.
Goldman, Peter B., Paul J. Hoff, and Neil A. Rice. "Being, Doing, and Representing: Secondary Characters and Third-Rate Fictions in *Fortunata y Jacinta*." *Crítica Hispánica* 13 (1991): 87–97.
Gómez-Feria Prieto, Ildefonso. "Un trastorno delirante celotípico en una novela de Pérez Galdós." *Informaciones Psiquiátricas* 144 (1996): 193–7.
Gordon, M. "'Lo que le falta a un enfermo le sobra a otro': Galdós' Conception of Humanity in *La desheredada*." *Anales Galdosianos* 12 (1977): 29–37.
- "The Medical Background to Galdós' *La desheredada*." *Anales Galdosianos* 7 (1972): 67–77.
Gullón, Germán. "La obra como texto vivo: *Doña Perfecta*, de la novela (1876) al drama (1896)." *Anales Galdosianos* 36 (2001): 155–66.
- "Originalidad y sentido de *La desheredada*." *Anales Galdosianos* 17 (1982): 39–50.
- "'Sustituyendo el azogue del espejo': la novelización de la ideología decimonónica en *Doña Perfecta*." *Galdós y la historia*. Ed. Peter A. Bly. Ottawa: Dovehouse, 1988. 131–44.
Gullón, Ricardo. "*Doña Perfecta*, invención y mito." *Cuadernos Hispanoamericanos* 250–2 (1970–71): 393–414.
Hafter, Monroe Z. "'Bálsamo contra bálsamo' in *Ángel Guerra*." *Anales Galdosianos* 4 (1969): 39–48.
- "Galdós' Presentation of Isidora in *La desheredada*." *Modern Philology* 60 (1962–63): 22–30.
Hall, J.B. "Galdós's Use of the Christ-Symbol in *Doña Perfecta*." *Anales Galdosianos* 8 (1973): 95–8.
Harvey, W.J. *Character and the Novel*. London: Chatto and Windus, 1965.
Hoar, Leo J., Jr. *Benito Pérez Galdós y la Revista del Movimiento Intelectual de Europa (Madrid, 1865–1867)*. Madrid: Ínsula, 1968.
Hoddie, James H. "The Genesis of *La desheredada*: Beethoven, the Picaresque and Plato." *Anales Galdosianos* 14 (1979): 27–50.
- "Reexamen de un enigmático texto galdosiano: *El doctor Centeno*." *Cuadernos Hispanoamericanos* 521 (1993): 47–67.
Jaccoud, Sigismond. *Tratado de patología interna*. Madrid: 1885.
James, Henry. *The Portrait of a Lady*. Boston: Houghton Mifflin, 2001.
- *Theory of Fiction*. Ed. James E. Miller Jr. Lincoln: University of Nebraska Press, 1972.

Jones, C.A. "Galdós's Second Thoughts on *Doña Perfecta*." *Modern Language Review* 54 (1959): 570–3.

José Prades, Juana de. "Los libros de Dickens en España." *El Libro Español* (October 1958): 515–24.

Kirsner, Robert. *Veinte años de matrimonio en la novela de Galdós*. Eastchester: Eliseo Torres, 1983.

Kronik, John W. "Galdós and the Grotesque." *Anales Galdosianos Anejo* (1978): 39–54.

Krow-Lucal, Martha G. "The Meaning of Theater in *La desheredada*." *Revista de Estudios Hispánicos* (Puerto Rico) 9 (1982): 151–6.

Labanyi, Jo. *Gender and Modernization in the Spanish Realist Novel*. Oxford: Oxford University Press, 2000.

– "Introduction." In Pérez Galdós, *Nazarín*, vii–xxiv.

Lakhdari, Sadi. *'Ángel Guerra,' de Benito Pérez Galdós. Une étude psychoanalytique*. Paris: L'Harmattan, 1996.

Lerner, Isaías. "Para una nueva lectura de *Doña Perfecta* de Galdós." *Lexis* 1 (1977): 211–27.

Liébault, Ambroise-Auguste. *Du sommeil*. Paris: 1866.

López, Ignacio-Javier. *Caballero de novela. Ensayo sobre el donjuanismo en la novela española moderna, 1880–1930*. Barcelona: Puvill, 1986.

– *Galdós y el arte de la prosa*. Barcelona: PPU, 1993.

– "Génesis, texto y contexto del galán galdosiano: Joaquín Pez en *La desheredada*." *Cuadernos Hispanoamericanos* 427 (1986): 111–21.

– "El poder de Pigmalión: Galdós y la creación del personaje." *Ínsula* 561 (September 1993): 9–11.

López-Baralt, Mercedes. *La gestación de 'Fortunata y Jacinta'. Galdós y la novela como re-escritura*. Río Piedras, Puerto Rico: Huracán, 1992.

Lukacs, George. *Ensayos sobre el realismo*. Buenos Aires: Ediciones Siglo Veinte, 1965.

– "The Intellectual Physiognomy of Literary Characters." *International Literature* 8 (1936): 55–83.

Mañas Martínez, María del Mar. "Obdulia Zapata y Frasquito Ponte: algo más acerca de 'el romanticismo y los románticos." *Actas del cuarto congreso internacional de estudios galdosianos (1990)*. Las Palmas: Ediciones del Cabildo Insular de Gran Canaria, 1993. 2:135–56.

Martin, Wallace. *Recent Theories of Narrative*. Ithaca: Cornell University Press, 1986.

Mata Fontanet, Pedro. *Filosofía española. Tratado de la razón humana en sus estados intermedios*. Madrid: Carlos Bailly-Bailliere, 1864.

Maudsley, Henry. *Natural Causes and Supernatural Seemings*. London: Kegan Paul, Trench and Co., 1886.

– *The Physiology and Pathology of the Mind*. London: Macmillan, 1867.

- *Responsabilidad del hombre en las enfermedades mentales.* Tr. Antonio A. Ramírez F. Fontecha. Madrid: M. Minuesa de los Ríos, 1881.
- *Responsibility in Mental Disease.* 2nd ed. London: Henry S. King, 1874.
Mazzara, Richard A. "Some Fresh *Perspectivas* on Galdós' *Doña Perfecta.*" *Hispania* 40 (1957): 49–56.
McCarthy, Mary. "Characters in Fiction." *On the Contrary.* New York: Farrar, Straus and Cudahy, 1961. 271–92.
McGovern, Timothy Michael. *Dickens in Galdós.* New York: Peter Lang, 2000.
McKnight, Natalie. *Idiots, Madmen, and Other Prisoners in Dickens.* New York: St Martin's Press, 1993.
Menéndez y Pelayo, Pereda, Pérez Galdós. *Discursos leídos ante la Real Academia Española en las recepciones públicas del 7 y 21 de febrero de 1897.* Madrid: Viuda o hijos de Tello, 1897.
Mesonero Romanos, Ramón de. *El antiguo Madrid.* Madrid: Establecimiento Tipográfico de Don. F. de P. Mellado, 1861.
- *Escenas matritenses.* Ed. Federico Carlos Sainz de Robles. Madrid: Aguilar, 1956.
- *Memorias de un setentón, natural y vecino de Madrid.* Madrid: Ilustración Española y Americana, 1881.
Miralles, Enrique. "Introducción." In Pérez Galdós, *La desheredada*, ix–lxxxi.
Montero-Paulson, Daría J. *La jerarquía femenina en la obra de Galdós.* Madrid: Pliegos, 1988.
Montesinos, José F. *Costumbrismo y novela.* 2nd ed. Madrid: Castalia, 1965.
- *Galdós.* 3 vols. Madrid: Castalia, 1968–72.
Moreno Castillo, Gloria. "La unidad de tema en *El doctor Centeno.*" *Actas del primer congreso internacional de estudios galdosianos.* Las Palmas: Ediciones del Excmo Cabildo Insular de Gran Canaria, 1977. 382–96.
Muir, Edwin. *The Structure of the Novel.* 5th ed. London: The Hogarth Press, 1949.
Nimetz, Michael. *Humor in Galdós: A Study of the 'Novelas contemporáneas.'* New Haven: Yale University Press, 1968.
O'Byrne Curtis, Margarita Rosa. *La razón de la sinrazón: la configuración de la locura en la narrativa de Benito Pérez Galdós.* Las Palmas: Ediciones del Cabildo Insular de Gran Canaria, 1996.
O'Dea, Thomas F. *The Mormons.* Chicago: University of Chicago Press, 1957.
Oliver, Walter. "Galdós' 'La novela en el tranvía': Fantasy and the Art of Realistic Narration." *Modern Language Notes* 88 (1973): 249–63.
Onions, C.T., ed. *The Oxford Universal Dictionary on Historical Principles.* 3rd ed. Oxford: Clarendon Press, 1955.
Ortega Munilla, José. "Madrid." *Los Lunes de El Imparcial* (30 July 1883): 1–2.

Ortiz Armengol, Pedro. *Apuntaciones para 'Fortunata y Jacinta.'* Madrid: Universidad Complutense, 1987.

– *Vida de Galdós.* Barcelona: Grijalbo Mondadori, 1995.

Páez Martín, Jesús. "Métodos de caracterización de personajes en *La desheredada.*" *Actas del cuarto congreso internacional de estudios galdosianos (1990).* Las Palmas: Ediciones del Cabildo Insular de Gran Canaria, 1993. 1:441–56.

Palomo Vázquez, María del Pilar. "Galdós y Mesonero (una vez más: costumbrismo y novela)." *Galdós. Centenario de 'Fortunata y Jacinta' (1887–1987). Actas (Congreso Internacional, 23–28 de noviembre).* Ed. Julián Ávila Arellano. Madrid: Universidad Complutense de Madrid, 1989. 217–38.

Pardo Bazán, Emilia. "*Ángel Guerra.*" *Nuevo Teatro Crítico* 1.8 (1891): 19–63.

Pattison, Walter T. *Benito Pérez Galdós: etapas preliminares de 'Gloria.'* Madrid: Puvill, 1979.

– "How Well Did Galdós Know English?" *Symposium* 24 (1970): 148–57.

– "The Manuscript of *Gloria.*" *Anales Galdosianos* 4 (1969): 55–61.

Penuel, Arnold M. "Narcissism in Galdós' *Doña Perfecta.*" *Hispania* 62 (1979): 282–8.

Peñate Rivero, Julio. "Sobre el *Manicomio político-social* galdosiano y el sentido de sus cuatro variantes, a partir de *El espiritista.*" *Sociedad de Literatura Española del Siglo XIX. Actas del 1 coloquio. 'Del Romanticismo al Realismo' (Barcelona, 24–26 de octubre de 1996).* Eds Luis F. Díaz Larios and Enrique Miralles. Barcelona: Publicacions de la Universitat de Barcelona, 1998. 515–27.

Pereda, José María de. *Tipos y paisajes.* 4th ed. *Obras completas.* 17 vols. Madrid: Imp. y Enc. de Jaime Ratés Martín, 1920. Vol. 6.

Perés, Ramón D. "*Ángel Guerra.*" Reprinted in Marisa Sotelo Vázquez, *ANGEL GUERRA de Benito Pérez Galdós y sus críticos (1891).* Barcelona: PPU, 1990. 101–14.

Pérez, Francisco. "Dos novelistas galdosianos." *Crítica Hispánica* 3 (1981): 165–71.

Pérez Galdós, Benito. *Ángel Guerra.* In *Obras completas,* 5:1195–537.

– *Los apostólicos.* In *Obras completas,* 2:107–216.

– "Aquél." In Correa Calderón, 2:535–9.

– *Los artículos de Galdós en La Nación (1865–1866, 1868).* Ed. William H. Shoemaker. Madrid : Ínsula, 1972.

– Tr. Charles Dickens. *Aventuras de Pickwick.* Ed. Arturo Ramoneda. 2 vols. Madrid: Júcar, 1989.

– *Cádiz.* In *Obras completas,* 1:843–957.

– *Las cartas desconocidas de Galdós en 'La Prensa' de Buenos Aires.* Ed. William H. Shoemaker. Madrid: Cultura Hispánica, 1973.

– *Compassion*. Tr. Tony Talbot. New York: Frederick Ungar, 1962.
– "Cuarenta leguas por Cantabria." In *Obras completas*, 6:1443–57.
– "Cuatro mujeres." In Correa Calderón, 2:355–60.
– *Cuentos fantásticos*. Ed. Alan E. Smith. Madrid: Cátedra, 1996.
– *La de Bringas*. Eds Alda Blanco and Carlos Blanco Aguinaga. Madrid: Cátedra, 1983.
– *La desheredada*. 2 vols. Madrid: Biblioteca Nacional. MS 21783.
– *La desheredada*. Ed. Enrique Miralles. Barcelona: Planeta, 1992.
– *La desheredada*. In *Obras completas*, 4:983–1181.
– *The Disinherited*. Tr. Lester Clark. London: The Folio Society, 1976.
– *El doctor Centeno*. 2 vols. Madrid: Biblioteca Nacional. MS 22227.
– *El doctor Centeno*. In *Obras completas*, 4:1311–468.
– *Doña Perfecta*. Madrid: Biblioteca Nacional. MS 14416.
– *Doña Perfecta*. Ed. Rodolfo Cardona. Madrid: Cátedra, 1984.
– *Doña Perfecta*. Tr. Alexander R. Tulloch. London: Phoenix House, 1999.
– *Ensayos de crítica literaria*. Ed. Laureano Bonet. 2nd ed., rev. and ampl. Barcelona: Península, 1999.
– *La familia de León Roch*. In *Obras completas*, 4:779–980.
– *Fisonomías sociales*. In *Obras inéditas*, Vol. 1.
– *Fortunata y Jacinta*. Cambridge: Harvard University. MS SPAN 93.
– *Fortunata y Jacinta. Dos historias de casadas*. Ed. Francisco Caudet. Madrid: Cátedra, 1983.
– *Fortunata and Jacinta. Two Stories of Married Women*. Tr. Agnes Moncy Gullón. Athens: The University of Georgia Press, 1986.
– *Gloria*. In *Obras completas*, 4:513–699.
– *Gloria. A Novel by B. Pérez Galdós*. Tr. Clara Bell. 1882. New York: Howard Fertig, 1974.
– *Memorias de un desmemoriado*. In *Obras completas*, 6:1671–714.
– *Misericordia*. Eds Luciano García Lorenzo and Carmen Menéndez Onrubia. Madrid: Cátedra, 1982.
– "La mujer del filósofo." In Correa Calderón, 2:322–8.
– *Nazarín*. Ed. Yolanda Arencibia. Las Palmas: Ediciones del Cabildo Insular de Gran Canaria, 1995.
– *Nazarín*. Ed. and tr. Jo Labanyi. Oxford: Oxford University Press, 1993.
– "La novela en el tranvía." In *Cuentos fantásticos*, 71–104.
– *Obras completas*. Ed. Federico Carlos Sainz de Robles. 6 vols. Madrid: Aguilar, 1963–69. [Editions used: vol. 1: 11th ed., 1968; vol. 2: 10th ed., 1968; vol. 4: 7th ed., 1969; vol. 5: 3rd ed., 1961; vol. 6: 5th ed., 1968.]
– *Obras inéditas*. Ed. Alberto Ghiraldo. 11 vols. Madrid: Renacimiento, 1923–31.
– "Prefacio del autor." *Misericordia*. Paris: Thomas Nelson and Sons, 1913.
– *Lo prohibido*. Ed. James Whiston. Las Palmas: Ediciones del Cabildo Insular de Gran Canaria, 1998.

– *Los prólogos de Galdós.* Ed. William H. Shoemaker. Mexico: Andrea, 1962.
– *Rosalía.* Ed. Alan E. Smith. Madrid: Cátedra, 1983.
– *The Shadow.* Tr. Karen O. Austin. Athens: Ohio University Press, 1980.
– *La sombra.* Ed. Rodolfo Cardona. New York: Norton, 1964.
– *El terror de 1824.* In *Obras completas,* 1:1719–818.
– *That Bringas Woman.* Tr. Catherine Jagoe. London: J.M. Dent, 1996.
– *Tormento.* Madrid: Biblioteca Nacional. MS 21298.
– *Tormento.* In *Obras completas,* 4:1469–584.
– *Torquemada en el purgatorio.* In *Obras completas,* 5:1018–111.
– *A Translation of Ángel Guerra by Benito Pérez Galdós.* Tr. Karen O. Austin. New York: Edwin Mellen Press, 1990.
– "Un tribunal literario." In *Ensayos,* 140–67.
Phelan, James. "Character, Progression, and the Mimetic-Didactic Distinction." *Modern Philology* 84 (1987): 282–99.
Price, Martin. *Forms of Life. Character and Moral Imagination in the Novel.* New Haven: Yale University Press, 1983.
Priestley, J.B. "The Two Wellers." *The English Comic Characters.* New York: E.P. Dutton, 1966. 198–223.
Ràfols, Wifredo de. "From Institution to Prostitution: Bureaumania and the Homeless Heroine in *La desheredada.*" *Anales Galdosianos* 37 (2002): 69–87.
– "The House of Doña Perfecta." *Anales Galdosianos* 34 (1999): 41–60.
– "Lies, Irony, Satire, and the Parody of Ideology in *Doña Perfecta.*" *Hispanic Review* 64 (1996): 467–89.
Ramón y Vega, Antonio. *Compendio de práctica médico-forense.* Madrid: Tip. Manuel G. Hernández, 1888.
Ramoneda, Arturo. "Introducción." In Pérez Galdós, tr, *Aventuras de Pickwick,* 1:5–23.
Randolph, E. Dale A. "A Source for Maxi Rubín in *Fortunata y Jacinta.*" *Hispania* 51 (1968): 49–56.
Real Academia Española. *Diccionario de la lengua española.* 19th ed. Madrid: 1970.
Ribbans, Geoffrey. "Unas apostillas más a Rufete y Canencia." *Anales Galdosianos* 29–30 (1994–95): 101–3.
– *Conflicts and Conciliations. The Evolution of Galdós's 'Fortunata y Jacinta.'* West Lafayette, Indiana: Purdue University Press, 1997.
– "*La desheredada,* novela por entregas: apuntes sobre su primera publicación." *Anales Galdosianos* 27–8 (1992–93): 69–75.
– "*Doña Perfecta*: Yet Another Ending." *Modern Language Notes* 105 (1990): 203–25.
– *History and Fiction in Galdós's Narratives.* Oxford: Clarendon Press, 1993.
– "The Making of a Minor Character: Galdós's Plácido Estupiñá." *Symposium* 46 (1992): 147–57.

– "Woman as Scapegoat: The Case of Dulcenombre Babel in Galdós' *Ángel Guerra*." *Bulletin of Hispanic Studies* (Glasgow) 76 (1999): 487–97.

Ricard, Robert. "Place et Signification de *Tormento* entre *El doctor Centeno* et *La de Bringas*." *Aspects de Galdós*. Paris: Presses Universitaires de France, 1963. 44–60.

Rimmon-Kenan, Shlomith. *Narrative Fiction: Contemporary Poetics*. London: Methuen, 1983.

Robin, Claire-Nicolle. *Le Naturalisme dans 'La desheredada' de Pérez Galdós*. Paris: Les Belles Lettres, 1976.

Rodgers, Eamonn. "The Appearance-Reality Contrast in Galdós' *Tormento*." *Forum for Modern Language Studies* 6 (1970): 382–98.

– *From Enlightenment to Realism. The Novels of Galdós 1870–1887*. Dublin, 1987.

Rodó, José Enrique. "Una novela de Galdós." *Obras completas*. Ed. Emir Rodríguez Monegal. Madrid: Aguilar, 1967. 874–9.

Rodríguez, Alfred. *Aspectos de la novela de Galdós*. Almería: Artes Gráficas, 1967.

– "El 'Don Simplísimo' de Galdós: variaciones sobre una fijación tipológica." In *Aspectos*, 110–27.

– *Estudios sobre la novela de Galdós*. Madrid: José Porrúa Turanzas, 1978.

– "Génesis de un personaje de *Doña Perfecta*." In *Estudios*, 13–26.

Rodríguez, Alfred, and Thomas Carstens. "Tomás Rufete y Canencia: los dos ancianos locos que introducen las *Novelas contemporáneas*." *Anales Galdosianos* 26 (1991): 13–17.

Rodríguez, Alfred, and Luz María Rodríguez. "*Lo prohibido,* ¿una parodia galdosiana?" *Bulletin of Hispanic Studies* (Liverpool) 60 (1983): 51–9.

Rogers, Philip. "Mr Pickwick's Innocence." *Nineteenth Century Fiction* 27 (1972): 21–37.

Romero Tobar, Leonardo. "*La desheredada* en la novela." *Actas del tercer congreso internacional de estudios galdosianos.* 2 vols. Las Palmas: Ediciones del Excmo Cabildo Insular de Gran Canaria, 1990. 2:197–205.

– *La novela popular española del siglo XIX*. Madrid: Castalia, 1977.

Rosenberg, Brian. *Little Dorrit's Shadows. Character and Contradiction in Dickens*. Columbia: University of Missouri Press, 1996.

Round, Nicholas G. "The Fictional Plenitude of *Ángel Guerra*." *Galdós' House of Fiction*. Eds A.H. Clarke and E.J. Rodgers. Llangrannog: Dolphin, 1991. 143–67.

Rubio Cremades, Enrique. "El costumbrismo como documentación novelesca en *Fortunata y Jacinta*." *Galdós en el centenario de 'Fortunata y Jacinta.'* Ed. Julio Rodríguez Puértolas. Palma de Mallorca: Prensa Universitaria, 1989. 103–10.

– "Galdós y las colecciones costumbristas." *Actas del segundo congreso inter-*

nacional de estudios galdosianos. 2 vols. Las Palmas: Ediciones del Excmo Cabildo Insular de Gran Canaria, 1979–80. 1:230–57.

Ruiz Aguilera, Ventura. *La Arcadia moderna.* Madrid: Imp. de Rojas y Comp., 1867.

– *Proverbios cómicos; nuevos proverbios ejemplares.* Madrid: Librerías Principales, 1870.

– *Proverbios ejemplares.* Madrid: Librería de D. Leocadio López, 1864.

Ruiz de la Serna, Enrique. "Los personajes de Galdós." *Estampa* 2.93 (22 October 1929).

Ruiz Salvador, Antonio. "La función del trasfondo histórico en *La desheredada.*" *Anales Galdosianos* 1 (1966): 53–62.

Russell, Robert H. "The Christ Figure in *Misericordia.* A Monograph." *Anales Galdosianos* 2 (1967): 103–30.

Sainte-Beuve, C-A. *Nouveaux Lundis.* 13 vols. 2nd ed. Paris: Calmann Levy, 1884. Vol. 9.

Sainz de Robles, F.C. *Ensayo de un diccionario español de sinónimos y antónimos.* Madrid: Aguilar, 1959.

Sánchez, Roberto G. "Las Troyas: un episodio en *Doña Perfecta* que anuncia el posterior Galdós." *Homenaje a Antonio Sánchez Barbudo: Ensayos de literatura española moderna.* Eds B. Brancaforte, E.R. Mulvihill, and R.G. Sánchez. Madison: Department of Spanish and Italian, University of Wisconsin, 1981. 51–9.

Santaló, Joaquín. *The Tragic Import in the Novels of Pérez Galdós.* Madrid: Playor, 1973.

Santana, Mario. "The Conflict of Narratives in Pérez Galdós's *Doña Perfecta.*" *Modern Language Notes* 113 (1998): 283–304.

Santiago Obeso, Julio. "Tomás e Isidora Rufete: dos personajes galdosianos para entender una época de la asistencia psiquiátrica en España." *Actas del séptimo congreso internacional de estudios galdosianos (2001).* Las Palmas: Ediciones del Cabildo Insular de Gran Canaria. Forthcoming.

Sarraute, Nathalie. "The Age of Suspicion." *Approaches to the Novel. Materials for a Poetics.* Ed. Robert Scholes. San Francisco: Chandlers, 1961. 207–17.

Scanlon, Geraldine M. "*El doctor Centeno*: A Study in Obsolescent Values." *Bulletin of Hispanic Studies* (Liverpool) 55 (1978): 245–53.

Schmidt, Ruth A. "José Ortega Munilla: Friend, Critic, and Disciple of Galdós." *Anales Galdosianos* 6 (1971): 107–11.

Schnepf, Michael A. "Galdós's *El doctor Centeno* Manuscript: Pedro Polo and Other Curiosities." *Romance Quarterly* 41 (1994): 36–42.

– "Galdós's *La desheredada* Manuscript: José Relimpio y Sastre." *Hispanófila* 34.100 (1990): 7–13.

Scholes, Robert. *Elements of Fiction.* New York: Oxford University Press, 1968.

- "Reading Like a Man." *Men in Feminism*. Eds Alice Jardine and Paul Smith. London: Methuen, 1987. 204–18.

Shoemaker, William H. "Galdós' Literary Creativity. D. José Ido del Sagrario." *Estudios sobre Galdós*. Madrid: Castalia, 1970. 85–122.

- "'Los Pepes' of Galdós in 1868 and 1887: Two Stages of His Style." *Hispania* 53 (1970): 887–98.

Sinnigen, John H. and Lilia Vieyra Sánchez. "*Nazarín* y *Halma* en *El Siglo diez y nueve*." *Anales Galdosianos* 37 (2002): 143–83.

Skultans, Vieda. *Madness and Morals. Ideas on Insanity in the Nineteenth Century*. London: Routledge and Kegan Paul, 1975.

Smith, Alan E. "Catálogo de los manuscritos de Benito Pérez Galdós en la Biblioteca Nacional de España." *Anales Galdosianos* 20.2 (1985): 143–56.

- "Introducción." In Pérez Galdós, *Rosalía*, 9–14.

Smith, Paul C. "Cervantes and Galdós: The Duques and Ido del Sagrario." *Romance Notes* 8 (1966–67): 47–50.

Smith, V.A. and J.E. Varey. "'Esperpento': Some Early Usages in the Novels of Galdós." *Galdós Studies*. Ed. J.E. Varey. London: Tamesis, 1970. 195–204.

Snow, C.P. "Galdós." *The Realists: Eight Portraits*. New York: Scribner's, 1978. 217–55.

Sobejano, Gonzalo. "Muerte del solitario: (Benito Pérez Galdós: *Fortunata y Jacinta*, 4a, II, 6). *El comentario de textos, 3. La novela realista*. Ed. Andrés Amorós. Madrid: Castalia, 1979. 203–54.

Standish, Peter. "Theatricality and Humour. Galdós's Technique in *Doña Perfecta*." *Bulletin of Hispanic Studies* (Liverpool) 54 (1977): 223–31.

Suleiman, Susan Rubin. *Authoritarian Fictions. The Ideological Novel as a Literary Genre*. New York: Columbia University Press, 1983.

Tarrío, Ángel. *Lectura semiológica de 'Fortunata y Jacinta.'* Las Palmas: Ediciones del Excmo Cabildo Insular de Gran Canaria, 1982.

Tolosa Latour, Manuel. [El Doctor Fausto] *Niñerías*. Madrid: Tipografía de Manuel Ginés Hernández, 1889.

- "Siluetas contemporáneas: Pérez Galdós." *La Época* (26 March 1883): 3.

Turner, Harriet S. "Rhetoric in *La sombra*: The Author and His Story." *Anales Galdosianos* 6 (1971): 5–19.

- "The Shape of Deception in *Doña Perfecta*." *Kentucky Romance Quarterly* 31 (1984): 125–34.

Ullman, Joan Connelly and George H. Allison. "Galdós as Psychiatrist in *Fortunata y Jacinta*." *Anales Galdosianos* 9 (1974): 7–36.

Unamuno, Miguel de. *Niebla (nivola)*. 12th ed. Madrid: Espasa-Calpe, 1968.

Valis, Noël M. "Una opinión olvidada de Palacio Valdés sobre Benito Pérez Galdós." *Boletín del Instituto de Estudios Asturianos* 36 (1982): 691–714.

Varey, J.E. "Charity in *Misericordia*." *Galdós Studies*. Ed. J.E. Varey. London: Tamesis, 1970. 164–94.

- *Pérez Galdós: Doña Perfecta*. London: Grant and Cutler, 1971.

Villasante, Olga. "El manicomio de Leganés. Debates científicos y administra-
tivos en torno a un proyecto frustrado." *Revista de la Asociación Española
de Neuropsiquiatría* 19 (July-September 1999): 469–79.

Walton, L.B. *Pérez Galdós and the Spanish Novel of the Nineteenth Century.*
1927. New York: Gordian Press, 1970.

Welsford, Enid. *The Fool: His Social and Literary History.* 1935. Gloucester,
Mass.: Peter Smith, 1966.

Whiston, James. "Change and Creativity in Galdós's Writing: the First Draft of
the *Lo prohibido* Manuscript." *New Galdós Studies. Essays in Memory of
John Varey.* Ed. Nicholas G. Round. London: Tamesis, 2003. 27–41.

– *The Early Stages of Composition of Galdós's 'Lo prohibido.'* London:
Tamesis, 1983.

– "Language and Situation in Part I of *Fortunata y Jacinta.*" *Anales Galdosianos* 7 (1972): 79–91.

Willem, Linda M. "A Dickensian Interlude in Galdós' *Rosalía.*" *Bulletin of
Hispanic Studies* (Liverpool) 69 (1992): 239–44.

– *Galdós's 'Segunda Manera.' Rhetorical Strategies and Affective Response.*
Chapel Hill: University of North Carolina, Department of Romance Languages, 1998.

– "Latent Narratives: Sideshadowing in *Fortunata y Jacinta.*" *Anales Galdosianos* 36 (2001): 299–306.

– "Moreno-Isla's Unpublished Scene from the *Fortunata y Jacinta* Galleys."
Anales Galdosianos 27–8 (1992–93): 179–83.

Wilson, Rawdon. "The Bright Chimera: Character as a Literary Term." *Critical Inquiry* 5 (1979): 725–49.

Wright, C.C. "*Las aventuras de Pickwick*: Notes on Benito Pérez Galdós as
Translator of Dickens." *Revista de Estudios Hispánicos* (Puerto Rico) 9
(1982): 263–70.

Wynter, Andrew. *The Borderlands of Insanity and Other Allied Papers.* London: Robert Hardwicke, 1875.

Yáñez, María-Paz. "Algo más sobre José Ido del Sagrario." *Homenaje a Alfonso Armas Ayala.* 2 vols. Las Palmas: Ediciones del Cabildo Insular de Gran
Canaria, 2000. 2:849–64.

– "Autores y lectores de un texto llamado Fortunata." *Actas del XI congreso
de la Asociación Internacional de Hispanistas. (Irvine, California, 24–29 de
agosto de 1992).* Ed. Juan Villegas. 5 vols. Irvine: University of California,
1994. 5:252–63.

Zahareas, Anthony N. "*Doña Perfecta* and Galdós's Aesthetic Solutions to
Historical Problems." *Anales Galdosianos* 36 (2001): 319–30.

Index